AN
OUTDOOR
JOURNAL

Also by Jimmy Carter

EVERYTHING TO GAIN (with Rosalynn Carter)
THE BLOOD OF ABRAHAM
NEGOTIATION: THE ALTERNATIVE TO HOSTILITY
KEEPING FAITH: MEMOIRS OF A PRESIDENT
A GOVERNMENT AS GOOD AS ITS PEOPLE
WHY NOT THE BEST?

Jimmy Carter
AN OUTDOOR JOURNAL

ADVENTURES AND REFLECTIONS

BANTAM BOOKS

TORONTO · NEW YORK · LONDON · SYDNEY · AUCKLAND

AN OUTDOOR JOURNAL
A Bantam Book / June 1988

Grateful acknowledgment is made for permission
to reprint an excerpt from McClane's *New Standard Fishing
Encyclopedia*, Holt, Rinehart & Winston.

Library of Congress Cataloging-in-Publication Data

Carter, Jimmy, 1924–
An outdoor journal.

Includes index.
1. Fishing. 2. Hunting. I. Title.
SH441.C36 1988   799   88-3334
ISBN 0-553-05301-9

Published simultaneously in the United States and Canada

To Rosalynn

CONTENTS

A BRIEF WORD   1

CHILDHOOD   3
    A Childhood Outdoors   5
    Fishing with My Daddy   18
    Learning to Hunt   36
    Dangers in the Woods   51

AMERICAN SEASONS   61
    Notes of a Fly-fisherman   63
    Trout Fishing and a Birthday: Spruce Creek   72
    Arkansas Rain, Ice, and Ducks   83
    The Rainbows of Yellowstone—and Japan!   92
    Ruffed Grouse, from Georgia to Michigan   103
    The Forty-ninth State, but First in Fishing   113

HOME-GROWN   131
    The Noble Turkey   133
    Catching Bass on Television   145
    The Prince of Game Birds   153

CROSSING BORDERS   171
    Salmo Salar   173
    Queen Charlotte Steelheads   185
    Bonefishing on Anegada   198
    Fishing in Europe   206
    New Zealand Adventure   218
    A Visit to Nepal   228

FULL CIRCLE   257
    On Turniptown Creek   259

INDEX   267

AN
OUTDOOR
JOURNAL

A
BRIEF WORD

Writing this book has been a labor of love. Over the last six years I have stolen an hour or so every now and then to reminisce about my early years out-of-doors or to transform a few scratched notes on fishing and hunting into several paragraphs and, eventually, a chapter. This delightful task was always like a vacation from my other writing, speeches, teaching at Emory University, international conferences, and work for my favorite organizations.

These hunting, fishing, and mountain climbing experiences have been all too rare since we moved back to Plains from the White House. And yet it has amazed me how often these trips of only a few days or even hours have turned into real adventures, magnified in importance and stretched in time by the pleasures of anticipation and the precious memories that never seem to fade away. The recollections of my early childhood have been especially moving: life on an isolated farm that would be primitive by modern standards; the intimate feeling I had walking alongside my daddy behind a bird dog, or my pride when he included me in a grown man's world on trips to the Okefenokee Swamp; or sitting in a boat with Mama, who always teased me because she could catch more fish—a habit she continued even after I had grown up to be President.

These narratives have been sharpened and clarified by my editor, Nessa Rapoport, although (or perhaps because) she has never spent a night in a swamp, heard a shotgun fired, or seen a rainbow trout coaxed into a landing net. I have received a delightful bonus from her probing questions and good advice.

There are many characters in this journal, friends of ours who have helped Rosalynn and me find excitement and joy, improve our skills, and become more deeply immersed in God's beautiful world. I hope my readers also benefit from knowing men and women like Joe Strickland, Jack Crockford, Wayne Harpster, Richard Adams, George Harvey, and Rachel Clark— people who have never lost the pioneer spirit and who have helped teach us what genuine companionship means. They and others like them comprise a special family of those who love the outdoors, who relish undisturbed quiet and beauty, who seek to be tested by the harsh experiences of the natural world, who like to stretch their hearts and minds, and who later enjoy reflecting on what they've seen and touched. This book is a tribute to them.

PLAINS, GEORGIA
JANUARY 1988

CHILDHOOD

A CHILDHOOD OUTDOORS

"Why do you hunt and fish?" I'm often asked.

The easiest answer is: "My father and all my ancestors did it before me. It's been part of my life since childhood, and part of my identity, like being a southerner or a Baptist."

I could add that, during the proper seasons, the urge within me to be in the woods and fields or along a stream is such a strong and pleasant desire that I have no inclination to withstand it. As a child and an adult, I would hunger for a chance to escape for a while from my normal duties, no matter how challenging or enjoyable they were, and to spend a few hours or days in relative solitude away from civilization. Such retreats have always been as much an escape *into* something delightful as *away* from things I wanted to avoid or forget for a while.

This impulse is not the same as laziness or abandonment of responsibilities. All my life, even from the early years, my dreams kept me hard at work: to attend the United States Naval Academy and become a submariner, to be a pioneer officer in the nuclear program, to develop a successful business back in Plains, to advance my political career from state senator to governor, to run for (and win) the presidency, then to build a presidential library and a Center within which Rosalynn and I could work productively for the rest of our lives.

And yet, right through those busy years, there has never been any significant amount of time when I have stayed away from the natural areas that mean so much to me. During the most critical moments of my life I have been renewed in spirit by the special feelings that come from the solitude and beauty of the out-of-doors.

I spent eleven years in the U.S. Navy, much of the time at sea, and still remember with nostalgia the feeling of liberation when we cleared the last channel buoy and headed for the open water. On long cruises the paperwork and routine family obligations were minimal or nonexistent. In the close confines of any ship, and particularly a submarine, personal privacy is carefully respected by all the members of the crew. Before submarines were equipped with nuclear power and snorkels, they stayed mostly on the surface. Our hours on the bridge, in the conning tower, or in the sonar room allowed each of us to know the ocean and the heavens in a unique way.

As sonar officer, I was expected to be familiar with all the sounds of the depths and could identify shrimp, dolphin and other fishes, and different species of whales as we recorded their chatter and songs on our extremely sensitive listening devices. Primary navigation was by sextant, and we most often had only a few seconds on the bridge or at the periscope to take a quick sight on a star or planet that might peep through an opening in the clouds. Underwater currents, temperature gradients, and the topography of the bottom were other factors crucial to our work—indeed, to our survival. But when our duties were done, there was plenty of time for sleep, reading, or long hours of quiet contemplation. Somehow the complexities of life seemed to sort themselves out, and my own priorities came into better perspective.

Life on land, of course, is different, but not in the way it can affect the spirit. In forests, mountains, swamps, or waterways I also gain a renewal of perspective and a sense of order, truth, patience, beauty, and justice (although nature's is harsh). Even on one-day weekends at home during the frantic 1976 presidential election, my family found time together to hunt arrowheads in remote fields or to fish in our pond for a few hours. I probably know the inside of the Camp David wooded compound more intimately than most of the permanent caretakers, and the nearby Hunting Creek—just six minutes down the mountain road from the main gate—saw Rosalynn and me regularly. We often landed in the helicopter at Camp David, changed clothes while the White House press corps departed to a nearby Maryland town, and then secretly took off again, to land forty minutes later in a pasture alongside Spruce Creek in Pennsylvania for a couple of days of secluded fly-fishing. These jaunts were among our best-kept secrets in Washington.

As a President of the United States who enjoyed fishing, I realized that I was sharing a love of this art with several of my predecessors: George Washington, Chester Arthur, Calvin Coolidge, Herbert Hoover, Dwight Eisenhower, and, most notably, Grover Cleveland. In fact, they and I have fished in some of the same streams.

In the wintertime our family found a similar kind of isolation and pleasure on cross-country skis, exploring the many trails in the state forest areas around Camp David. There were a number of summer camps in the region whose hiking and riding trails were never used during the colder months of the year. They stretched before us, pristine, and our cross-country skis made the first marks on the undisturbed open paths that wound up and down through these mountain areas of northern Maryland. Here we became avid students of the sport, largely self-taught.

In my eagerness I had two serious spills going down hills

that were too steep for me, once slashing my face in a dozen places when I dived into a half-inch sheet of surface ice. Only heavy makeup saved me from embarrassment during the following week or two as I went about my presidential duties. Then, about a month before I left office, a submerged boulder caught my right ski. My left collarbone broke cleanly when I fell.

Several years later, when Rosalynn and I took up downhill skiing on the slopes of New Mexico and Colorado, we were careful to get expert instructors to help us master the technique more quickly and reduce the danger of serious accidents. Both kinds of skiing, quite different in character, let us savor a new relationship with nature.

I have never been happier, more exhilarated, at peace, rested, inspired, and aware of the grandeur of the universe and the greatness of God than when I find myself in a natural setting not much changed from the way He made it. These feelings seem to be independent of the physical beauty of a place, for I have experienced them almost equally within a dense thicket of alders or rhododendron alongside Turniptown Creek in North Georgia and in the high mountains of Alaska or Nepal.

Although actually carrying a gun or rod has become increasingly unnecessary as a motivation for my sojourns into remote places, I still go on hunting and fishing expeditions several times a year. There is special pleasure not only in these moments, but also in my thoughts and conversation in the months before and afterward.

To find game and to become a proficient wing shot or to be able to present the proper fly to a rising fish demands the greatest degree of determination, study, planning, and practice; and there is always more to discover. In the woods or on a stream, my concentration is so intense that for long periods the rest of the world is almost forgotten. I also immerse myself in books and magazines to acquire an understanding of nature, plants, insects, birds, fishes, and mammals, and the complicated interrelationships among them. I will read almost anything on these subjects, they interest me so much.

But reading is never enough. Books and articles must be supplemented continually by personal experiences, shared when possible with more accomplished friends who are willing to teach what they know—preferably in a kind, not overbearing, manner! When I was a boy, my daddy provided this instruction as though it were his natural and pleasant duty. I would have considered it inappropriate and somewhat disloyal to seek advice or information elsewhere unless Daddy specifically asked someone to take me hunting or approved of my fishing with another adult. However, instruction by others was frequently available to me without my having to ask.

During the summer months I sold boiled peanuts every day in the town of Plains, near our home. When I had served my regular customers and pretty well covered the town, there was often time before returning home to hang around the checkerboards, whittling benches, or barbershop and listen to the never-ending discussions and arguments about farming, weather, philosophy, town gossip, and hunting and fishing. The few acknowledged masters of the woods and fields had solidly established reputations, and everyone was more inclined to listen when they spoke. Those who trained the best bird dogs, observed the niceties of hunting etiquette and still brought home the most quail, were consistently successful in a dove field, caught fish when others couldn't, or were wise in the ways of the fields and swamps were usually treated with respect no matter what their financial or social status. Thinking back on it, I don't remember any really prominent citizens who were in the master class of outdoorsmen. Perhaps the persistent recounting of exploits, for which only a loiterer could spare the time, was also a necessary component in the establishment of a notable reputation. In any case, a great number of leisure hours were a prerequisite for developing the outstanding skills a person could boast about.

And yet, over the years, no one could get away with inflating his accomplishments; there were too many witnesses to the actual performance in this tiny community. For instance, a special string of fish or a trophy bass had to be displayed or weighed in the local grocery store in order for a claim to be believed. Performance on a dove field could be observed by as many as a dozen other hunters in the immediate vicinity. Although it was expected that some ultimate secrets were withheld, the storytelling and debates were entertaining and sometimes helpful. For me they became a kind of classroom. Daddy was usually busy and seldom joined these bull sessions, but later I would ask him to confirm some of the more questionable statements and claims or to assess the veracity of the participants.

As a voracious reader, I searched for adventure books by Zane Grey, Jack London, and others, and liked, too, the flowery writing of John Muir. Thoreau's memoirs were fascinating and sometimes disturbing—he was against honest labor, seemed to have no religion, and favored civil disobedience. Thoreau had lived almost all his days in cities but wrote beautifully about two years spent at Walden Pond. In contrast, my own early years were spent in the country, and I had no knowledge of city life.

I also read a lot of the hunting and fishing magazines but never remember buying one when I was a boy. The Plains drugstore had a good stock, and I was a frequent visitor to the home of the druggist's son, Pete Godwin, where dozens of magazines were always available, stripped of their covers which had been returned for credit. At the end of each month a few of the dated periodicals circulated within a small circle of Pete's friends. Among those we enjoyed were *Field and Stream, Outdoor Life, American Sportsman, Boys' Life*, and many nature articles in the *Saturday Evening Post* and *Collier's*.

I was always eager to test this new information or advice in the woods and streams nearby. When there was no opportunity to hunt I used my BB gun or .22 rifle to hone my shooting skills. Shotgun shells were too expensive to waste, but a dime would buy a giant cylindrical container with five hundred shots for the air rifle. My friends and I would spend hours throwing up tin cans for one another to shoot at, varying the distance and direction to simulate as best we could the explosive rise of quail or the swift passing flight of doves. An open bucket in the yard was an excellent target for bait casting. I would vary the distance and my arm delivery to correspond with the circumstances we would face in the creeks and ponds.

I learned these skills as a boy, but there is no age limit to the enjoyment of outdoor excursions. Some of my most memorable moments have been spent teaching my own children and grandchildren how to catch their first fish at the age of three or four. On the other hand, among my cherished fishing and hunting companions is D. W. Brooks, who as an octogenarian still demonstrates his personal superiority in inducing wary fish to take a well-placed fly or in successfully following up a beautiful bird-dog point.

The joy of fishing was well described more than three hundred years ago by Izaak Walton, when he referred to angling as "that pleasant labour which you enjoy, when you purpose to give rest to your mind, and divest yourself of your more serious business, and (which is often) dedicate a day or two to this recreation."

As for the lives of those who are not fishermen, this best known of all piscators deplores their lot:

> Men that are taken to be grave, because nature hath made them of a sour complexion; money-getting men, men that spend all their time, first in getting, and next in anxious care to keep it; men that are condemned to be rich, and then always busy or discontented; for these poor rich men, we Anglers pity them perfectly, and stand in no need to borrow their thought to think ourselves so happy. No, no, sir, we enjoy a contentedness above the reach of such dispositions.

Such "contentedness" can be attained in the company of others or alone; I am thankful that it is not necessary to choose between those states. There are times during the fall and winter hunting months when my only desired companions are my two bird dogs. Fly-fishing in a small mountain creek requires solitude; Rosalynn may be upstream or down, in a separate pool, often out of sight. But there are other times. Sitting in a small bateau in our own farm pond, choosing for our supper the mature bluegills and bass we've caught and returning the others to grow some more, gives us long and precious hours of uninterrupted conversation about all kinds of things, an opportunity quite rare in the lives of many married couples. Usually, on hunting trips or when fishing from a boat on large streams or lakes, I am with family and friends, and it is good to share with them the frustrations and successes, the hardships and delights, the plans and memories. Outdoor people constitute a close fraternity, often international in its membership. Like music and art, love of nature is a common language that can transcend political or social boundaries.

What about the taking of life? Every hunter and fisherman, I am sure, sometimes has twinges of uneasiness when a beautiful and swift quail or waterfowl is brought down, or when a valiant trout finally is brought to the net. Those of us who habitually release trout know that on occasion even a barbless hook will kill. For people who might find these feelings overwhelming, my advice would be: "Don't hunt or fish." Indeed, if someone has a moral or ethical objection to taking an animal's life for human use, it is logical that he or she be a dedicated vegetarian and not require others, perhaps in a fish market or slaughter-house, to end lives for their benefit; many make that decision.

Although these sentiments are admirable, I have never suffered from such compunctions, except on one or two occasions during my younger childhood days. I was brought up in an agricultural society, where chickens, hogs, sheep, goats, and cattle were raised for food. There was no real distinction in my mind between those animals and the quail, doves, ducks, squirrels, and rabbits that also arrived on our table after a successful hunt. Nevertheless, there were limits on hunting activities, observed and imposed by my father.

Even before I had my first gun, Daddy made me a flip. With rubber bands, cut from an old inner tube, connecting a leather pouch to the two prongs of a forked stick, I could propel small projectiles with considerable velocity. I practiced regularly, shooting small pebbles and chinaberries at various targets, including birds, with no effect except that a few of the green glass telephone-pole insulators around our house were shattered. One day, while my mother and father visited on the front porch of a friend, I aimed at a robin sitting on a fence that surrounded the yard. The chance shot killed the bird, and I approached the adults with the dead robin in my hands and tears running down my cheeks.

After a few awkward moments, Daddy didn't help by saying, "We shouldn't ever kill anything that we don't need for food."

Mama partially salvaged my feelings by adding, "We'll cook the bird for your supper tonight."

When I grew older, it would have been considered effeminate, or even depraved, to discuss such feelings with my friends. As an adult, however, I became aware of debates on the subject. I'll always remember how surprised most hunters were at the storm of protest that arose early in 1972 when a photograph was published of a smiling Senator Ed Muskie in hunting clothes, holding a gun in one hand and a dead Canada goose in the other. He was bombarded with criticisms and threats; the photo may have contributed to his defeat during the subsequent presidential primary season.

On my first Christmas home as President, I went quail hunting on our farm with one of my sons. That night our family enjoyed a nice quail supper, a fact that the ever-present White House reporters included in their routine news articles. The following Sunday morning as we approached the entrance to the First Baptist Church in Washington, I was amazed to find the sidewalk populated with demonstrators protesting my murderous habit.

In the church, I answered some questions about it from my Sunday School students by referring them to Biblical references about God's sending manna and quail to the people of Israel, who killed and ate them. Even more pertinent was the intriguing account in the twenty-first chapter of the Gospel according to John, when our resurrected Lord advised his disciples on how and where to catch fish, cooked some on a charcoal fire and ate with them, and presumably joined in counting their catch: 153 large ones.

I have been made to feel more at peace about my hunting and fishing because of my strict observance of conservation measures, including the deliberate protection of overly depleted game and the initiation and support of programs to increase the population of species that seem scarce. It was because my father liked to hunt that he was an active worker in the Chattahoochee Valley Wildlife Conservation program, directing my work as a child in this effort. We planted feed patches, controlled burning, and attempted to improve habitat in our woods and along fencerows and terraces. I also know that many of my fellow hunters and fishers, in personal practice and through formal organizations, are the very people most dedicated to these same worthy goals; they are the prime founders and supporters of Ducks Unlimited, Trout Unlimited, and similar institutions whose purpose is to protect habitat and increase the population of their quarry. Working with professional game and fish specialists and donating substantial time, influence, and funds, they have been quite successful. For instance, when I was young we seldom saw a white-tailed deer in Georgia, but now there are more of these animals there than at any time in history; wild turkeys, too, are making a remarkable comeback.

It is the strict circumscription of hunting and fishing—those unwritten rules of ethics, etiquette, and propriety—that define the challenge. Therefore, the game sought must be abundant enough that your gun and rod do not deplete or permanently reduce a desirable population of the species. At the same time, there should be a relative scarcity or elusiveness of the game or fish, and not too much disadvantage for the prey in that particular habitat, so that both skill and good fortune will be necessary in achieving your goal. Our home is in an area well populated by deer, turkey, quail, doves, ducks, fish, and other animals of many kinds, but I have often spent many hours without any success whatever, either because I did not encounter any game or because bad luck or my lack of skill led to failure. These experiences, still enjoyable despite the results, only enhance the pleasure of my times of success.

Success, when it comes, must be difficult and uncertain. The effortless taking of game is not hunting—it is slaughter. My only experience in hunting the rail, or marsh hen, happened to be at the time of a maximum spring tide near one of Georgia's coastal islands. Much of the marsh grass was covered with water, and the birds had little cover. I soon reached the legal limit without missing a shot, and still remember the facile experience with distaste. I've never wanted to shoot another rail.

On the other hand, I have hunted and fished with neophytes who shot fifty embarrassing times without touching a feather or who cast a fly thousands of times without much likelihood of a strike, while others around them were repeatedly demonstrating their prowess. And yet the newcomers were undeterred, eager for some private advice and another chance. I finally took my first Atlantic salmon after three and a half days of steady and fruitless casting; that year I was one of the few successful East Coast salmon fishermen. Curt Gowdy, my fishing partner, and I timed the number of our casts in a ten-minute period and then estimated that I had caught that fish after presenting a fly more than eleven thousand times, mostly while balanced perilously on large slick boulders in a rushing torrent or shivering in a boat during extended cold and steady rains. In all that time, I don't remember a dull or unenjoyable moment!

Even in the best of times there is an element of difficulty, doubt, discomfort, disappointment, and even danger involved in such pursuits, and often great distances must be covered during very early hours, even in the dark night. It is almost inherent in the seeking of wild things in their native habitat that you must forego many of the comfortable trappings of civilization. Although sporting goods stores offer adequate supplies to substitute for many of the normal conveniences, there is a limit to what you can tote, and living without some of the manufactured luxuries is a necessary part of being absorbed within a woodland or wilderness.

Even ancient records show that there has almost always been a scarcity of available game near centers of human habitation, and that for many centuries hunting and fishing were considered the unique privileges of the rich and powerful. The historic accounts of national revolutions, as well as the delightful tales of Robin Hood and his merry men in Olde England, indicate that these special rights were both jealously guarded by a few and deeply resented by common people who were deprived of both food and pleasure. I have been fortunate all my life to live in a community where working people have had almost unlimited access to game and fish, and later to have the means to travel when my interest was aroused by distant places.

Not that you must hunt or fish in order to enjoy unknown regions and new adventures. During the time I was governor, Rosalynn and I lived fairly close to the North Georgia mountain streams. It was not long before some of our younger friends asked us to join them in canoe trips through the white-water areas. We started off on the Chattahoochee River above Atlanta, just to get acquainted with the paddle and learn how to handle moderate turbulence. Then we graduated to the much more challenging Chattooga, a truly wild river on which the movie *Deliverance* was being filmed—a story by James Dickey about the devastating encounter of four Atlanta businessmen with terrible rapids and some grotesque mountain hoodlums.

As we proceeded down the river, the rapids become increasingly challenging. Soon we were taking the more difficult "section two" and "section three" rapids in open two-person canoes. One day my partner and I successfully traversed what is known as Bull Sluice, a double five-foot waterfall where the canoe descends almost vertically at times. This unprecedented achievement was written up in a nationwide magazine for canoeists. Eventually Rosalynn and I even tackled the lower section four in a small rubber raft. We made it, but I was covered with bruises and had trouble walking for several days afterwards!

Then we graduated to kayaks, spending several evenings in an Atlanta university swimming pool learning how to roll all the way over and continue on without "bailing out." Unsurprisingly, this proved much more difficult in a moving stream with a shallow and rocky bottom, but we persisted and greatly enjoyed this new sport and an opportunity to see parts of our state that would otherwise have been inaccessible.

My recently gained knowledge and pleasure is never at the expense of my earlier memories or habits. I've hunted mallards in the rice fields and pin-oak woods of Arkansas and fished for steelhead in the Queen Charlotte Islands, for Atlantic salmon on the Matapédia River in Quebec, for giant rainbow trout in Alaska and New Zealand, and for bonefish and marlin in the Caribbean, but I still find the same excitement ten minutes from my home in Plains, perhaps with renewed pleasure and a deeper gratitude.

Now, as my bird dog strikes the scent of a covey on the edge of a deep gully in Webster County, I remember my father taking me there as a little boy, and my own son Chip bringing down his first quail on the same spot. With the rise of a large-mouth bass or the slow but steady disappearance of my cork on a bream bed below the Pond House in May, I can almost hear my mother's voice at the other end of the boat as she chortled over catching the most and biggest fish in spite of my best efforts. In my early life she would say, "You always pull too soon, Jimmy, when you get behind." Later: "You may be President, but you still haven't learned how to catch fish." Some of the memories are painful because my parents and other dear companions are no longer with me, but they're still especially vivid and will always be precious.

Although we hope to be active for many years, Rosalynn and I are already making careful plans to enjoy the final years of our lives. One of our most important priorities is the opportunity to spend more and more time in interesting and beautiful places—places that are quiet, simple, secluded, and relatively undisturbed.

We won't have to go far to observe the beauties of nature. In our own yard we see gray and flying squirrels, rabbits, chipmunks, opossums, raccoons, quail and many other birds, snakes and other reptiles. Deer frequently graze within fifty yards of our front door, and without going farther we regularly harvest wild plums, peaches, mulberries, black and white muscadines, cherries, blackberries, persimmons, and mayhaws.

Wherever life takes us, there are always moments of wonder. I remember going to the roof of the White House to watch the thrilling flight of Canada geese overhead, their weird calls barely penetrating the night sounds of Washington, and their breasts illuminated by ghostly reflection of the city lights. A few years earlier, we and our children had lain on our backs on the governor's mansion lawn in Atlanta to watch millions of monarch butterflies on their southward journey to distant Mexico.

When I look at how fragile and lovely the natural world is, I can understand the feeling of Henry David Thoreau: "The earth was the most glorious instrument, and I was audience to its strains." In the late twentieth century, his conviction that "in the wilderness is the salvation of mankind" is more true than ever.

FISHING
WITH
MY DADDY

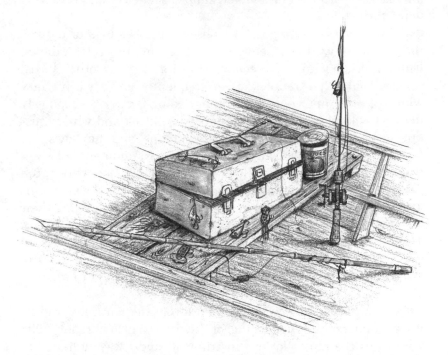

Growing up as a farm boy, I wanted either a fishing pole or a gun in my hand whenever possible—when school was out, when it was too wet to work in the fields, when the crops were laid by in the summer, when harvest time was over in the fall and winter, when chores around the house and barn were all done, or, in my earliest years, when some willing adult was free to go with me to the woods or swamps if my daddy wasn't free. Looking back, it seems that there were a lot of "whens" in the way, and yet there were fewer obstacles then than now.

My father was the dominant person in our family and in my life. He was a relatively stern man when discipline and work were on his mind, and duty always came first. I rarely disobeyed Daddy, both because of my respect for him and because I knew that punishment for my transgressions would be certain and sometimes severe. Most often, the penalty was my being confined to home and school. These periods were usually for a day or so, but there was one occasion when I was deprived of liberty for a month. Our school principal had reported to Daddy that some of my classmates and I had directly defied his orders and left school to enjoy an afternoon jaunt in nearby Americus, our county seat. We had aggravated the situation by writing an article about our good times that was published in the local newspaper.

For more serious offenses than pranks like these, I was whipped with a spirea or peach switch. At the age of four, my first such punishment was for taking a penny out of the Sunday School collection plate instead of giving my offering. So unforgettable was the experience that I've never stolen anything since. A few years later I got a switching for shooting my sister Gloria in her behind with my BB gun, and another time for hiding in my tree house, refusing to answer Daddy's calls, and pretending that I had run away from home. The few whippings from him—perhaps half a dozen in all—were truly memorable events. I admit now that I deserved them, but at the time I resented the severity of the punishment.

Until the mid-1930s, Plains was widely recognized as a major medical center. The Wise brothers, all physicians, operated a clinic that did pioneering work in radiology, surgery, and anesthesiology. They always had a group of young medical doctors in residency practice, some of whom later became famous in their specialties. (One was chief surgeon at Emory University Hospital in Atlanta.) Dozens of nurses also received their training in Plains; my mother was one of them. As a registered nurse she ministered to the neighbors in our relatively remote rural community of Archery, at times performing some of the services of a medical doctor for those who could not hope to pay for their treatment.

The result was a close-knit social community of doctors,

nurses, and their spouses who worked long and hard, balancing their daily lives with frequent parties on the weekends. A fair share of the parties were held either at our home or in a clubhouse near our pond. On several occasions I used Daddy's mules to pull a partygoer's automobile out of the pond following a particularly successful frolic. It was easy to leave a car out of gear on the steep hill or to take a wrong turn when heading back toward the road and home. We children were, of course, excluded from this part of our parents' lives, but were sometimes kept awake by music and singing in other parts of the house.

Although he was tough, my father was also fair, generous, and fun-loving. He was a successful farmer who did much of his own carpentry and blacksmithing, and excelled at business, baseball, tennis, dancing, playing poker, and as an outdoorsman. It was a special blessing that he never thought hunting or fishing was a waste of time for either him or me. Daddy considered both activities a normal and necessary part of his life and of my growing up, and he shared my pride when I was able to put fish or game on the table.

I was born in 1924, and so much of my boyhood was during the Great Depression. Daddy worked very hard in growing and selling products from our farm, always seeking the more profitable retail markets for eggs, milk, sausages and cured hams, syrup, and even homemade ketchup from our tomatoes. Since I had much more time off than he did, even including my schoolwork, in my early childhood we usually went our own separate ways in the woods and on the streams. He on occasion would join his friends when adult frolicking was part of the excursion, and I more frequently would go with my black friends who lived near our home in the Archery community a few miles west of Plains. Although we unconsciously honored the proprieties of the segregated Deep South, my life of work and play was naturally and inseparably entwined with that of my black neighbors.

During the days I was not in school, I worked in the fields with the other "hands." My father made sure that I and everyone else on our 350-acre place knew that the well-being of our animals came first. When we returned to the barn lot after sundown, exhausted from a long day of fieldwork, no one went home for rest or supper until after the mules and horses were well watered, fed, and bedded down for the night. Without electricity, these jobs required a lot of pumping and toting.

We also kept sheep, donkeys, goats, beef cattle, hogs, geese, chickens, guineas, ducks, and milk cows; I was taught how to care for them all. As far back as I can remember I had a pony of my own, for my own pleasure, to run errands, or at times to help me carry drinking water to fieldworkers from a nearby spring. Daddy considered one of my duties to keep the pony properly exercised, and he could often take away my appetite by asking, "When's the last time you rode your pony?"

Today, the most vivid and pleasant memories of my childhood are of those times when Daddy and I were able to fish and hunt together, or ride along in a pickup truck talking about it. He seemed to love me more and treated me as something of an equal when we were in a dove field, walking behind a bird dog, or on a stream. In each pursuit of game or fish I had to go through a kind of apprenticeship, beginning when I was four or five years old, learning how to bait a hook and watch a cork or practicing with a flip or slingshot.

My father never seemed to care much for fishing on the branches or creeks around home. Since we didn't have our own fishpond until the year before I finished high school, I did most of my earlier fishing either with a next-door neighbor named Rachel Clark or with some of the playmates near my own age, particularly A. D. Davis. All my fishing partners were black. Rachel's husband, Jack, was in charge of our farm's barn and lots, and only rarely worked in the fields. He supervised care of the livestock and milked the cows morning and night. There was a large garden between our house and theirs, which Jack and I worked together, his family and ours sharing the vegetables produced. When I was a few years older and had to help milk the cows, Jack gave me more detailed instructions in how to train and use a bird dog and how to understand the niceties of quail hunting.

Jack was a good raconteur and a friend, but Rachel was my hero in the Clark family and a special person in my life. She was light-brown, small in stature, laughed a lot with a kind of quiet chuckle, almost always had a dip of maccaboy snuff in her lip, and in a strange way seemed a little above doing housework or other menial labor for anyone else. In the field, though, she was a star. No man on the farm could equal her in shaking and stacking peanuts or in picking cotton. She always set the standard of performance for all of us. With her steady persistence and nimble fingers she seemed to move like a vacuum cleaner between her two rows of cotton, picking two or three bolls every time I plucked one, even during my most ambitious moments after I was big enough to hold my own as a man. At the end of these hottest of all summer days came weighing time, and the inevitable question among all of us in the field was: "How much did Rachel pick today?" I always tried to get the row next to hers, so that she could help me if I started to fall behind.

Rachel was also known as the finest fisher in the neighborhood, and there was no doubt that she deserved this reputation. She knew the best spots in all the creeks and was especially successful on the smaller "branches," which were not so heavily fished in those days. During the Depression years, particularly among the poorer families, hunting and fishing were not looked on as sports but as necessary rest times from fieldwork and a valuable means to supplement the standard farm diet with meat. Although some fresh meat was available during slaughtering time in the winter, "fatback," or salt pork, was the only kind of meat most people could afford to buy. Nowadays it is almost impossible to walk through the thick underbrush and briers alongside my old streams, but back then there were clear paths by all of them because of the heavy fishing. Sometimes the paths would depart from the creek to avoid a bog or some other obstacle, but they always managed to dip back in to the stream where there was a good hole to fish.

Whenever I asked Rachel to allow me to go fishing with her, she let me earn my way by digging the earthworms or periwinkles, or by finding the more succulent caterpillars on the large leaves of catalpa trees. I also contributed by adding some store-bought canned goods to our common lunch pail. Then we were off to Choctawhatchee or Kinchafoonee Creek or to Hog Branch, sometimes walking five miles or more before we arrived at the creek bank. We carried one or two cane poles, but Rachel immediately cut some small saplings in the woods and would soon be fishing as many as half a dozen lines at once.

Some would be tightline with a heavy sinker in the swifter current, and most others were with corks in the slower-moving or eddy water.

Try as I might, I could never manage more than two lines, and they often tangled with each other or with underwater snags or overhead limbs. A much more significant difference between us was that I was constantly slapping at mosquitoes and yellow flies, while they didn't seem to bother Rachel. I tried dousing my head with citronella a few times as a repellent, but soon gave it up as hopeless.

As Rachel and I moved up or down the stream from hole to hole, we tried to catch redbellies (redbreast sunfish), the powerful little stumpknockers (spotted sunfish), catfish, jack (chain pickerel), an occasional "trout" (largemouth bass), and, when the water was muddy or rising, eels. Some of our incorrect names—such as "trout" instead of bass, and "bream" for various sunfish—came from British forefathers who had arrived as Georgia's first European settlers. It was not even a matter of comment that Rachel invariably caught a lot more than I did; I was never tempted to be jealous or envious, so great was her skill. I carried my fish on a stripped willow limb threaded through their gills; Rachel put hers in a kind of creel made out of a white flour sack. When we were not toting them from one place to another, we tried to keep the fish refrigerated in the cool creek water.

At the stream we watched an occasional otter and quite often flushed wood ducks, but neither they nor even the water moccasins ever disturbed us enough to interrupt our fishing. Rachel and I kept everything we caught except mud turtles, but I would give her the dogfish (bowfin) and snapping turtles, which my mother wouldn't cook. Nor would Mama clean any fish when I got home. That was my job, but well worth the pride I felt when our family sat down to enjoy the grits, hush puppies, and my fish.

The family had a couple of rules about eating fish. As a result, I never ate wheat bread with fish, and there was an absolute injunction against drinking any kind of milk with a fish meal. My childhood impression was that in some way these combinations could cause serious illness, even death.

*   *   *

As for my playmates, we would fish in the nearest of the streams, the Choctawhatchee (which we called "Chock-li-hatchet"), although mostly after a heavy rain when the creek was rising and fieldwork was impossible. Sometimes a white friend, Rembert Forrest, would come to visit me and join us. His home was about four miles north of ours as the crow flies—or as we walked—through the swamps, or about seven miles around by the road. This was a different kind of fishing, using set hooks baited with tough scraps of meat. In the muddy water our catch was almost exclusively catfish and eels.

On these excursions we took meal, lard, grits, sweet potatoes, and coffee or sassafras roots with us, often spending the night on the creek bank around a fire, checking the set hooks by lantern light every half hour or so and cooking when we were hungry. When we saw one of our short switches bobbing up and down or bent down into the current, we would pull in the fish, rebait the hook, and move on to the next hole. We usually ate the eels first, because the delicious fillets would become soft if kept very long, while the catfish would be good to take home when we left the creek.

We had no idea then that we were participating in a remarkable natural drama. All the eels we were catching, some as much as three and a half feet long, had been born as tiny transparent creatures in the Atlantic Ocean, probably in the Sargasso Sea. After a year or more, the maturing females had made an extraordinary journey, finally to live and grow to full size in our small inland streams thousands of miles from their birthplace. The smaller males apparently remained in the ocean and saltwater estuaries, where, somewhere south of Bermuda, mating and spawning occurred when the females returned after an absence of as much as ten or fifteen years, there to die as the cycle ended.

It was only in recent times that the mystery of the eel was solved, after ages of scientific speculation that little ones formed from scrapings of the skin of adults, grew from horsehair, or sprang in some spontaneous and miraculous way from mud, slime, or horse dung. Also, we did not realize that in Europe and other countries, the same eel is considered to be one of the foremost aquatic delicacies. In fact, we thought we were the only ones who knew how delicious they were.

If the rains were heavy enough, the creeks would leave their banks and flood the surrounding swamps, sometimes several feet deep. When this happened, as it did a number of times each year, the flooding stopped all access to the good fishing holes until the high water fell again, leaving isolated "lakes" or pools in low places under the dense cover of magnolia, bay, gum, water oak, and poplar trees. Sometimes we would go into the swamp with hoes and a long-handled dip net to stir up the drying holes of water. Fish of all kinds would come to the top seeking to escape the densely muddied water, and we would quickly scoop them up, beating the raccoons, otter, turtles, snakes, and other creatures to some choice meals.

Near the time of the full moon in March, the word would spread around Plains: "The suckers are running." Although not comparable in scope to the salmon and steelhead spawning runs I would find so intriguing many years later, the runs of the suckers were exciting events in our community among those of us who wanted to participate in this seasonal effort to contribute to the family larder. I didn't know much about the life cycle of spotted suckers *(Minytrema melanops),* but it was obvious that these mature and powerful fish, sometimes weighing as much as four or five pounds, would not bite a hook when they were moving up the small streams to spawn. The use of nets was illegal; anyone seen bringing a net was roundly condemned by the rest of us because a net could completely block any passage of suckers upstream. I remember one altercation among adults on the creek bank that almost resulted in fisticuffs until the majority finally prevailed, and the net was put back into the pickup truck.

The only way to catch suckers at that time of year was to use a small gig or harpoon in the middle of the night. Because spawning streams were often the smallest of tributaries, not more than three or four feet wide, we had to stand in water that was seldom more than waist deep. Sometimes it was possible to straddle the entire current with a foot planted firmly on each bank. Shining a flashlight beam down into the water, we tried to spear the fast-moving fish as they went by, but it was much more difficult than might be expected. We thought ourselves lucky if, after hours of effort, we got two or three of them. Although the suckers were filled with tiny bones, the meat was firm, white, and tasty. If the fillets were slashed at half-inch intervals, the bones would be cooked enough to be edible. Most of us considered the suckers prime eating.

Some of these fish seemed to dwell permanently in the larger streams, such as Kinchafoonee Creek, and so could be caught with hook and line. This was a special kind of fishing which required a lot of patience, skill, and knowledge of the habits of the fish. When someone came upon a good pool, very deep with slow-moving water, it was generally adopted secretly as his "sucker hole." This information had to be carefully guarded because all fishing streams were considered public property; I never knew any landowner to prevent fishermen from walking the banks or catching fish at any place along the creeks running through a farm. There were hundreds of holes along each stream, of course, and it was relatively fruitless to fish indiscriminately for suckers. You had to have a private hole.

I never adopted one of my own but was invited every now and then to join others at theirs, provided I contributed to the preparations. For weeks we would feed the fish, usually with compressed peanut- or cottonseed-meal cake, until eventually they would tend to congregate in that particular spot. Those of us who knew the hole's location took great care not to leave any empty bags, trampled underbrush, or other indications on the creek bank that might betray us.

When we thought the fish were ready, we used small hooks baited with a gob of red worms or dough and a little cork adjusted carefully to place the hook just on the bottom of the creek. Then we watched the float with close attention. The sucker bites were so tender and tentative that it was almost like fishing for ghost fish, and it was important to know just when to pull. The bobbles of the cork were nearly undetectable, sometimes consisting just of vibrations that made a spider web of concentric circles around the cork. The hook then had to be set with a hard and steady pull. Most of the time nothing was there, but when a sucker was on, it was a battle royal. Few fish of that size could fight so furiously.

I never was much of a sucker fisherman, and my catch on most occasions was nonexistent or much smaller than that of my fishing companions. However, for a boy, such fishing was a real adventure, combining secrecy and intrigue, the patience of waiting until there was a prospective catch, a special technique, the power of the hooked fish, and the enjoyment of the resulting meal. I would hate to depend on Izaak Walton's instructions on fishing for salmon or trout, but his description of fishing for river carp is very similar to our efforts at the sucker holes. First, to bait them ahead of time, then to use small worms or a small wad of "paste" on the hook. He also describes some of the frustration I have often felt: "You must put on a very large measure of patience; especially to fish for a river carp: I have known a very good fisher angle diligently four or six hours in a day, for three or four days together, and not have a bite."

One of the turning points in my life was when I got my first bait-casting outfit. This purchase, using some of the earnings from my boiled peanut sales, was the culmination of months of desire, conversation, study of outdoor magazines, and comparative analysis of advertisements for rods, reels, and lures. Finally, when I was ready to get serious, I turned to the Sears, Roebuck catalogue and placed my order for a four-foot Shakespeare rod and a Pflueger reel.

When at last the rural mail carrier made the precious delivery, I took a few Heddon and Creek Chub wooden plugs and began to haunt the local millponds in search of largemouth bass. At that time private farm ponds were rare. The millers would permit us to fish in the millponds if our families were among the customers who brought wheat or corn to them to be ground into flour, meal, or grits. Since Daddy spread his business around, there were two or three millponds where my friends and I were welcomed.

We boys would ride our ponies or bicycles the long distances to the mill and, as a necessary courtesy, stop to ask permission to fish in the pond or in the very large pool that almost always formed just below the millrace. The atmosphere inside the mill was fascinating, with the great turning pulleys, flat belts driving a multitude of little machines, and the final grain products sifting down at different places from the rotating grinding wheels and oscillating screens. We always stuck our hands into the falling meal, quite hot from the friction of the millstone, and ate with relish. I never ate cold meal in Mama's kitchen or heated any in the stove; it would not have been the same. After a few minutes we were ready to fish, but some of the lonely millers were quite loquacious and had to spend a while talking even with little boys, discussing the weather, giving fishing advice based on recent experience, or idly inquiring about our families.

At the pond we would begin casting, from the shore or from a boat, trying to place the plugs as near as possible to snags, brush, or lily pads where the bass were most likely to be hiding. At first I spent a substantial portion of my time unsnarling backlashes or retrieving my treble-hook bait after an inaccurate cast. My friends and I could not afford to lose a plug. If we were hung up too solidly to shake the hooks loose, we would have to ruin a good pool by swimming over to release them.

With practice, while fishing or throwing at a bucket in our backyard, I became more and more able to keep the plugs in the water where they belonged. We had good luck fishing this way for bass, because there wasn't much competition. Most fishermen used cane poles and fished deep with worms or minnows, and the per capita use of bait-casting gear was quite low. There was always a great contest between me and my fishing companions over who could catch the most and largest bass. We eagerly tried new plugs whenever they were announced in the fishing and hunting magazines to see if we could improve our catch.

One that proved exceptionally effective was the Hawaiian Wiggler, a metal-headed rubber-skirted plug with a single weedless hook. It seemed to go anywhere without getting snagged; depending on the model, the arrangement of the skirt, and the speed of retrieval, the lure could be placed at almost any depth we desired. Bass were mesmerized by it. Because the lure rode over the submerged snags, we began to cast increasingly in the creeks, which were filled with logs, limbs, and brush. Although we didn't catch as many fish, the quest was more exciting, as the jack or bass, using submerged hiding places, obstacles, and the current to their advantage, had much more of a fighting chance. Also, there was a greater mystery about what might be found in a deep running stream buried in the shadowy woods than in a man-stocked millpond.

Another lure that added a new dimension to fishing was the Jitterbug, a floating wooden plug with a wide concave tin mouth. When retrieved, it would wobble back and forth and disturb the surface with its antics. We would cast it into a likely place, let it lie still for perhaps half a minute until all the wavelets subsided, and then give it a good twitch or short pull. This would result in the most explosive strikes as the larger bass came up expecting to make a juicy meal of an injured fish, a frog, or some other small animal swimming above its head. The surface wobblers and popping lures were especially effective at night. The powerful thrust of a feeding fish from out of the dark depths, sometimes leaping into the air at my feet or almost under our boat, never failed to startle and thrill me.

About once a year my daddy took me on a fishing trip to a more distant place, usually farther south in Georgia. We made a couple of such visits to the Okefenokee Swamp in the southeastern corner of our state, near the Florida line and not far from the Atlantic Ocean but cut off from the east coast by sand hills. The swamp is a shallow dish of six hundred square miles of water and thousands of islands, mostly of floating peat, on which thick stands of cypress and other trees grow. These peat islands are the "trembling earth" from which the area got its Indian name. Stained with tannin, the water has a reddish-brown color, but was considered by all the fishermen to be pure enough to drink.

We stayed at the only fish camp around the western edge of the swamp, owned by a man named Lem Griffis. His simple pine-board bunkhouses, with screens instead of windowpanes, could accommodate about twenty guests. As we sat around an open fire at night, Lem was always eager to regale us with wild tales about the biggest bear, the prettiest woman, or a catch of so many fish they had to haul in water to fill up the hole left in the lake. His stories were honed by repetition so that the buildup and punch line equaled those of any professional entertainer. We listened and laughed for hours even when we were hearing the same yarn for the second or third time. His regular guests would urge, "Tell us about the city lady who thought her son might drown."

Lem would wait awhile until enough others joined in the request, and then describe in vivid and heart-rending tones the anguish of a mother who was afraid to let her only child near the swamp. "I finally said, 'Ma'am, I can guarantee you the boy won't drown. I've been here all my life and never heerd of anybody drowning in this here swamp.' The lady was quite relieved." There was always a long pause, until Lem finally added, "The 'gators always get them first."

The camp was located near the shore of Billy's Lake, out of which flows the Suwannee River, a beautiful stream that eventually wanders out of Georgia and across the entire Florida peninsula into the Gulf of Mexico. Sometimes we cast or trolled in the lake among the numerous alligators, whose heads would surface quite near us and then submerge quietly as the alligators moved on without a ripple underneath the water. When we inadvertently hooked a small one—two or three feet long—we hastily cut our line, trying to save as much of it as possible. We did catch largemouth bass and jack, and quite often had an especially fierce struggle with a mudfish, or bowfin. After such a good fight, we were always disappointed to see what it was, but at Lem's request we would keep some of the largest ones for him to trade off with his neighbors, who liked to eat them.

To me, the most fearsome creature was the alligator gar, a vicious-looking fish with savage teeth. Since we were not fishing with steel leaders, the gar frequently severed our lines. I was almost willing to sacrifice a spoon or other lure in order to avoid having to remove the creatures from my hook and risk losing a finger. They seemed to cruise just under the surface; when one approached the boat we always slapped a paddle in the water to force it to leave. Lem told some frightful stories about the gar fish, and I was inclined to believe him. Later, I checked the fishing encyclopedia and found that the largest alligator gar ever caught was more than ten feet long and weighed 302 pounds. For once, Lem hadn't embellished his descriptions.

We also had good luck still-fishing in Billy's Lake with cane poles for warmouth perch or bream, using pond worms, crawfish tails, or catalpa worms for bait. Most of the time, however, we preferred to go into the more remote wilderness areas of the Okefenokee. Lem's sons were our guides as we moved deep into the swamp each day. Our boats were long and narrow, specially built to squeeze between the snags and cypress roots along the water trails that had been chopped out to connect the numerous small open places among the trees. Because a very slow but steady current moved throughout the swamp toward Billy's Lake, there was no stagnant water there. Fish were plentiful and we caught a lot of them, but one of the attractions of the trip was to see Lem's sons use a casting rod. Whenever we stopped on one of the floating islands for lunch, they would take the boat a short distance from shore and, on each cast, place the lures within an inch or two of their chosen target point, underneath an overhanging bush, between the roots, or among the lily pads. They knew just what kind of lure action would appeal to a fish, and it was amazing to see how quickly they caught enough bass for all of us to eat.

As we moved along these waterways we saw many kinds of birds, including ducks, terns, herons, egrets, ibises, kingfishers, hawks, pileated woodpeckers, and on rare occasions, a bald eagle. The reflection on the surface of the still, dark water was practically perfect, and in some of our photographs it was later impossible to tell which side was up or down. When we were still, the silence would at first seem absolute, but then we would begin to hear a myriad of sounds coming from the surrounding swamp. The Griffis boys could identify the cry of each bird and animal. I remember particularly the bellow of the bull alligators and the deathly silence that for a few moments always followed.

Late one afternoon, one of the other guest fishermen shot an enormous snapping turtle and brought it back to camp. Lem and his boys hung it up on a tree limb and dressed it, easily removing the edible portions by running a sharp knife around the inside edge of the ridged shell. After cutting up the choice-looking meat into small pieces, we set a large washpot half-filled with water on the campfire and added the turtle, two or three chickens, some onions, and later a few vegetables and seasoning. In a couple of hours we all ate several bowlfuls of the turtle soup, a supper few of us would ever forget.

We returned home from the Okefenokee with enough cleaned and iced fish to supply all our kinfolks and neighbors. Sometimes Daddy would take a portion of our catch to the freezer locker in Plains to be kept for a future party and fish fry for his friends. One of my favorite aspects of each trip was telling Mama and my sisters about my part for a few days in a man's world. I proudly described our experiences, most of them not needing much enhancing to make them interesting.

A few miles north of the Okefenokee was the small village of Hortense, not far from where the Little Satilla River joins the Big Satilla. This was one of my father's favorite fishing spots; he tried to go there every year with some of his associates in the farming, peanut, and fertilizer business. On two occasions he took me with him, when I was about ten or twelve years old. We stayed in a big and somewhat dilapidated wood-frame house on a small farm near the banks of the Little Satilla. The house had been built to accommodate at least three generations of a family, but now there were just a man named Joe Strickland, his wife, Shug, and two daughters, one a pretty girl in her teens named Jessie. Joe was the guide for our group of about six people. The women cooked our meals and plowed mules in the small fields during the day while we were fishing. It was the first time I had seen women plowing, which I found quite surprising, but they all seemed to take it as a matter of course.

The Little Satilla is a serpentine stream in the flattest part of Georgia's coastal plain, weaving back and forth from one bend to another. A number of oxbow lakes had been left behind when the river changed its course. We fished in the area of what was called Ludie's Lake. On the outside of almost every bend of the stream there was a deep hole, often cut into a steep bank, and on the opposite side of the river was usually a sand bar. There were not as many bushes and snags in the water as we had around Plains, and the bottom was sandy and firm.

I had never done this kind of fishing before. We spent our time in the stream, wading halfway across it to fish in the deep water under the overhanging banks, using the longest cane poles we could handle. I wore cutoff overall pants with no shirt, and tied my fish stringer to one of the belt loops. Joe and I were the only ones barefoot; all the other men had on old tennis shoes or brogans to protect their tender feet. We fished with large pond worms and caught mostly "copperheads," which were very large bluegill bream whose heads, when mature, assumed a bronze color, perhaps from the tannin stain in the water.

The group of us would string out along the river, my daddy and I usually fishing within sight of each other. We always had a fairly good idea of what luck each fisherman was having. For some reason I have never understood, the men would shout "Billy McKay!" when they had on a nice fish. The words would roll through the woods as all of us smiled; the enthusiasm of the voices was contagious. Each night after supper I went to bed early, but the men stayed up to play poker and to have a few drinks. Sometimes they made enough noise to wake me up, but I didn't mind. It seemed to make me more a member of the party if they weren't trying to stay quiet just for me. Most often I was tired enough to go right back to sleep.

While we were in the river Joe moved quietly from one of us to another, just to make sure we were properly spaced and to give advice about the water and some of the bypasses we had to take around obstacles. He tried—successfully—to build up a reputation as something of a character and always gave the group something to talk about during the months between our visits to Hortense.

Once we were walking single file along a path toward the river and Joe called, "Watch out for the barbed wire!"

One of the men said, "Joe, you didn't look down. How do you know wire's there?"

Joe said, "My feet will flatten briers or thorns, but I can feel barbed wire when I step on it."

Another time, when we had to cross the river, Joe walked down the bank, entered the water with his pole and lunch over his head, and moved smoothly across toward the other side with the water never higher than his armpits. The next man, whom I called Mr. Charlie, was the oldest in the group, and he stepped off in the water and immediately went down out of sight. He came up sputtering, and shouted, "Joe, how deep is it here?"

Joe replied, "Oh, I reckon it's about fifteen foot." Joe could tread water like a duck, and just wanted to demonstrate his prowess so that none of us would forget.

Then came my most memorable day. Late one afternoon, after a good day of fishing, Daddy called me over and asked me to keep his string of fish while he went up the river to talk to one of his friends. I tied it on with mine on the downstream side of me while I kept fishing, enjoying the steady pull of the current on our day's catch. It wasn't long before I watched my cork begin to move slowly and steadily up under a snag and knew I had hooked a big one. After a few minutes I had a large copperhead bream in my hands, but as I struggled with it and wondered how I was going to hold the fish while untying the stringer, a cold chill went down my spine. I realized that the tugging of the current on the stringers was gone, as were all our fish! My belt loop had broken.

I threw my pole up on the nearest sand bar and began to dive madly into the river below where I had been standing.

Then I heard Daddy's voice calling my nickname, "Hot," he said, "what's wrong?"

"I've lost the fish, Daddy."

"All of them? Mine too?"

"Yes, sir." I began to cry, and the tears and water ran down my face together each time I came up for breath.

Daddy was rarely patient with foolishness or mistakes. But after a long silence, he said, "Let them go." I stumbled out on the bank, and he put his arms around me.

It seems foolish now, but at that time it was a great tragedy for me. We stood there for a while, and he said, "There are a lot more fish in the river. We'll get them tomorrow." He knew how I felt and was especially nice to me for the next couple of days. I worshipped him.

At Joe's home we ate fish and whatever was in season. Both times I went, our breakfasts consisted of biscuits, grits, green beans, and fried fish. It was the first time I had eaten green beans early in the morning, but soon it seemed like a normal thing to do. With plenty of butter and sugar-cane syrup to go with the piles of hot biscuits, we never got up from the table hungry.

When I left Joe's place to come home, his daughter Jessie told me that she had brought me a going-away present. She then handed me a baby alligator about a foot long, whom I immediately named Mickey Mouse. When I returned to our house I installed him inside a large truck tire, partially buried in the ground and covered with boards. For a number of weeks

I fed him earthworms, crickets, wasp larvae, and anything else he would eat. My friends were quite envious of my new pet. Unfortunately, the cats and dogs around the farm were also interested. One morning I went out to feed Mickey and found the boards pushed aside and the little alligator missing. Daddy was very considerate and said he was sure the 'gator had escaped into the nearest swamp. I was not quite naïve enough to believe him, but from then on I stayed on the lookout for my 'gator whenever I was fishing or exploring along the neighborhood creeks.

Almost fifty years later, after I left the White House, I stopped by Hortense, Georgia, to try to find the place we used to visit. I couldn't remember the roads or even Joe's last name when I inquired of some folks in the service station. I did recall the pretty daughter, but one of the men told me: "We had a lot of pretty daughters around here." At least I remembered the bare feet, barbed wire, good catches, lost fish, Mickey Mouse, and green beans for breakfast. When I described some of these things to the postmistress, she said, "You must mean Joe Strickland. Miss Jessie still lives at the same place, but in a new house." I followed her directions and found the cottage in what had been the large yard of the old house, just a few steps from the Little Satilla River.

Miss Jessie responded to our knock on her door, saying, "Won't y'all come in!" even before she knew who we were. We had a good time reminiscing about old times. Both her parents had died long ago, and she was intrigued that I remembered so much about them. She said she remembered my visits: "I told a lot of people while you were in the White House that the President had fished with my daddy."

To which I replied, "When I was in the White House, I told several people the same thing about yours. Many of the most highly publicized events of my presidency are not nearly as memorable or significant in my life as fishing with my daddy and yours when I was a boy. Certainly, almost none of them was as enjoyable!"

LEARNING
TO
HUNT

Before I was big enough to handle my own gun or even a BB rifle, I was serving proudly as a pickup boy for my father during the frigid hours of the winter dove shoots. Daddy would always call me long before daylight, about 4:30 A.M. sun time. Outside it was remarkably still, except for the roosters, who had often begun to crow. We carried to the truck his guns and a seat made of an empty shotgun-shell box, holding a half case of shells and some lightwood splinters. Sometimes, after ceremonially checking to be sure it was empty, he would let me carry one of the guns.

Our first stop was at a prearranged gathering place, either one of the stores downtown in Plains or perhaps a farmer's house. I'd be filled with a great excitement as we went in to gather around a potbellied stove or a warm hearth fire. Most of the time I was the only child there. There was a feeling of exclusive masculinity within the group when the men talked about hunting and laughed a lot at jokes and ribald accounts of sex adventures that they assumed I could not understand. The men drank big cups of coffee, sometimes laced with spirits, while I was offered a Coca-Cola or perhaps a cup of hot chocolate. It was at such moments that my father was most exalted in my mind.

After a half hour or so, we traveled in as few vehicles as possible to the designated field, where its owner, our host for the morning, described the layout and gave instructions on how to reach the different "stands." With lanterns or flashlights we found our way by the edge of woods, or along a fence, hedgerow, or brush-covered terrace, expecting that some of the latecomers would fill in the less desirable spaces in the center of the open spaces to keep the doves moving if they flew in to light. The fields were relatively small then, because land-breaking and cultivation were done with mules and horses; the large plots of today's tractor cultivation simply did not exist. With shouts and light signals we made sure we were not too close to our neighbors, identified them, and settled down to wait for the first signs of daybreak. If the weather was too cold to bear, Daddy kindled a small fire and trusted me to gather enough sticks around our site to keep it going.

The night was still pitch-black. We could hear the call of owls in the more distant deep woods and then the small killdeers landing and taking off in the field. Later came the sound of crows in the distance and unseen songbirds among the nearby trees. We were so still that some of them would land almost on top of us. Sometimes the song of a lonely bobwhite quail intimated in its urgent call that it had been separated from the covey and not reunited before last night settled in. Then, as daybreak approached, we would hear the earliest whistle of unseen doves' wings overhead.

After a few minutes the sound of the first shots reverberated across the brightening field, usually around 6:00 A.M., and the dove shoot was underway. The hunters were well within gun range of one another; spent birdshot rained down harmlessly all around us after their skyward trajectory was completed. If anyone grew careless and endangered a neighbor by shooting too low, it was a serious matter indeed, warranting an angry shout of condemnation and a damaged reputation.

Without being told, I learned very early not to comment on Daddy's missed shots, except to phrase a quiet excuse for him. "That one swerved just as you shot, Daddy." "He was pretty far away." "I saw the feathers come out of him." "I think he went down way over yonder in those bushes." "They're sure flying high this morning." I didn't have to do this too often, because Daddy was an experienced hunter and a good marksman; he brought down plenty of doves.

Many years later, after we had returned to Plains from my time in the Navy, I took my own sons hunting. The first time the youngest, Jeffrey, went with me to pick up doves, he didn't know how to protect the sensitivities of his father. During the past two decades I had rarely shot doves and was having a very frustrating morning. Time after time I fired my 20-gauge shotgun, but the doves never wavered in their flight.

Without my noticing, Jeff had picked up the empty shells and carefully arranged them in the dirt.

A couple of my friends walked by us and asked, "How are you doing?"

"Not too well," I replied.

Then Jeffrey spoke up: "Daddy has shot eleven times and ain't hit nothing."

Thanks a lot, son.

When I was a child my main job was to mark where my father's birds fell and to run and pick them up when other birds were not coming in. This assignment wasn't easy if a bird was wounded but still able to run and fly short distances. Even those lying still were sometimes indistinguishable in the light-gray frostbitten grass or among empty corn shucks, which looked almost like doves with closed wings. On one memorable occasion, a redtail hawk swooped down just ahead of me and flew up with our dove. Daddy waited until it was safely away from me and then brought down both birds with a long shot. We talked about that for a long time afterwards, with my father cautioning me not to forget that ordinarily hawks do a lot of good and should not be killed. I believe that he felt somewhat guilty about shooting this one, but he never said so.

Even at a great distance, we could identify the other hunters, mostly from their hats. Only a few times in my life did I ever see my father outdoors without a hat, and most of the other men considered themselves partially undressed if they were bareheaded. Headgear became quite distinctive, almost like hallmarks, among the men of our community. This was, of course, before the days of the now ubiquitous and standardized baseball caps, whose only distinguishing feature is whether they bear advertisements for farm tractors, bulldozers, fertilizer, pesticides, snuff, or chewing tobacco.

After a couple of hours the shooting became more sporadic; the experienced hunters with the best stands usually had a good mess of doves by then. Most often my father and I were among the first to leave. Daddy wanted to be at his work, and after I was five years old and going to school he had to deliver me to the classroom. These were among my proudest moments: At times I would leave a few feathers casually attached to my jacket or trousers to prove that I had been hunting with my daddy. I don't remember any explanation or excuse ever being offered to the teachers for my tardiness—hunting was a routine part of life in those days.

A little later, Daddy let me use an old single-shot .410 shotgun that he had borrowed from a neighbor, and placed me on the dove field near him. Watching me carefully, he would call out a warning when a dove approached my stand and give me constructive advice after I had missed the bird. "You shot too soon." "Lead them a little more." "Let your gun keep on swinging until after you pull the trigger." "Hold your cheek firmly down on the gun stock." "Try to keep both eyes open if you can." I soon began to hit a dove every now and then, with gratifying congratulations from my father.

By the time I was ten years old I had graduated from flips, slingshots, and BB guns to own a .22 caliber Remington pump rifle and a bolt-action 4-shot model .410 shotgun from Sears, Roebuck. I was holding down my own stand on the dove fields, sometimes going with older friends even without Daddy along.

And Rachel's husband, Jack Clark, was taking me out hunting every now and then for bobwhite quail, which were plentiful around our house.

We did not call them quail in those days but either "birds" or "pottages" (from the *partridges* of our European forebears). When Daddy said, "I'm going bird hunting," we never thought he meant doves, ducks, turkey, or anything else but quail. We all considered this pursuit to be the ultimate in hunting: The combination of bird dogs, guns, etiquette, the stark beauty of the late-fall and winter woods, the fascinating stories derived from the always unpredictable excursions, the close comradeship among the hunters as they walked along behind the dogs (for safety, Daddy would never shoot with more than one other person at a time), and the delicious quail recipes that were sources of pride within each farm family, all combined to give these experiences a special flavor.

On our farm the production of crops and livestock was paramount, but never incompatible with good hunting. We always had two or three bird dogs, one of them often a puppy that was being trained. We never owned a cat, although some were permitted to live around the barn or outhouses to catch mice and do battle with the large wharf rats which, before Warfarin and D-con, were almost impervious to any existing control methods except a .22 rifle. Our dogs, on the other hand, were considered almost members of the family. They were not babied as personal pets, were never fed so much as to become overweight, and were not allowed by Daddy inside our house. But within those bounds the bird dogs were special, and we let them know it.

Although they were taught to obey orders meticulously, they were not trained in a fancy way. Daddy didn't teach them to "lie down," "sit," "heel," or "stay," because these commands were not considered necessary on the farm. Dogs were shut in a kennel only when a bitch was in heat; otherwise, they ran loose. At a relatively early age they were taught to stop instantly when ordered to "whoa," and to come when they heard "here." "Careful" and "close" were important commands when birds were believed to be nearby, and "Come in here" with a hand signal was used to indicate the side of the trail to be covered next by the dog. Repeated use of the word "dead" kept the dog in the immediate area of a downed bird, and "fetch" was used to have the bird brought to the dog's owner.

Daddy was quite stern with a dog who would not obey, often saying, "If a dog won't mind, he's not worth having." I hate to think of his assessment of my own two bird dogs today; they will point quail but are with me in the coverts too seldom to be well trained. Daddy was gentle, however, with a young dog or one he believed to have made an honest mistake in the field. My father did not believe in the methods described by the sporting magazines for teaching dogs to point in the yard. Ours learned from experience, among the plentiful wild game around our home.

When trained, they were dear to us and had a remarkable monetary value as well. Even during the Depression years on the farm, when cash money was scarce and most trade was by barter or on credit until harvesttime, urban standards applied to the price of good bird dogs. Although Daddy would no more consider selling one of our best dogs than one of us children, I remember that once he was offered several hundred dollars for a locally renowned liver-spot female pointer—equivalent in some of those poorest crop years to the net annual income from a two-horse farm.

Some of the most disturbing family times were when one of our prized dogs was missing; then my normally calm father grew uncharacteristically distraught. If the dog had gotten lost during a hunt, everyone went to the area to whistle and call until it was found. If we were still unsuccessful before nightfall, Daddy would lay one of his old sweaters or hunting coats on the ground where he had last seen the dog and place a pan of water beside it. In most cases the missing animal would be lying on the garment the next morning. But if one of our dogs just didn't show up by feeding time, the presumption was that it had been stolen or bitten by a rattlesnake. In most cases, a snakebite was not eventually fatal, and the dog would come home and lie around for a week or two with face or head swollen to more than twice its normal size, often developing a large sore before it finally recovered.

Bird dog theft was the worst threat of all. In our part of the country it was regarded as much worse than stealing horses— almost as bad as kidnapping children. If a stranger showed too much interest in one of our dogs, we would be particularly careful in watching it for a few days. The thief who succeeded could never keep a stolen dog anywhere around its former home, because good dogs were as well known within the community as people and would be recognized immediately if sighted. The general presumption was that some "foreigner" from far-off Albany, Columbus, or Atlanta was guilty.

Daddy was not a superstitious man, but he believed in fortunetellers when it came to finding a lost bird dog—or at least he did not want to overlook the possibility that they might help. There were always a few around, and he would go from one to the other, following the cryptic advice he received as long as there was any chance. It seemed to me that he and his friends were inclined to remember the successes and forget the failures, so that each time another dog was lost they were hopeful all over again. One time Daddy took me with him to see a large black woman who lived alongside a country road with some brightly painted crescent moons, stars, and an enormous human hand tacked to the trees in front of her house. The lines in the palm of the wooden hand were carefully drawn, with words beside the main ones to signify LIFE, LOVE, PAST, and FUTURE. I remember that she made us wait for a while before she would see us, which was a strange experience in itself for white people in a black woman's yard. When finally my father was invited in, I slipped through the door behind him into the darkened room. The fortuneteller, by her comments, seemed to identify the dog. After asking several questions, she said, "Mr. Earl, you ain't never gonna see that dog ag'in."

He paid her a dollar, and we left. We rode in silence for a while, and then Daddy said, "I expect she's right."

She was.

By the time I was big enough to tote a real shotgun, my use of our dogs was unrestricted, because my father and Jack had carefully trained me on hunting safety, proper manners, and the right way to treat each dog. With my bolt-action .410, I began to hunt by myself with just one dog at a time, usually a close-ranging setter bitch named Lady. One day, about a quarter of a mile east of our house, Lady pointed in a grove of scrub oak trees. I approached carefully, a large covey of quail flushed, and I fired somewhat blindly in the direction of the birds. One fell. This was one of my life's proudest moments. I picked up the quail and ran all the way home.

Daddy was working in the blacksmith shop, where I breathlessly described to him my great adventure. He shared my pride and then looked around and asked me: "Where's your gun?"

I had no idea. When I went back to look, I couldn't find the place where the covey had flushed. It was especially embarrassing that we had to ask several other people to help before we finally found the shotgun lying among some leaves where I had dropped it. I was thankful that my daddy never mentioned the abandoned gun again, at least to me.

I also hunted squirrels and rabbits by myself, the former with the .22 rifle and the latter with my .410 shotgun. For the first few years I still-hunted for squirrels, sitting quietly in the woods where there was a good stand of oak or hickory trees, or perhaps one of the increasingly rare chestnuts that had survived the blight, and waiting for one of the bushy-tailed creatures to show itself. When he ran or leaped through the trees, I would watch carefully until he stopped. If he saw me, the squirrel would often flatten himself against the tree trunk or a limb and then move around to keep the tree always between us. I learned to carry with me a long string, which I would tie to a bush. Then I'd move quietly to the other side of the tree, yank the string, and watch for the squirrel to hide from the noisy bush and move into view on my side.

Two or three gray squirrels made a good meal for our family. Fox squirrels were half again as large but not so common, and Daddy told me never to shoot at the flying squirrels, which were too small to eat and somewhat rare. They moved around mostly at night, but every now and then I would see one during daylight hours.

One day Daddy brought me a Boston bulldog puppy, whom I named Bozo. We were inseparable. He turned out to be not only a great pet but also the best squirrel dog in the neighborhood—better than any of the hounds owned by our neighbors. From then on, I walked through the woods with Bozo hunting squirrels. When he treed one, barking furiously, it was a simple matter to get on the other side of the tree and find my quarry.

Bozo became well known among other squirrel hunters in the neighborhood. Early one morning, two of my father's friends came by and borrowed my dog to go hunting. That night, Daddy drove up in his pickup and called me out in the yard. Bozo was lying in the back, dead. He had jumped out of the hunters' car while it was parked in front of a garage in Americus, become confused on the city streets, and been run over by a truck. Mama and Daddy tried to comfort me, but I didn't want to talk to anyone. I went down in the woods by myself to some places we had hunted together and said some prayers that my dog was safe and happy in heaven. Bozo was the only dog I ever owned as a child, and I kept his picture tacked to the wall of my room until I went off to college.

Rabbits were too plentiful around our fields, house, and garden, providing a lot of good hunting and eating for the people who lived around Archery. The only time I didn't shoot rabbits was while hunting quail. Daddy said if I let the bird dogs run rabbits and I shot them, the dogs would think that was part of their job and it would divert them from their primary responsibility.

This was one rule of my father's that Jack Clark found fit to ignore when he and I were hunting alone. He shot rabbits even in the presence of our dogs, and they didn't seem to acquire any worse habits. Mama would not cook a rabbit in the summertime—something to do with diet or pests or disease—but they were considered all right when the weather was cold.

Daddy was not a coon hunter and we never owned hound dogs, but on occasion he would go along on a fox hunt—primarily a white man's sport. In our area the fox hunt began by turning the hounds loose at night, then sitting around a campfire and listening to them. There is something special about a fire of any kind, particularly a campfire in the deep woods. Just looking at the colored flames and flickering shadows seems to arouse some instinct from prehistoric times, when gathering around a fire was the source of the clan's comfort and even survival, and where the earliest human conversations were heard on earth. During the leisurely hours of a fox hunt there was plenty of time for silence, a lot of philosophizing, drinking, and the identification and assessment of hounds' voices. The hunters did not expect to catch the foxes, and they knew that a good portion of the next day would have to be spent trying to find all the dogs.

Some of the men were consummate liars, although their tales were always begun in a quiet and unassuming way, as though they were true. Only at the end of a story, or maybe a few minutes afterward, would the listener realize he had been bamboozled.

"The other day I had the damndest experience of my life," one would start. "I was walking along Kinchafoonee Creek down near the Murray place looking for an old sow of mine, and seen a squirrel go out on a little limb that was lying out in the creek. It was kind of in an eddy, and there was a hickory nut caught in a fork of the limb. Just as the squirrel reached down to get the nut, a tremendous bass came up out of the water and swallowed the damn squirrel. I almost fell over backward, and had to sit down and think about what I had seen.

"After about five minutes there was a disturbance in the water, and I saw that bass come up and carefully put another hickory nut in the same place." Long pause. "First time I ever seen a fish squirreling."

Hunting coons and possums was a different proposition entirely. It was done for meat, the participants were usually black, and most of the night was spent walking through thick woods and swamps. Even as a young boy I was a sought-after companion when our adult neighbors went hunting for raccoons or opossums, because I was one of the best and most daring tree-climbers around. Mama wouldn't let me stay out all night before a day of school, but at other times I was free to join the hunters.

For that night, three or four men would pool their hound dogs. After the dogs went through a standard ceremony of sniffing and a little snarling and snapping, we were off with a lantern or two, carrying a five-cell flashlight we used only after the dogs had treed an animal. With just a little light from the sky we did without the lanterns in order to save kerosene; it was surprising how well we could see after our eyes became adjusted to the dark. When we hunted on our place, I was familiar with the territory and never got lost, but when we went farther afield it was not easy to know where we were. On clear nights I marked the stars and moon and kept up fairly well with our twists and turns, but in the cloudy or rainy times I had to depend on the others not to get lost. We always hoped that at least one of us hunters knew approximately where we were.

In the woods we walked single file, with enough room between us to keep the bent limbs ahead from springing back to hit the one next in line. But there were other hazards. Busting shins against a log or stump or running into one of the viciously thorned swamp blackberry vines could not be avoided for long. Every now and then we would stop to listen to the dogs; if they weren't hot on a scent we just kept moving along on our own chosen route. One of the men would whoop and holler on occasion so that the dogs would know where we were. Often one of the dogs would check in until it could see us and then disappear again. We all learned to recognize each hound's voice, so that it soon became superfluous to say, "That's old Red," or "Joe's onto somethin'." Still, we never failed to say it anyway.

When the tone or timbre of a dog's baying tightened up, we grew instantly alert and began to move in its direction. The hound's owner went forward and took charge, encouraging the dog with frequent shouts to move on and also to bay more often, giving us a more uninterrupted description of what was going on. The other dogs, previously scattered through the woods, would then converge on the leading hound. When we got close to the pack of dogs, we squatted down and waited for the finale: the treeing of the raccoon or opossum. There was a lot of guessing (in the form of absolutely positive assertions) about what was being chased, but most of the time it was impossible to be sure. Coons were more inclined toward the deep swamps, while possums preferred the kinds of trees that grow only in more sunshine around the edges of fields or along fences or hedgerows, such as persimmon or black cherry. If the dogs treed in a place for a while and then began another chase, we were pretty certain it was a coon, because coons were more willing and able than possums to leave a tree with a pack of dogs under it.

When we made our final move in to the furiously baying dogs, our path was a straight and fast one through briers, bogs, and streams. Sometimes it was difficult for me to keep up with the excited men. Under the tree, we would turn the beam of the flashlight up and search diligently until we saw the bright reflecting eyes shining back. There were times when we would find two or even three coons or possums in the same tree. They were never shot. Instead, the men would lift me up into the lower branches, I would climb until I reached the right limb and then shake it until the animal fell. If necessary, one of the grown men would help me. On some occasions this process would take more than an hour, but if the dogs' masters were very hungry for fresh meat or if it was almost daybreak, they would shorten the process by cutting down a relatively small and nonmarketable tree to bring their quarry to the ground.

Opossums, on the ground, would usually lie still and pretend to be dead, but the raccoons would back up, face their attackers, and fight until captured. Normally, the coon or possum was soon caught and put into a burlap bag, ideally with minimal injury to all concerned. Then we would induce the excited hounds to begin another chase. But if we made a mistake and let a live bobcat hit the ground, the dogs were in serious trouble. There was a standard joke about the man who climbed a tree and grabbed a bobcat by mistake. After a few minutes of furious scratching and clawing, the man yelled out, "Just shoot up here amongst us—I'd rather take my chances with the bullets!"

Our minimum goal was to catch one animal for each family represented in the hunt, but sometimes luck wasn't with us and some of the men went home empty-handed and disappointed. First priority went to whoever owned the dog that struck the trail of the animals we caught. At our house we didn't eat these animals because Mama wouldn't cook them, but I have eaten them many times at other places. It was advisable to keep them caged up for a week or two and fed sweet potatoes or similar vegetables until any remnant of their dubious wild diet was gone. Then one could be sure they were "fitten to eat."

A white family that lived about a half mile from our house had some good hounds and loved to hunt with them. It was also generally known that some pretty good moonshine was produced on their farm; from our front porch we would watch the steady stream of automobiles and pickup trucks visiting there for a few days whenever a new batch had been cooked off. The revenuers caught Mr. Bob fairly regularly, and he was fined and sometimes gone for a few months, but his business seemed to thrive in between these interruptions. He was not condemned by his neighbors. Although Prohibition had been repealed, our state was still dry and there was a good bit of sympathy for a few respectable people who were willing to provide for some of the human needs in the neighborhood, in spite of legal risks to themselves.

Whiskey stills were artfully concealed in the most remote locations, near a stream of good water and where the necessary fire and smoke were screened as thoroughly as possible from any aerial observation. A few times the revenue agents came to notify Daddy that they had discovered a moonshine still on some of his land, and later we would go to the secluded spot and look at the equipment the revenuers had demolished. Sometimes the 'shiners were caught; most of the time they escaped. They devised all kinds of ways to tell that someone had come down a path leading to the still. Then they would abandon the place, or observe it from a distance until it was destroyed or the intruder was identified as an innocent passerby who failed to reappear after a suitable interval.

One night we were coon hunting with a couple of our black neighbors and Mr. Bob when the dogs struck a trail and began to follow it down one of the branches west of his house. We all sat down to listen, but Mr. Bob seemed to become more and more nervous as treeing became imminent. When we finally went to the dogs, they were under a tree right at his moonshine still. There was a lot of joking, laughing, and some embarrassment because I was there. We got the coon, and all swore to keep mum about the exact location of its capture. I honored my oath; I didn't even tell my father about it until after I was graduated from college.

Although the Plains area was not on any major flyway, we still had plenty of good duck hunting during the cold winter months. I seldom went to the larger lakes of the Flint and Chattahoochee rivers, which were about fifty miles east and west of our home; even the nearby millponds were not as attractive as the more natural and isolated places. Our swamps, with their remoteness, good cover, and plentiful supply of acorns and other feed, provided an excellent home for the indigenous wood ducks, and during the winter months we would have some scattered flights of migrating teal and mallards come in to stay for a few days. In most of the flat swampy areas, there were a number of permanent "lakes" left where the creek had changed its course, and the eddy or backwater portions of the streams also provided plenty of water for ducks to hide and feed.

We had some favorite places for duck hunting in the swamp lakes and would usually seek them long before dawn, leaving home to go in to shoot during the early morning hours. At other times a friend and I drifted down the larger creeks in a small flat-bottomed plywood boat I built, one of us steering with a few quiet paddle strokes in the stern while the other sat in the bow with the shotgun, ready for startled waterfowl to flush. We didn't get as many ducks while moving down the streams as we did in the swamp lakes, but there was a chance to see much more of the creek wildlife as we traveled long miles through the center of the swamp as silently as possible.

Looking back on my hunting days, it seems obvious that the excitement and challenge of hunting was closely related to the acquisition of food. There was never any question about the morality of hunting, but neither was there any acceptance of killing for the sake of a trophy. Landowners, large and small, thought of wild game as one of the important products of the farm, and studied and applied good conservation practices to enhance the value of this harvest in the proper seasons.

These measures were even confirmed by our religious beliefs. At least once a year in all the churches, the minister offered a sermon on stewardship, in which the responsibilities and joys of landownership were emphasized. Even during the Depression years, when many marginal farm families were on the verge of starvation, their prayers of thanksgiving for the land, streams, and woods were devout and sincere. Often, when I am in a particularly beautiful or isolated place, a vivid image comes to my mind of bowed heads, quiet prayer, and old-fashioned church hymns, as I remember the habits of my youth.

DANGERS
IN
THE WOODS

I had two main worries when I was in the deeper woods and swamps by myself or with other boys: getting lost, and being bitten by a rattlesnake or water moccasin. Being bitten was a more constant anxiety—always threatening to be fatal, because the venom was likely to have several hours to act before the victim could expect to get from a remote swamp to a hospital to receive antivenom serum. All of us learned quite early in life to be vigilant in the fields and along the streams, constantly looking before each step, so that it became a lifetime habit almost like breathing.

For some reason, I was never very worried about the poisonous moccasins when I swam in the local creeks, even when we knew such snakes to be in the vicinity. We convinced ourselves that moccasins couldn't bite in the water. But when my friends and I went down the streams in small boats, we might pass under water moccasins sunning on overhanging limbs or small trees. We would see several of the snakes on an average outing but kept the canoe well clear of them. A continuing debate was what we would do if one of the reptiles should drop into the boat—whether to jump overboard or perhaps to beat a hole in the bottom of the craft with a paddle while trying to kill the startled and angry snake. I always planned to leave the boat.

One day my cousin Hugh, a neighbor named Kit, and I were hiking through the woods and stopped at the little pool that my daddy had built in the swamp about a mile behind our house, an oblong wooden box about four feet wide and deep, and twelve feet long, with a small stream running through it. That was where he had taught me to swim, before I was four years old. Since the little pool was near several large fields, it was convenient for a quick cooling off whenever we had a chance. This time we saw a large moccasin swimming around. While we started hitting at the snake with sticks, Hugh stumbled over the edge of the pool and fell in. He scrambled out so quickly that we always accused him afterwards of not even getting his clothes wet. After that scare, of course, we let the cottonmouth get away.

We frequently found snakes around our yard or under the house, and except for king snakes and rat snakes, which we thought hunted rattlers and rats respectively, we generally killed them. Even if they weren't poisonous, they were unwelcome, since most of them lived on eggs or baby chicks and ducklings.

Rattlesnakes like the warmth of sunlight and would often be found lying in open pathways or around the edges of cultivated fields. One disturbing characteristic of these snakes is that their odor seems to be very similar to that of the bobwhite quail, and trained bird dogs will sometimes point them (which is probably why so many dogs get bitten). Early during one bird season, in November, one of our dogs came to a firm point in a patch of blackberry bushes while I was hunting with my mother's brother Lem. When we walked in ahead of the dogs for the covey rise, we found a large rattlesnake instead. It was coiled to strike, and its rattlers began to sing as we stood, amazed, within striking distance. A shock, almost of paralysis, went through my body. Uncle Lem quickly shot the snake, and I nearly became nauseated when I saw it thrashing around in the grass. I even thought for a few minutes about giving up bird hunting for good.

Twenty-five years later, Rosalynn and I confronted a similar danger. During the mid-1960s, we built a small fishpond on our Webster County farm about seven miles northwest of Plains, stocked it with bluegills and largemouth bass, and made plans to enjoy fishing there during the following year. Weeds and briers soon began growing up around the edges, and so we went over to clean out a pathway near the water. As Rosalynn was pregnant that summer, she could do only light work. While working on the dam we saw an otter swimming across the small lake and realized that our yearling fish were already being harvested rapidly by one of their most voracious natural enemies. We went to the pickup truck, got my .22-caliber rifle, and moved quietly back onto a bluff overlooking the head of the pond. I shot the otter and then led the way around the edge of the water back toward the dam. All of a sudden, behind me, Rosalynn began screaming in obvious terror.

When I whirled around, she was about fifteen yards away, backed up as far as she could go and almost surrounded by overhanging swamp blackberry vines, which grow five or six feet tall and are always covered with especially cruel thorns. Between her and the pond was a large water moccasin, crawling directly toward her, either angry or confused. He was less than five feet from her when I saw him. There was no limb or other club around, so I had to resort to the rifle. My first shot broke its back, and the vicious snake began to thrash around at her feet, apparently still lunging toward her. It was pure luck that my second shot blew its head off. Rosalynn collapsed in my arms when I reached her. We'll never forget that snake writhing in its death throes almost under her.

Another close call would have had more historic consequences. One day during the second year I was President, we were home for a weekend. Rosalynn and I were walking up and down the rows of one of our favorite fields, hunting arrow-heads. The crop had been harvested, and several subsequent rains had packed the earth, leaving many small pieces of flint completely bare and often exposed on little pedestals of dirt. Our eyes were fixed on the ground, looking for Indian artifacts. As I reached the end of the field and changed direction, I found my foot within eighteen inches of a huge rattlesnake, coiled among some dead grass and poised to strike. Its rattles began to sing a deadly song and I leaped backward and fell down, yelling for Rosalynn to be careful. When we were well clear of the snake and the danger was over, we examined the reptile. It was an old one, with twelve rattles. No harm was done, but the spine-tingling sensation lasted a long time. I could just imagine the headlines describing my dire fate if I hadn't been lucky enough to see that snake before it struck me.

During bygone days and also quite recently, I have known of several people who were bitten by rattlesnakes in the Plains community. A few of them died. Although these were isolated instances that occurred over a lifetime in the woods, during snake season in the South—when the weather is warm—it is good to be constantly alert. We always wear boots or heavy chaps, and I carry a stout stick when I'm hiking. It is easy to overemphasize the danger, because any close encounter with a rattlesnake makes a lasting impression.

Rattlers were a regular part of our lives except when cold weather forced them to hibernate, and the subject of many hours of conversation even during the winter months. These loathsome creatures are still fascinating to many people. In the winter the snakes hibernate in gopher holes, deep in the ground. Hunters insert a rubber hose down into these burrows, put their ear against the opening, and listen for the telltale buzz of an angry rattlesnake. A small amount of gasoline poured into the hole will force the snake to emerge, whereupon it can be picked up with a loop on the end of a stick and dropped into a canvas bag. Each year in South Georgia there are two "rattle-snake roundups," attended by thousands of visitors who come to see the captured snakes. I went to this event in Whigham, Georgia, when I was running for governor and looking for crowds so that I could shake hands with as many potential voters as possible. All the snakes were bought by Ross Allen, operator of a large reptile show in Florida. In addition to displaying the creatures for tourists, he milks the venom from the snakes' fangs and sells it to pharmaceutical companies for the preparation of antitoxin used to counteract bites.

ॐ

Although an encounter with a poisonous reptile is more dramatic in the telling, it is, strangely, even more frightening to be lost. Because of the few times it has happened to me, I've developed a strong determination while wandering in wild or wooded areas to remain aware of distances, directions, topography, landmarks, stream flow, altitude, and other markers that might help me reach my destination or at least return to my starting point. I carry a compass in unfamiliar territory, and even in cities I feel somewhat uncomfortable if I don't know the direction of north.

When I was quite young, perhaps ten years old, my friend Rembert Forrest and I were fishing up and down Choctawhatchee Creek about three miles from home. There was no road to the creek; we had walked across fields and through woods to get there. The stream flowed generally toward the southwest, and since we knew about how far we were at all times from the place we had entered the swamp, we weren't worried about our ability to return home before dark. Late in the afternoon, while climbing over a newly fallen tree, we found that one of its limbs had pinned down the largest snapping turtle we had ever seen, weighing perhaps thirty or forty pounds. We decided we would carry it home to show to my folks and, using our fish stringers, tied its legs to a sapling. We then put the two ends of the pole on our shoulders and began to walk single file out of the swamp and southward toward home.

It was a cloudy day and we couldn't see the sun, but it was obvious when it went down. We began to hurry to avoid getting caught out at night, with my parents' not knowing where we were. After a half hour or so we were pleased to cross some human tracks in a field, but soon realized that they were our own. We had walked in a big circle, probably because of the load we were carrying.

We almost panicked for a few minutes but finally decided

to drop the turtle and try to walk in as straight a line as possible more to the west, where we knew there was a north-south road and a few houses. It was a much longer way home, but a shorter and more certain route to civilization. We would pick out a large tree outlined against the sky and walk to it, then another in the same direction, each time being careful not to detour in such a way as to risk another circular route. Around nine o'clock we came to more open fields and then to the road, where we turned south until we arrived at a house.

It was only then that I knew where we were, and I was very concerned to learn from the family that people were already searching for us. There were no telephones or electricity anywhere in this rural area, and the only vehicle these people had was a wagon. Rembert and I began to trot down the road. After a mile or so we met a truck with Jack Clark in it. He picked us up and we drove about six more miles back to our house. Daddy's anger was tempered by relief, and my punishment was not very severe—restriction to the yard for about a week, I believe.

Adults can get just as lost, often in familiar territory. My oldest son, Jack, was a star basketball player, and on a Friday night in the winter of 1964 our family planned to attend a game at the Plains High School gymnasium. Business was slack that time of the year at the warehouse, and so I locked the doors early and went out to a beaver pond near the Sumter-Webster county line to hunt ducks. It was very cold for South Georgia, with ice around the edge of the water; I had on insulated chest waders and warm clothes. Parking my pickup truck near the bridge, I walked less than half a mile northward into the Choctawhatchee swamp. Soon I was standing immobile in waist-deep water near the stump of a dead oak tree in the middle of the pond, not far from the beavers' den. I enjoyed the total solitude of the place and the apparent fearlessness of the crows, kingfishers, woodpeckers, and the sparrows and songbirds, some of whom would practically light on my shoulder. When the shadows lengthened, the beavers began to swim across the water with small willow limbs in their mouths. All the wild creatures seemed to ignore my presence, while I enjoyed theirs.

Shortly before sunset I shot a wood duck and then a

mallard, noted where they had fallen, and was preparing to leave the pond when it began raining steadily. Thunder rolled and lightning flashed as I waded over to pick up the ducks. I found the smaller one but couldn't see the mallard. Just as it was becoming too dark, I saw the other bird floating only a few feet away in an opening among the willows about twenty yards from the beaver dam. I pushed through the thick limbs, but with my next step I never felt bottom. As I sank, the icy water filled my waders and covered my head. Grabbing the bushes, I struggled back to where my feet found a hold on the bank, and broke a long limb to retrieve the duck. Although obviously quite cold, I was not particularly worried until I discovered that my flashlight would not work.

By then, it was too dark to see anything, even a tree right in front of my face. I held the gun crosswise at arm's length in front of me and bumped along through the swamp. I was wet and shivering, having great difficulty walking with waders full of water, and soon realized that I had no idea where I was or which direction to take. My body was almost instantly saturated with cold sweat. This was one of the worst moments of my life; for a while I couldn't think clearly.

There is no way to describe the mixed feelings of hopelessness, fear, and anger when a man realizes he is lost. Finding the way out is uncertain at best, and there is a sickening realization that your civilized skills are useless. The physical discomfort is exacerbated, at least, by the potential embarrassment of impending search parties and publicity. You imagine the headlines: JIMMY CARTER LOST IN THE WOODS. At worst, there is the vision of a dead, frozen body lying in the swamp. Rational thought is difficult. For some reason, you want to crash frantically ahead even though the right direction is unknown.

Finding a high place a foot or so above the water, I lay down on my back and elevated my feet enough to permit some of the water to run out of my waders onto the ground. Then I tried to analyze my predicament more calmly.

I knew the beaver pond drained into a number of small, somewhat parallel streams, all of which tended to converge and eventually run into the large creek. Stepping back into running water, I put my hand down in it to determine the direction of its movement and slowly followed the tiny stream. Stumbling, falling, and bumping into things, I was able to feel with my hand which course to follow, into larger and larger currents. Eventually the sound of the creek could be heard up ahead. Keeping the murmur of the creek on my left, I turned right toward the bridge and road and eventually encountered the steep embankment of the roadbed. I had to stop several times as I climbed it, but was finally leaning against the pickup, totally exhausted. It was hard for me to breathe, and I had to rest before I was strong enough to open the truck door. The heater took some of the chill off as I drove slowly home.

The next time I was in those woods, it was surprising to find how close I had been to the road, and how easy it was to move through the same swamp in the daylight, while warm and dry. I never went duck hunting again by myself without a waterproof flashlight and a compass, and before I go into strange territory I always try to study a map or aerial photograph.

Rosalynn is quite at home in the woods, but amazingly, she became lost in an eleven-acre tract just behind our house on the edge of Plains. A few years ago at the beginning of the Christmas holidays she walked out late one afternoon to find some holly berries, palmetto leaves, and smilax for decorations, but when she decided to return home she had lost direction. She pushed her way through brush and briers, ran into a barbed-wire fence, and became entangled in and had to crawl out of an almost impenetrable palmetto thicket. Finally she stopped, thought to listen to the sounds of traffic, and then walked in as straight a line as she could toward the highway. The next day when we went back together, she couldn't imagine where she had been. The wooded area looked relatively open and friendly to her, and the only palmetto patch was not more than fifty feet in diameter.

These kinds of experiences never dampened our love for the outdoors or our enjoyment of long hikes in the woods. They just taught us in unforgettable ways some of the habits and safety rules that our farming forefathers had been required to know so well as they hunted and trapped in deep woods when there were few fences or roads to help guide them on their way. Nowadays, when Rosalynn and I are moving through the North Georgia mountains or the South Georgia swamps, we ask each other questions about directions and landmarks. It is a good way to pass the time when we feel like talking, and helps us to stay alert and learn from each other.

The forests appear much more formidable from outside than within. It can be difficult to break through the outer fringes, because large tree limbs grow almost down to the ground, and, where sunlight can reach under the tall trees, there is usually a thick stand of smaller ones. Crowded between them are many kinds of bushes and briers. And intertwined in this plant thicket are vines, with all the growing things competing for the sun's rays that come through the open spaces. To pierce this maze can be a fearsome prospect, even for an experienced woodsman. A few yards from the edge, however, the crown of trees obstructs most of the sunshine, and the bed of leaves and needles helps to prevent the emergence and growth of smaller plants. Often it takes a little planning and effort for us to penetrate the fringe, but the interior woods are surprisingly open, and it is usually easy to walk freely and enjoy this special cathedral-like environment.

AMERICAN
SEASONS

NOTES
OF A
FLY-FISHERMAN

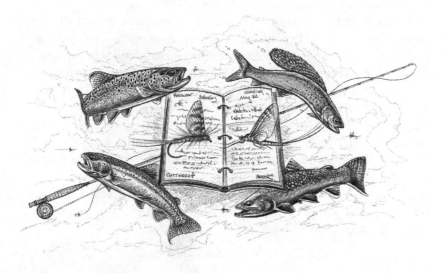

I didn't neglect my fishing in the navy, but now that I've learned more about the different opportunities, it is obvious that I missed a lot.

I remember once when I was on the bridge of the U.S.S. *Pomfret,* a World War II submarine, we were cruising on the surface of the Pacific Ocean late at night, hundreds of miles from the nearest land. I was bored and struggling to stay awake until another of the ship's officers would relieve me. All of a sudden I was struck a heavy and painful blow on my right arm which both amazed and frightened me. I couldn't imagine what had hit me, until I heard something flopping around on the deck at my feet. It was a large flying fish, about sixteen inches long. The two lookouts and I had quite a discussion about this phenomenon, since we had never seen a fish flying so high—some fifteen feet above the surface.

The next morning I talked it over with the captain, who gave us permission to rig up a net and electric light on the main deck, only about three feet above the glassy-smooth water. The sailors and I had a good time catching a couple of dozen fish. Then the cooks filleted them and gave us one of the best meals I've ever had at sea.

In more orthodox fashion, I fished many times for striped bass along the New England coast. My usual fishing partner was the submarine's hospitalman, whose name was Blackmon. He and I used casting rods to fish from the Connecticut and Rhode Island breakwaters or jetties at night, sometimes from midnight until daybreak, with artificial lures or small eels for bait. Since it was often freezing cold and our lines were stiff, we were constantly plagued with backlashes that almost defied untangling in the dark with our frozen fingers.

It was then, in the late 1940s, that we first learned about spinning reels. Both of us promptly bought them; we fashioned our own Fiberglas rods and then were able to make long casts, with rare backlashes. Sometimes we rented or borrowed a small boat and trolled in the Thames River near New London. We caught a lot of fish, the largest one an eighteen-pound striper that Blackmon landed.

Rosalynn and I live in South Georgia in the Coastal Plains region, which was formerly covered by the Atlantic Ocean. Its climate is balmy, the landscape relatively flat, annual rainfall about fifty inches, and the farming regions highly productive. There is a tremendous aquifer underneath our land, with many millions of gallons of water moving very slowly up from the south, then turning eastward and emptying into the sea, taking thousands of years for any particular drop of water to complete the journey. Numerous springs well up from the ground to form our streams. Good drinking water can often be found in shallow dug wells; I remember that most of the open wells of my boyhood were only about twenty feet deep.

The streams run slowly in the level land, and it doesn't take the warm sun long to heat the water to a moderate temperature. Despite our other blessings, therefore, we southern fishermen have to go farther north to find such cold-water species as trout, salmon, char, or grayling. This is why, in spite of years of experience in warm-water lakes and creeks, I was still somewhat piscatorially retarded when we moved to Atlanta and the governor's mansion, just a few miles from the frigid waters of the Chattahoochee River. I soon asked Jack Crockford, director of Georgia's Game and Fish Department, to introduce me to the fly rod and trout fishing. Not only did we enjoy fishing the river from the shore, canoes, and floating tubes, but Rosalynn and I found time to sample some of the smaller streams in the North Georgia mountains.

Since this was one of the most gratifying developments of my life, when I was President I sought out opportunities to continue the sport. Early in my term our family took a delightful raft trip down the Middle Fork of the Salmon River in Idaho, fishing as we traversed one of the most beautiful scenic regions of our country. Later, when we watched some of the movies made of the voyage, I was distressed by my poor style, particularly when I attempted a longer cast. Rosalynn and I resolved to learn more about this exciting pastime.

Although I had fished for bass, bream, catfish, and other warm-water fish since I was a child, and still enjoy it just as much as ever, there is something special about fly-fishing for trout. By taking up this sport fifteen years ago, I entered a world of cold and pure flowing water, rocks and waterfalls, quiet streams often nestled in meadows of mint and wild flowers, cool mountain valleys, personal solitude, and the exquisite science of imitating and presenting a myriad of sometimes tiny insects that comprise the elusive trout's diet.

There is also the enigma of the individual trout's habits and preferences; when I find him zealously feeding, he will totally reject any fly I offer to him, no matter how similar it might seem to those he is taking or how naturally it floats down and past him. I have come to realize over the years that close observation and patience are prerequisites for success.

My eagerness to wade out into the current, or just to get a hook in the water, is most often best suppressed while a painstaking analysis of a stream is made: its depth, main flow-path, eddies, submerged obstructions, shadows on the surface, flotsam going by, overhanging banks and foliage. Only then am I able to make an educated guess about where fish might be lying, or perhaps actually sight an unwary quarry, all without revealing my presence by movement, shadow, or sound.

Fortunately for us modern-day fishermen, beginning a little more than a hundred years ago the eggs and fry of three major species of trout were transferred internationally to distant streams—brookies and rainbows from the Americas and browns from Europe. Now, with proper habitat, the introduced trout are thriving and even believed by many nonhistorians to be native to the area.

The only trout originally found in the eastern states was *Salvelinus fontinalis,* known as brook trout. Requiring water that is both pure and cold and being somewhat gullible when presented an attractive fly imitation, this most beautiful species has become almost extinct in many of the major streams of the East. I have caught them in the smaller, more inaccessible streams of Maryland, Virginia, Pennsylvania, and a few in North Georgia, but always carefully released them in hopes that their population might increase. Like the browns and rainbows, brook trout have been introduced in many other areas in the world. Very large brook trout, in the ten-pound class, can still be caught in eastern Canada and in Argentina. The world record, caught on rod and reel, is fourteen pounds.

Rainbow trout, *Salmo gairdneri,* were originally native only to the Pacific coast but were brought to the eastern states in 1874. Today there are few cold and clear streams in the United States where rainbows cannot be found. Rosalynn and I have also fished for them in New Zealand, Japan, and Switzerland. These fish are more hardy than the brookies, a little more cautious about taking artificial lures, and are spectacular fighters and leapers when hooked. However, rainbow trout are wanderers, tending to leave smaller streams where introduced and to move downstream until turned back by warm water or pollution. Migratory rainbows, known as steelhead, are extraordinary fighting fish. Like Atlantic salmon, they spend a great part of their life in large lakes or the ocean, returning several times to their native streams to spawn. The largest steelhead caught on rod and reel weighed forty-two pounds.

Perhaps the most prevalent trout now is the brown, *Salmo trutta,* which is not native to the Americas but was brought over from Germany and England in 1884 and first introduced to the streams of Michigan and the Northeast. The brown has proven to be a hardy species, able to withstand warmer water temperatures, relatively shy, inclined to stay in a particular location, and more attracted to insects on the surface than other trout. These characteristics, along with a relatively long life, large size when mature, and a courageous fighting spirit, have made the brown a favored species. The world's record brown trout is thirty-six pounds.

Rosalynn and I have fly-fished for several other species, including lake trout, cutthroat trout in western streams, and grayling in the Yellowstone area, Alaska, England, and continental Europe. Grayling require the coldest and purest of waters and are seldom found in our country except in Alaska. The largest ever caught weighed six pounds.

The enormous size of record fish can be quite misleading. It is entirely possible for an expert to fish for a lifetime on the more popular streams of our country and never catch a trout that weighs as much as three pounds. In most areas, trout are measured by length, with fish of just fifteen or sixteen inches being a source of pride. The smaller mountain streams often produce mature native trout of eight to twelve inches. In remote areas of Alaska, Canada, New Zealand, and Argentina, the fish are likely to be much larger, and fishermen are increasingly protecting these trophy trout from being killed. When caught they are handled carefully, photographed, and released to reproduce or perhaps to be caught again.

There is no way to understand tales about fly-fishing without knowing something about what trout like to eat. I have spent many hours studying the life cycles of the food most prevalent in our fishing waters. There are three orders of stream insects that provide the basis for trout survival: mayflies, stoneflies, and caddis flies. It is not necessary in this book to describe the differences among them, but any successful fisher for trout would have to know. These aquatic insects share some common characteristics that help to explain the fishing methods used to catch trout on a fly rod.

They are born from tiny eggs that hatch on the bottom of lakes and streams, protected by trash or rocks from the many predators that seek them for food. As nymphs, the insects then live for a year in their native water, successively shedding their protective shells up to twenty times as they increase in size. Some move quite rapidly and others slowly. When mature, the nymphs swim to the surface or crawl out on the shore, emerge from their last shell, unfold their wings after a few seconds and, when dry enough, fly into nearby trees and bushes to finish drying and sometimes to undergo another metamorphosis.

After a day or two, these winged insects gather in large numbers above the water, flying up and down in their aerial mating dance. Having copulated, the female swoops down to deposit her fertilized eggs in the water, and then this generation, male and female, dies as the eggs sink to the bottom to begin another cycle. These final stages of life, between the water and the air, are known as hatches, and often the trout go into a frenzy of feeding when the succulent insects are most prevalent and vulnerable. In well-populated pools I have often seen several dozen trout feeding simultaneously. At other times a single trout may be the only one periodically surfacing to feed. The challenge for a fly-fisherman is to recognize the particular insect that is hatching and, with a reasonable imitation, present the artificial fly to the feeding trout in a natural and believable fashion.

Sometimes mayflies hatch in enormous quantities. In August 1980, Rosalynn and I took a delightful voyage down the Mississippi River on an old paddle-wheeler, the *Delta Queen*, from St. Paul, Minnesota, to St. Louis, Missouri. I spent a number of hours on the bridge with the captain, discussing steamboat history and the various points of interest along the shore. All around us, mayflies were hatching in unbelievable numbers. At times the captain had to keep the powerful window wipers going to remove the large adult insects that otherwise would have totally obscured our vision of the channel ahead. Each day, while the ship was traversing one of the many locks, I would get my exercise by running several miles either along the levees or across the dams that separated the river into successive downward steps to permit navigation. On one occasion, the pathway was covered at least two inches deep by the bodies of just-hatched mayflies. I wasn't sure, but they seemed to be what fly-fishermen call Light Gray Drake.

The hundreds of species of flies vary widely in size, from those much smaller than a mosquito to stoneflies as large as two inches in length, and in color from almost snow-white to black, with many yellows, goldens, browns, greens, and numerous shades of gray in between. For a particular pool or lake the hatches occur periodically; the dates and times of day can be predicted by knowledgeable fishermen. Weather conditions cause variations of only a few days in the timing of hatches for a particular year. For instance, in our favorite Pennsylvania streams the caddis hatch will begin about April 15 and occur from 11:00 A.M. to 2:00 P.M.; the Hendricksons come on May 1, starting each day around 2:00 P.M.; the large Green Drake during the last days of May, almost simultaneously with the Sulfurs and Light Cahills; and the tiny Tricorythodes will be hatching from July 20 until the end of the season, usually beginning when it warms up in the morning.

Once a hatch is on, the trout become highly selective, their metabolism quickly attuned to flies of a particular size, color, and configuration. Most often they will simply ignore those that deviate from this pattern. Many flies and nymphs, known as midges, are almost too small to see, but for some unknown reason seem to be special favorites of the trout. One of the most frustrating and debilitating experiences of my sporting life is to present a dozen different imitations to feeding trout, all of which are totally ignored, while they are regularly gulping down some unidentified and nearly invisible insect.

As can be surmised, about 75 percent of aquatic insects are consumed by trout in the long-lasting nymphal stage, and submerged fly imitations are undoubtedly the most effective way to catch fish. These are known either as wet flies or nymphs, depending on how the fly is made to travel underwater. The taking of the lure can be a vicious strike or so gentle as to be almost undetectable. For centuries, this subsurface presentation was the only one used, but in the nineteenth century in England the dry fly was introduced, an artificial fly that floats on the surface to imitate the emerging or hatching insect. This exciting new fishing technique was quickly adopted in our country, and is now by far our favorite way of fishing because the path of the floating fly can be followed (if it is large enough to see) and the taking of the lure by trout is visible and often explosive.

Of course, trout feed on many other morsels, including smaller fish, salmon roe and other eggs, frogs, worms, mice or moles, and a wide range of terrestrial insects that fall into the water. I have imitated all these in various ways, but this latter class—including crickets, beetles, jassids, grasshoppers, and ants of all sizes—provides one of the most important sources of dry fly patterns. In fact, if I had to go the rest of my fishing days with only one fly (heaven forbid!), I think I would choose a black ant imitation made of deer hair.

Fly-fishing at its best includes some of the elements of primal hunting: understanding the habitat of the trout, stalking an outstanding specimen while concealing your own presence, thoughtful assessment of what is always a unique situation, planning strategy, and intelligent execution of it with enough deception to prevail. Then perhaps a salute or apology to a worthy adversary and—a significant difference—the ability to release the prey, unharmed.

Over the years I have accumulated an impressive library covering various aspects of fly-fishing, including information about aquatic insects and other trout food, how to tie artificial flies, and how to present the fly most attractively and seductively. I first set up my fly-tying vise and other paraphernalia in the room next to our bedroom in the White House that both Harry Truman and I also used as an office. Then, from my books, I learned how to create a few of the standard patterns.

Just down the mountain from Camp David was the small but well-stocked stream where Rosalynn and I found time during the weekends to catch a few trout. We also slipped away from presidential duties long enough to fish the upper reaches of the Potomac River for smallmouth bass, and explored trout streams in Maryland, Virginia, West Virginia, and southern Pennsylvania.

On one weekend at Camp David we invited about a dozen of the most notable fly-fishermen on the East Coast to visit. Rosalynn and I spent a delightful two days with them, discussing many of the aspects of the sport. A number of our guests had written the books we read or were frequent contributors to the sporting magazines. We had a good program of slide shows, casting and fly-tying demonstrations, and lectures on trout habitat, conservation, and the history and customs of fly-fishing in various countries around the world. One of the highlights of the weekend was a demonstration by the Camp David chefs of how to fillet a trout, removing every bone and leaving the rest of the fish intact; they outdid themselves with some special recipes.

Shortly thereafter, we had an invitation from the Spruce Creek Hunting and Fishing Club for a day of fishing on a portion of their leased stream. This was only about as far north of Camp David as Washington was south of it, so we helicoptered in, to a field adjacent to the water. Our hosts met us, then graciously left us alone to fish. Before we left to return to civilization, Wayne Harpster, who owned the land, came to invite us to return at any time. So began one of the most cherished friendships of our lives. Thereafter, whenever it was possible, we went back to Spruce Creek, landed in Wayne's pasture near the stream, stayed overnight in an old but comfortable house, and enjoyed some of the best fishing in the eastern states.

These were the kinds of fishing expeditions Rosalynn and I squeezed into the interstices of a busy presidential life. They were always too brief but especially welcome. For a few hours we enjoyed the solitude we badly needed. Or, if we were fishing with expert companions, we were able to learn more and more about how to fish effectively under different conditions.

Since leaving the White House we have, predictably, found more opportunities to fish; we modify our busy schedules just enough to take advantage of them. After all these years, I still feel a lot like a boy when I'm on a stream or lake, enjoying the unique beauty of the moment, using all my wits and talents, making mistakes, catching a wily fish, and relishing the memories of bygone times.

TROUT FISHING
AND A BIRTHDAY:
SPRUCE CREEK

Only a family that had spent the last fourteen years campaigning full-time or serving in major public office could understand how we relished this vacation. It was late in May 1981, four months after we had moved from the White House back to Plains. Now Rosalynn, Amy, and I were taking our first private motor trip since Amy had been born more than thirteen years earlier, spending two days in a camper van moving through the Great Smoky Mountains and up the Shenandoah Valley, on our way to Spruce Creek, Pennsylvania.

As we crossed each mountain stream in northern Virginia,

West Virginia, Maryland, and southern Pennsylvania, we examined it carefully to assess the quality of the fishing water following the recent heavy rains. Some currents were muddy and silted while others were pure and clear; I was sure that Spruce Creek, our destination, would be among the better ones.

Wayne Harpster, our host, still operates a dairy farm on much of the Spruce Creek Valley land along the upper reaches of the stream. Using special tillage practices he maintains a sod cover that minimizes erosion of the hilly but highly productive land. His hundreds of acres of corn and pasture are not cultivated at all. Wayne has followed this energy-saving and profitable procedure for more than a dozen years. I wish that all outdoorsmen and farmers of valuable bottom lands would come to appreciate his wisdom as much as we did when we arrived and found the creek in excellent condition. Although high and slightly discolored, the water was not muddy with soil washed from his fields.

Wayne is also, not insignificantly, one of the best trout fishermen I know. While living in the White House we had come several times to spend a day or two in one of his farmhouses on the west bank of the creek, and for more than a year we had planned to return in the last week of May to celebrate two important events: Wayne's birthday on May 29 and the annual hatch of Green Drake mayflies, *Ephemera guttulata*.

When I called Wayne from Plains the night before we left home, he reported that the Green Drakes had arrived on schedule. The first heavy hatch had occurred on Sunday night, May 24, but was expected to continue each evening for at least a week, well after our arrival.

Now, Rosalynn, Wayne, and I sat on the front porch of the cottage, assembling our rods, checking our leaders, and dressing our lines. In the late afternoon, we could see the large Green Drakes—called "shad flies" by some of the local fishermen—darting up and down in their mating dance, outlined against the dark branches of the hemlock trees on the far bank. (Despite its name, there have never been any spruce trees in the valley.) An occasional trout was rising, although we could not yet see any of the big flies on the water. The sight was so tantalizing to my fisherman instincts that I couldn't wait until after our early supper for my first cast but floated a small yellow-bodied Adams far under the overhanging limbs and soon netted and released a nice wild brown trout. It was a good omen for the coming days.

As dusk approached we found ourselves in a heavily wooded area, waist-deep in the cold water, casting Green Drake imitations upstream into the riffles and along the overgrown banks. This was mostly for practice, because the evening hatch had not yet begun. There had never been any stocked fish here, but we knew there was a heavy population of native browns in the rich limestone stream. At about 8:00 P.M. the cloud of mayflies began dipping to the water's surface for the females to deposit their eggs, and trout started rising regularly to take the floating insects. Whenever our casts were accurate and the floats natural, we caught fish. Even after the final darkness required us to depend on rough estimates of distance and direction, Rosalynn and Wayne continued catching trout, although during the last half hour I missed on every strike, disgusted that my judgment and reflexes were so poor.

Back at the cabin, making a routine check of my tackle, I discovered that my hook was broken off at the bend and realized how foolish I had been not to have checked my fly and tippet regularly, even in the darkness. Most of our catch that evening had been eleven-inch to thirteen-inch brown trout, but Rosalynn netted and released a beautiful sixteen-inch brownie.

During the next few days our three sons and their families joined us. All were avid fly-fishers except Amy, who, not yet mature, still believed there were higher priorities in life. After our years in public life, Rosalynn and I valued privacy during our rare vacation times, but we also cherished good companionship; at our request Wayne had invited our friends Lloyd Riss and George Harvey to join us from nearby communities.

George had helped me for several years with my fly-fishing and knew how to be patient with my mistakes, having taught more than thirty-five thousand students the rudiments and advanced skills of fly-fishing and fly-tying. In fact, as a professor at Penn State he had offered the first such college course in this country. Now retired, he still shares his knowledge and wisdom—and his beautiful flies—with a few lucky friends. Lloyd Riss, a distributor of Penn reels and Fenwick rods, conducted many classes for his customers and had given Rosalynn a lot of advice in the Pennsylvania trout streams.

Both of these men are fine fishermen. During the previous autumn they had introduced us to the special fishing methods required by the swarming daytime Tricorythodes hatches—a diminutive mayfly that hatches throughout most of the summer along Spruce Creek. Because of the fly's small size the trout cannot afford to expend much energy in taking each one. Instead, the feeding fish comes off the bottom and hovers just barely under the surface; as a Trico drifts overhead, the trout alters its attitude in the water just enough to ease its lips upward an inch or two, to sip in the fly.

The Tricorythodes are almost invisible to the naked eye, particularly at any distance. To locate them, we would sit on a shady rock in the meadow and watch for the telltale signal of barn swallows and other birds diving repeatedly through the clouds of dancing insects. Only then would we move to the area, find the dimples in the creek caused by the sipping of the trout, and move cautiously upstream. From the bank or while wading very slowly and silently, we cast carefully constructed twelve-foot leaders tipped with the tiny fly (smaller than a mosquito) above the quietly feeding trout. At times, when I needed help, I induced George to fish near me in the stream, always a sobering experience to a relative newcomer struggling to master one of the most challenging techniques of angling. With almost perfect accuracy his line would straighten out two or three feet above the water, stop in midair, and then float gently to the surface as he checked and lowered his rod. The transparent leader with its hairlike tippet would fall in slightly sinuous curves, and the apparently unattached fly would float naturally toward a waiting and hungry trout.

For those of us who release trout, George crusades for fishing with barbless hooks. In the week of this trip we were convinced of the value of his advice: It is then much easier to slip the hook out of the trout's mouth without a rough wet wrestling match and without serious injury to the fish. And to the fishermen who express concern about losing too many hooked fish, George makes his point with a flourish: After a trout is on his line he ostentatiously lays the rod on the ground and ignores it for a minute or two, then lifts it again and reels in the fish. I've never seen him lose a trout.

In addition to our talk about fly-fishing strategy and tactics, my fishing companions commiserated with me over my loss in moving from the White House back home to Plains. They were not alluding to politics. I had owned two superb bamboo rods, which I'd kept at Camp David, one of them designed by Tom Maxwell and built for me after normal working hours by the craftsmen at H. L. Leonard Company as a gift for a fly-fishing President. It was the finest and best-balanced rod I've ever seen. The other was a special conservation award commissioned by one of the sporting magazines when my administration had moved successfully to protect more than 100 million acres of the Alaskan wilderness. These rods were among my most cherished possessions and had been packed with special care for the trip from Camp David to the White House for crating and then to Georgia.

Back home, when I opened the wooden crates containing my fishing equipment, the two rods were gone. A subsequent investigation indicated that they had been stolen. Such were the important matters we discussed by the rich limestone waters of the Pennsylvania creek.

Early next morning I was the first one up, eager to try the meadow stream above our cottage. For an hour or so I never saw a fish and had to be satisfied with the solitude, the beauty of the sunrise, and my practicing wading, casting, and tying on a wide variety of dry flies. Finally the sun warmed me and the water, and with a deer-hair black ant I began to take trout. The more frazzled and bedraggled the fly became, the more eagerly the trout seized it. On my last four casts I caught and released three fish. Delighted, I went back to the cabin to get Rosalynn and my sons out to share the good fortune. It was midday when we finally realized that we had forgotten to eat breakfast.

That night we fished well to a sparser Green Drake hatch. I was again using the large "shad fly," but soon it became obvious that the heavier hatch were Pale Sulfur Duns, the preference of the rising trout. The evening was very enjoyable except for the bad manners of one thoughtless fisherman who came from upstream, cast from the bank into one pool after another, and covered a long stretch of the creek without any apparent regard for the other fishermen interrupted by his flailing line. All of us just had to wait patiently after he passed for a semblance of calm to be restored and for the fish to resume feeding. It was one of the rare examples of gross discourtesy I have ever seen on a trout stream.

I invited Don Daughenbaugh to join us early the following morning. Don is a high school teacher in nearby Williamsport, Pennsylvania, who, for twenty years or so, had spent each summer as a fly-fishing specialist in the Yellowstone National Park area. We had met him there on one of our presidential trips, and he'd given Rosalynn her first fly-fishing lessons in the headwaters of the Snake River at the base of the Grand Tetons.

I was fishing again with a black ant, but Don caught three fish for every one I landed. He was using a very small "fore and aft" fly with one grizzly hackle at each end of the hook and peacock herl wrapped in between. Later I tied a few of them, and they proved surprisingly effective both in the riffles and smooth water, even at times when the yellow-bodied Adams or the redoubtable black ant would not work in the meadow pools.

Just as we were preparing to leave the stream, Don flicked the little fly behind a partially sunken snag near the left bank of the creek. A large trout took it and, with a tremendous whirling dive, immediately broke Don's leader. I marked the spot carefully, determined in the coming days to provide other opportunities for the big brown to test his shrewdness and strength.

That night brought my most frustrating fishing experience. I had decided to try out a new heavier rod so that, after the evening hatch of insects was over, Wayne and I could shift to some late-night fishing with large streamer flies to imitate small fish. The weather was good, but everything else went wrong. Because of a faulty reel it was very difficult for me to strip off line when casting, and I soon broke my leader twice when large fish made strong runs downstream. I had forgotten my small gooseneck flashlight and could tie only the simplest of knots without light, not even attempting the better but more intricate knots in the dark. All this made me lose my confidence; the trees, grass, and snags seemed to reach out for my tackle on almost every cast. Fish were feeding voraciously on an excellent Sulfur hatch, but they were not for me. I finally gave up and waited for the others to return from the creek, where, predictably, everyone else had had notable success. That night and the next morning I spent several hours by myself, assessing all my mistakes and getting some needed therapy by disassembling and servicing reels, tying flies, and putting together a new supply of leaders.

The next day was Sunday. After my sad experience everyone was convinced that I needed to go to church. Then Rosalynn, Amy, and I drove up to State College to visit with George and his wife, Helen. We found them hospitable but disconcerted by an unbelievable gypsy moth attack on the trees around their house. The little black caterpillars—which even trout refuse to eat—had covered the trees, roofs, streets, and yards, and hung from every limb by threads of webbing in the air. We had to go inside to escape them.

George ushered us into his workroom, where some of the best fly-tying in the world takes place. Each of his flies is a work of art. He gave me a needed lesson and also taught Amy and Rosalynn to tie a few flies. As we left he offered me a prized gift—a box of pre-World War II hooks made by S. Allcock & Company Ltd. in England. When we compared them under a magnifying glass with some of the most expensive hooks made today, their superiority was surprising. What a shame that hooks of this quality are no longer manufactured or sold.

That evening at Spruce Creek, Rosalynn and I fished together in the same section of stream near our cottage, "leap-frogging" each other as we moved up the creek, casting in alternate pools. I managed to enter the large pool on the opposite side from Don Daughenbaugh's well-remembered sunken snag and caught several trout as I fished a wide shallow area. It was then that I saw a large trout rising methodically, taking the light-golden mayflies as they floated across his lair. He was shielded by the sunken log and a nearby pile of limbs and trash. As I was nervous, it took me several minutes to change to a heavier five-pound test tippet and then ease quietly out into the center of the stream, my heart pounding as I mentally rehearsed how to cast a right-hand curve. Finally I was ready, took a deep breath, and launched my fly. It traveled perfectly, landing three feet above the trout; he swallowed it as he rolled beneath the snag. This would be my first really big trout!

Surprisingly, the fish then moved forward into the open water. Slowly but steadily I worked him nearer to me. As I turned to shout to Rosalynn about my good fortune, the trout effortlessly turned downstream, stripped off line, and went back under the mound of limbs and trash. He and I had a long tug of war as I waded closer and closer to the pile of debris. I could not pull him out but finally got close enough to run my hand down the leader and feel his mouth. As I tried to reach farther to lift him free, he thrashed loose. All I had to show for my labor was a broken leader.

For a few moments I forgot the church sermon and my Baptist training and said some choice words that disturbed the former quiet of the murmuring stream. To ease the suspense of the reader, let me report now that I tried again to catch him a couple of days later, got him to rise once more to a Pale Sulfur Dun, but finally had to admit that I had more than met my match. Maybe next time . . .

The following day Rosalynn, Chip, and I drove up above Williamsport as guests of Don Daughenbaugh and the Gray's Run Rod and Gun Club. The club, in a wilderness area where deer, bear, and other animals are often seen along the stream, offered a different kind of fishing, more like the freestone creeks we had enjoyed so much around Camp David.

During the morning we caught a few small fish, all brook trout except two browns, but in the crystal-clear deeper water we did see several very large trout. Determined to try for them, we returned after lunch, but none of our dry flies raised a fish. I finally decided to try a slightly weighted old Muddler Minnow variation of my own design, allowing it to swing across the tail end of the deep pool. The response was electric, inducing repeated strikes by the big brook trout, who moved out of the deep water literally to attack the fly. After losing two large fish, I finally netted and released one, then relinquished the rod to Rosalynn. Within a half hour she, Chip, and I had all caught and released brook trout weighing over two pounds. The several smaller ones we caught afterward were an anticlimax. As we left, one of our hosts was contemplating a change in the club's bylaws to outlaw the Muddler Minnow, but he decided first to try it a few times himself to see if its effectiveness was permanent!

I was glad the next morning to meet Joe Humphreys, who drove down to give Rosalynn and me some pointers on different fishing techniques. Joe has managed to fill the shoes of George Harvey at Penn State very successfully for the last several years. We talked about our recent experiences for a few minutes as I thumbed through his new book, *Trout Tactics,* and then I asked if he wanted to put theory into practice and go fishing. He replied with a question: "What's your favorite kind of fishing?"

When I told him, "Dry fly, rising trout, long leaders, fine tippet, deep water," he said, "Then let's try nymphs on the bottom in riffles and shallow pocket water!"

Joe quickly tied a couple of Gold-ribbed Hare's Ear nymphs and we headed for a riffly section of the stream. It was the first time I had fished this way. In a few minutes I was using Joe's tuck cast, putting the fly line several feet above the surface and checking it sharply to let the leader and fly drop down and enter the water first. This delivery put the fly as deep as possible before the current began to move the floating line downstream, with me trying to remember to keep my rod tip high as the nymph floated toward me. An old Georgia creek fisherman for redbreast and bluegill bream, I had little trouble detecting the subtle takes. In fact, the fish seemed to be waiting for us and took the nymphs regularly. The trout we caught were larger, on the average, than our usual daytime catch on dry flies. After a couple of hours I was very proud of my new experience but pretended to Joe to be somewhat chagrined that we hadn't matched his sixteen-pound brown trout, a Pennsylvania fly-fishing record.

That evening my fishing was as good as the previous night's had been bad. Everything went right. On my second cast, around and under a deep bank, I caught a seventeen-inch native brown beauty, and from then on I couldn't miss. With no broken leaders or foul-ups in the trees, hitting my targets, catching almost every rising trout I saw, I netted and released between twenty-five and thirty good-sized fish. Then I accepted an invitation from Wayne and his neighbors to join the weekly neighborhood poker game, where my luck still held. When I finally went back to the cabin I was tired, happy, and thankful.

Instead of fishing the next morning, we decided to visit with Bucky Metz, the foremost producer of the special chicken feathers with which trout flies are tied. Bucky had come to visit us at Camp David in our previous existence, and now Rosalynn and I particularly wanted to see his farm in nearby Belleville, in Amish country. Since George Harvey had found him about a hundred special hen's eggs several years ago, Bucky had developed the surest and largest supply of top-quality hackle in the world—those feathers which, when wrapped around the shank of a hook, produce a stiff circle of bristles that imitate the legs and wings of a mayfly. Special roosters of a dozen different breeds have these stiff-bristle feathers on their heads and necks which are used to make dry flies of various colors and patterns. The softer feathers, from young roosters and hens, absorb water and are used for tying wet flies.

Bucky explained his breeding program to us as we examined some of his chicken families. We were impressed with the personal attention he gives to each rooster and hen—indeed, to each individual egg. After each neck, or cape, is removed with a scalpel, spread out, and dried, Bucky examines it closely. I found him to be very tough, downgrading a cape if even a few of the smallest feathers had been rubbed off or damaged while the roosters spent their final weeks in the special cages. About fifty thousand of the famous Metz capes were being produced each year and made available to fly-tyers throughout the world. With this high-quality hackle, Bucky has made a major contribution to the advancing art of fly-fishing.

During our final afternoon at Spruce Creek, Rosalynn and I climbed the steep rocky slope above our cottage to enjoy the view and see the thick white and pink laurel blossoms growing near the top of the mountain range. It was an exhausting climb but worth the effort. Tired and somewhat sad after supper because our visit was coming to an end, I decided to do my last fishing along with Wayne Harpster, our host. It was a moonless night, drizzling rain. As we left the cabin later than usual, we noticed several Pale Sulfur Duns clinging to the window screen. They proved to be the augury of a good hatch and we both caught fish, but the dark came too quickly for me. Wayne was still perfectly at home and continued to net trout when I could scarcely see the banks of the stream. With years of experience, he knew exactly how to place the floating fly to cover each barely audible dimple in the water. As we moved upstream I listened intently while he repeated for me some of the advice about night fishing that he had gotten from his father as a boy in this same fine stream at the foot of the mountain.

Late at night, as we walked back toward the distant cottage lights, Wayne suggested that we stop briefly near a large willow tree, with deep pools immediately above and below us. I could not hear anything except running water, but he moved quickly to enter the upper pool. Convinced that we were wasting our time, I waded out into the almost chest-deep water of the lower pool and began to cast safely and futilely toward the middle of the stream. I couldn't see Wayne, but every few minutes I heard his soft laughter and the splashing of fighting fish. Finally he announced that they had stopped feeding. He had just landed the three largest trout of the evening.

When I said in admiration, "I don't see how you do it," he replied kindly, "You're really improving as a fisherman—when it's light enough to see." That night Rosalynn and I talked about how Wayne, George, Lloyd, Don, and Joe all seemed part of a large but close-knit family of sportsmen who love God's world with its changing times and seasons and want to preserve its beauty. After this week with them, I saw very clearly how far I still had to go to become a really good fly-fisherman. But I relished the challenge. And still do.

ARKANSAS RAIN, ICE, AND DUCKS

I was leaning against an overcup oak tree, shivering. It was not easy to bend my cold fingers; for a few minutes I tried to hold my loaded over-under 20-gauge Ruger carefully cradled in my right arm while thrusting both hands into the side pockets of a down-filled camouflage coat. I scanned the sky around me, visible only in small fragmented portions through the overlapping branches of hundreds of almost leafless trees. Every now and then the wind dislodged one of the last remaining leaves, which sailed northwestward before settling on the wooded lake.

The silence in Leonard Sitzer's woods was broken only by

the stiff breeze and the strange rasping sound of the dry leaves as they scudded swiftly over the surface of the ice. It was December 1985 near Weiner, Arkansas. My eyes and nose were running, and my neck ached from the constant looking upward. There were six of us, including Leonard, arranged in a semicircle, with most of us facing downwind. Despite our steady scrutiny, the usual flights of ducks were missing in the cloudless heavens. Someone beside me commented, "This would be perfect bluebird weather, except that it's thirteen degrees!"

More than an hour earlier we had broken our way into the heart of the dark eight-hundred-acre forest that Leonard had flooded before the opening days of the duck season. We were moving even more slowly than usual because the throttle control on our boat's motor was frozen in one position. My hunting companions were Leonard; Kaneaster Hodges, former U.S. senator from Arkansas and our host for these annual duck-hunting visits; Frank Moore, who had been in charge of our relations with Congress when I was President; two local friends; and Red, a large Chesapeake retriever with impeccable manners, a master of his trade. At our destination in the deep woods, we had gotten into the water and waded around in concentric circles, pushing the aluminum boat ahead of us, rocking the thin hull from side to side to crack the ice sheets.

The boat was under some overhanging brush and covered with camouflage netting. We now waited, surrounded by almost an acre of cracked ice where we could walk and where a duck might land. The Sitzer farm was in Poinsett County, in the northeastern corner of the state, about fifty miles west of the Mississippi River. The land was remarkably flat, even including the shallow valleys where the numerous parallel streams flowed southward, eventually to join the big Mississippi; any rise in the water level flooded broad areas in the surrounding fields.

Leonard Sitzer and his wife, Kathleen, were from the tough and hardworking German families who for several generations had been able to scratch a living from the sticky topsoil with mules and hand tools before there were any tractors. There was an almost impenetrable hardpan a few inches below the surface, so that even the trees were not able to put down deep taproots. Now, the Sitzer family produced more than 100,000 bushels of top-quality long-grain rice on their land each year and also grew hundreds of acres of soybeans, milo, corn, and other grain crops. All of these, not incidentally, were choice feed for the tremendous flights of migratory waterfowl that traversed the Mississippi flyway. They came from Canada and the Dakota area as winter set in, joined the native wood ducks, and stayed as long as they could find open water and feed in the harvested fields.

The first week I had ever hunted here was in early December 1982. Northeast Arkansas had received a record seventeen inches of rain, suffering terrible damage from the resulting floods. Water in the woodlands was much deeper than usual, and we'd had to take our stands among the trees on the highest ground, with water still almost waist-deep. The driving rain had poured down on us, but so had the ducks; we had the limit of mallards quite early each morning.

During the night the birds fed in the open fields, gleaning the rice and soybeans from beneath a foot or so of water. With the first breaking of daylight, most of them headed for cover in the flooded wooded areas, either along the rivers and bayous or in the normally dry stands of hardwood trees. The many diving ducks soon exhausted the limited supply of acorns and other mast that accumulated on the forest floor, but for several weeks they would continue to enjoy the more plentiful feed in the fields.

Almost all of our game then was mallards, although occasionally we saw wood ducks and a few teal flashing past overhead. At times there were great flights of brant and snow geese, flying in perfect formation and calling constantly with the eerie discordant sound that has thrilled hunters for millennia. Strangely, there were few Canada geese seen here, and no open season for the large gray beauties anywhere in Arkansas.

We usually preferred to hunt in the woods, but one day during my second year of Arkansas hunting, the wind had been blowing exceptionally hard during a rainstorm. Concerned that some of the trees with their shallow root systems might topple over on us after standing for several weeks in the flooded areas, we drove to the edge of the rice fields and slowly slogged several hundred yards across the soft ground, balancing precariously on each foot as we struggled to extract the other from the clinging muck to take another step. Finally we arrived at the blinds, which were made of welded oil drums, buried in the ground on top of a narrow terrace. A few weed stalks separated the closely spaced personal enclosures and helped to camouflage the hunters.

We bailed out most of the accumulated rainwater from the blinds, rearranged the decoys that were left around them from previous hunts, and then eased down into the narrow cylinders. Slightly offset on one side, they had the advantage of affording us a narrow place to sit but the disadvantage of requiring us all to face in the same direction—this morning, into the driving wind and rain. It took me a few minutes to realize that any ducks attracted to our decoys would be coming from behind us. Red lay down on his belly between my blind and Leonard's, and we bent the weeds over to give the retriever a little more cover. This may not have been necessary; some hunters claim that waterfowl are often attracted by dogs.

The visibility was poor, but we could hear ducks flying around us and every now and then some came within sight. Leonard was a master at calling mallards, having practiced for more than forty years with the tens of thousands who used his farmland as a temporary resting place on their way down from the frozen North to sunny climes. When he now played his enchanting tune, a few birds finally came in to alight, but most of them landed without our getting a shot. Either they were too far away or had flashed silently over our heads before we knew they were near. Then we did begin to drop a few, one or two of which were crippled. Directed by Leonard, Red would sometimes go completely out of sight in the rain, only to return with a duck carefully cradled in his jaws.

There was no way to keep the rainwater from trickling down inside our clothing, blowing as it was directly into our faces. Also, we were almost totally immobile in the small steel blinds. At last we were only one bird away from having our limit when two mallards passed high overhead, beyond normal range. Kaneaster whispered, "Take a chance." I aimed my 20-gauge double-barrel at the greenhead, and all of us breathed a brief and silent prayer that we would be able to leave the field for a warm and dry place. Everyone cheered as the #6 shot reached their target and the mallard fell, almost on the blinds.

His leg band, which I later mailed in, proved the drake to be a native of Manitoba.

Now, on my third trip, surrounded by ice and no ducks, I tried · to think of anything to keep my mind off the cold. At times I lowered my eyes and looked around, passing the time by identifying different trees, mostly by their bark. There were pin oak, water oak, red oak, a few sweet gum, some maple, black gum, one cypress, and two kinds of hickory I'd never seen, which I was discussing with Leonard.

Our conversation was interrupted by a low whistle from Kaneaster, signaling that he had sighted some mallards overhead. Leonard immediately raised the duck call to his mouth. It was clear from our experience this morning that the birds had to keep moving southward fast enough to be sure they could always find water and not just ice on which to land. Leonard's hand was gloveless, red and swollen, but he said the sounds wouldn't be right with a glove wrapped around them. When the melody for ducks echoed through the forest, I followed the direction of his gaze. Moving my head as little as possible, I saw four mallards pass several hundred feet overhead, heading north.

I eased my right foot out of the mud and kicked. The water, almost waist deep, splashed, but not very loudly. The waves went out only a few feet, where they were smothered by the large flat sheets of ice that surrounded me. We wanted the ducks to think they could find open water among the trees, and that their brothers and sisters were already down here enjoying the safety of the woods. After a minute or so, Leonard quit calling and said, "I doubt if they heard me in this wind."

As I watched to the north, I glimpsed the same ducks coming back toward us, much lower, now just a hundred feet or so above the treetops. I whistled, and the quacking started again from under the wild pecan tree. It was obvious that these mallards were interested in our place. The sun was ten minutes above the horizon, illuminating the birds perfectly. After they passed over, I said, "It looked like three drakes and one Suzy."

Suddenly a dozen mallards flashed by us from the east, not very high. I wasn't cold anymore. The calling was steady now, and soon there were ducks in sight in all directions, circling lower and lower. As they crossed near us, ever closer, they never seemed to mix the flights. The ducks were suspicious of the ice, having spent the previous day in the woods as the temperature dropped and the frozen film became ever thicker. When they had left these same woods in the late afternoon to feed in the nearby rice fields, their instinct or common sense surely must have told them that open water suitable for soft landings was going to be scarce the following morning.

Finally, a flight of the circling ducks set their wings, just above the treetops, and sailed down toward us, darting from side to side as they avoided the outstretched tree limbs. We watched intently, our backs to the wind. No one moved as we crouched against the trees. I fired first. A greenhead hit the water. Three other guns opened up as the ducks flared upward, their wings beating rapidly. I turned and fired the other barrel. One of my rare doubles.

We counted six drakes down, with no cripples. One other was a female, but no one would admit having shot her. The daily limit of waterfowl for an Arkansas hunter was 100 points; each female mallard, or Suzy, counted as 75, while drakes were only 25 points each. Under threat of severe penalties, hunters refrain from violating these limits. In some years, when certain species may have suffered from a poor breeding season, no hunting of them is permitted and special efforts are undertaken for as long as necessary to replenish the population.

Red had jumped off the nearby pile of brush into the water, but Leonard ordered him back. Six of the birds had fallen close enough for us to pick up ourselves. The other had landed beyond our "open" pond, skidding thirty or forty yards across the frozen surface. We had already seen how difficult it was for the dog to break his way through the solid sheet of ice, anchored every few feet by the trunk of a large tree or sapling. "If I had known the ice was so thick, I'd have left Red at home," Leonard said.

"I've got ice water running down my spine!" someone cried out. We all looked over at Frank Moore. Water was dripping from his heavy camouflage parka. He explained that he had whirled around when the ducks flew over, lost his balance as a submerged stick caught between his legs, and fired at a mallard almost straight overhead at the same time. The blast of his

12-gauge shotgun had toppled him over backward through the ice. We started forward to help him, but he said, "I'll be all right. The water will soon be as warm as my backbone. The worst thing is that my gloves are soaked and already getting stiff." One of us took him a pair of dry gloves, and I moved off to retrieve the most distant duck.

I tried to push my way through the three-quarter-inch ice, but there was no way to make any progress. It was too thin to support my weight but too thick to break easily. The footing was tricky with mud, stump holes, and sunken logs and brush, and I was even more careful than usual—still thinking about what had happened to Frank. Also, I was afraid that some of the jagged ice might puncture my waders. Finally I laid down my gun on a snow-covered log and pulled on a low-hanging limb. Frozen, it parted with a loud snap. Using it as a club, I began to pound on the ice in front of me until it cracked, then took a careful half-step, broke more ice, and tried again. It was slow-moving through the timber toward that duck. I began to sweat under my wool cap. At last I reached out with the limb and dragged the greenhead to me.

Within the next hour Leonard was able to call in two more pairs of ducks, but it was obvious that most of the thousands of mallards we had seen the previous morning had decided to spend the day on the nearby Cache River or the Bayou de View, where the moving water would keep the ice from forming a solid, impenetrable sheet. By now it was too late for us to leave the woods and drive to our blinds on the riverbank, more than twenty miles away. This was our second morning of hunting, and we had to leave the Newport, Arkansas, airport within two hours in order to catch our noon flight from Memphis back to Atlanta. With no more ducks coming in, it was again very cold. When Leonard said, "It's time to go," no one argued much—Frank least of all.

When we were all in the boat, Kaneaster grinned and said, "I have another surprise." He pulled out a small flask of schnapps, jokingly threw the top in the bottom of the boat, and passed it around. It helped to stop some of the shivering and teeth-chattering; we felt much better as the boat started toward the levee. Threading our way back through the trees, we were lost in our own thoughts. Large flights of ducks were passing high overhead, almost out of sight. The hum of the motor broke the stillness, but we could still absorb the beauty of the flooded woodland and contemplate the awe-inspiring cycles of nature, of which we were such a small part. We knew that 100 million ducks were migrating southward and that here near the Mississippi River we were in one of the major flyways.

At the landing, we thanked Leonard and Kaneaster for another great day together. "This is our sixth duck hunt," I told Kaneaster, "and you and Leonard have surprised us with two new records set this morning. I've never seen the Arkansas sun before, and this is the first time the entire group didn't get the full limit of mallards. Also, if it hadn't been for Frank we would have all stayed dry for a change."

Sitting there were a couple of game wardens in their warm automobiles. One of them said, "We've been right here, just covered up with ducks all morning. They've been going into the deep water south of here in the bayou, flying over us so low we could have knocked them down with a fishing pole." We looked at our watches, but it was too late to try for them.

After a quick cup of coffee in Leonard's small camper, we drove toward Kaneaster's home in Newport, leaving behind us one of the finest duck-hunting spots in the United States—at least until late in December, when the rice fields and ponds freeze and the ducks are forced to move farther south.

&

In Georgia I have rarely hunted any waterfowl except the ubiquitous mallard and the indigenous wood ducks that nest along our creek bottoms and around beaver ponds. As a boy I did more jump shooting, either walking quietly along the bank of a stream or floating down in a bateau and attempting to shoot flushing ducks. This was not a very fruitful experience; my friends and I had more success by waiting in our favorite beaver ponds or alongside a creek or swamp lake where ducks habitually fed or roosted overnight. In addition to wood ducks, perhaps the most beautiful of all species, we would sometimes see teal or mallards as a few of them migrated through our part of Georgia.

I don't think I've ever been to any place that was not

visited by mallards. One year a mallard hen even nested in the lowest crotch of a large ginkgo tree on the south lawn of the White House. I watched her closely as I jogged daily past her perch. All the groundskeepers were aware of her presence and careful not to disturb her in any way. Finally, after several weeks, we saw her and her brood of eight waddling toward the fountain pool one Friday morning; they were all gone by Monday. We presumed that she made it to the nearby Potomac.

As governor and President, I have always worked very closely with game biologists responsible for prescribing and enforcing strict game laws. Whenever possible I liked to visit nesting areas myself to listen to the specialists explain what was being done to maintain the waterfowl population at a maximum level.

Sportsmen who buy hunting licenses or contribute their time and funds to organizations such as Ducks Unlimited always demand that they be integrally involved in this process. The driving force behind these conservation measures is hunters, who are most often both personally interested in the benefits and also knowledgeable enough to monitor circumstances as they are and ought to be during each hunting season. We are all very proud of the fine results achieved over the last few decades.

THE RAINBOWS OF YELLOWSTONE— AND JAPAN!

Early in 1981, not long after I left the White House, my good friend and fly-fishing adviser George Harvey called from Pennsylvania to tell me that the Confederation of Fly-fishers would be meeting in West Yellowstone in August. He asked if Rosalynn and I might go out there to help dedicate a new fly-fishing museum. We regretted his invitation because we already had a busy schedule for that summer, and I had to work on my memoirs on a fairly regular basis to meet a self-imposed deadline.

As the months passed, however, we began to learn more about the fishing possibilities in the area. As it turned out, Jack

Crockford was able to spend some time in Hebgen Lake near where we would have been staying and also farther downstream on the Madison River in Quake Lake, float-fishing for "gulpers." He described to us how the large trout would come to the surface during a fly hatch and cruise along with their dorsal fins out of the water, gulping down several mayflies or caddis before submerging again. The trick for the fisherman, he said, was to place the proper fly in front of the trout on one of these visible feeding runs. He had been quite successful and recommended this trip as an intriguing new fishing experience for us.

When two famous fly-fishermen, Dave Whitlock and Charlie Brooks, sent us invitations to fish for large rainbows and grayling there, we began contemplating some major changes in our schedule. I had read their books about fishing techniques, insects in trout waters, and the streams around the Yellowstone areas, and Rosalynn and I saw this as an unprecedented opportunity to fish with and learn from some of the best fishermen in the country. Suddenly, the rest of our summer plans began to pale in comparison.

Fate was with us when we found that we could work in a few days at Yellowstone on the way to some less recreational engagements in China and Japan. Furthermore, since we would now have our fishing gear along, we made arrangements to do some fly-fishing in the mountain streams at the base of Mount Fuji during the latter part of our Japanese visit. Everything began to come together very well; I sent my final manuscript to the publisher in mid-August, just before leaving home with an exciting month ahead of us.

On a Tuesday afternoon Rosalynn, our son Chip, and I arrived at Yellowstone Village to find that George, Bucky Metz, and their wives would be our neighbors. We still had a few hours of daylight left, enough time to take a look around—with our fly rods, of course—and so all of us drove down alongside the Madison River almost to Quake Lake, stopping when we spotted fish rising in the stream, apparently not far from the shore.

When I waded out into the river and attempted to get a fly out to the feeding fish, however, I found them still beyond my maximum casting range. Every time I reached for more distance, my backcast collided with the steep and grassy roadbank behind me. Meanwhile George Harvey, with effortless ease, was making his backcasts sharply upward and still sending the line far out into the stream.

I tried to copy his technique, without success, and proceeded to wade ever a little farther in order to escape the grass. All of a sudden I found myself underwater. Only after quite a struggle was I able to regain my footing and scramble back to the bank. By then I figured it was too late to fish anymore, and we returned to our lodgings and an evening of good food, drink, conversation—and dry clothes.

Among the stories, the Harveys told us how they had helped support themselves during the Great Depression by tying flies for Abercrombie & Fitch and by putting on fancy fly-casting demonstrations. Helen Harvey would hold a match in her mouth while her husband demonstrated the accuracy of his casts by clipping off the matchstem with his hook. George added that he would also spell out his name in the air with his fly line, one letter at a time. We scoffed quietly at this last claim, but later in the week we were given a convincing demonstration of his skill.

Early the next morning Rosalynn, Chip, and I flew westward in a small helicopter with me at the controls, my flying carefully monitored by the regular pilot. It was the first time I had managed a helicopter since I was governor, when the National Guardsmen would sometimes invite me to act as copilot. Referring to the map, I went over a place called Henry's Lake. We could see the small boats below clustered around the upwelling springs, where very large brown trout tend to congregate. Then we proceeded over the Red Rock Lakes and adjacent wetlands that were specially protected game preserves for sandhill cranes and whooping cranes. We saw some large cranes on the edge of the water and soon afterward two bald eagles soared slightly below the helicopter, moving east. When we reached Sheridan Ranch, our destination, I was glad to let the pilot be the one to land on top of a narrow dam; it enclosed two sides of a large manmade lake which had been built before 1890.

As a result of an earthen dam's breaking near Toccoa Falls, Georgia, a few years earlier, a number of people had drowned in the flooding lake water. As President, I then made dam safety a nationwide issue, requiring that all earthen dams be inspected to be sure that people living downstream were safe. As part of this program the water level of the Sheridan Ranch lake had been lowered somewhat while the dam was thickened and strengthened.

We were delighted to meet Dave Whitlock right there on the dam. An Arkansan who lived on the White River, Dave was not only a good sportswriter but also a fine illustrator (as the reader of this book will confirm). He pointed out immediately that a number of nice rainbows were rising to a Callibaetis hatch. We fished first from a boat, using dry imitations to match the flies we could see, and caught several trout of thirteen inches or less. Although almost solid moss extended out about twenty-five feet all around the edge of the lake, Dave decided that we might do better casting from the shore for the larger fish. We decided to try some clipped deer-hair caterpillars we had and some black leeches that he provided.

The wind was blowing hard, and so we had to cast either low into the wind or high if the wind was behind us, as far into the lake as possible. Each time, we let the flies sink for a few feet and then retrieved them slowly in short jerks. Soon we were catching large rainbows, from sixteen to twenty inches in length. They were fierce fighters, performing some of the most impressive aerial maneuvers I had ever seen, sometimes leaping as much as three feet out of the water. We had to let them play for a while far out in the lake until they began to tire and then, with rod held high, bring them in through or sometimes over the top of the moss. If they didn't escape in the moss, they swam away vigorously as we released them.

During our lunch break around noon, we watched some sandhill cranes, large numbers of Canada geese in flocks, pelicans, and, most remarkably, osprey catching and flying away with trout in the head of the lake. With one claw holding the fish's head directly ahead and the other gripping its tail straight behind, the bird had its prey perfectly streamlined for flight, like a missile aligned precisely under a fighter plane.

After a couple of hours the helicopter returned with the Harveys. As we greeted them George proudly began to uncase a new boron rod, explaining that it was an innovative design he had been testing for the manufacturer. He put it together and held it erect, right in the path of the still whirling helicopter blades! Boron came out second. George found another rod and fished with us until it was time to go to the dedication ceremonies, to be conducted by local officials and the assembled fly-fishers. We were quite excited to meet some of the other famous ones we knew from their writings, including Ernest Schwiebert, Lefty Kreh, and Charlie Brooks, whom we would be joining later in the week for a try at grayling.

The weather was quite bad the following day, but we didn't have much time to waste and wanted to try at least once for the gulpers on Hebgen Lake. It was Rosalynn's first experience at tube fishing, and quite tiring for all of us because the wind blew us and our inner tubes across the surface of the lake, requiring us to paddle constantly with our rubber flippers just to stay in place. Although we didn't take any trout, we did catch several whitefish, after having a fine time watching them feed across the lake's surface and trying to place our dry flies where we thought one was heading. Rosalynn hooked a very large one with which she tussled for fifteen or twenty minutes, the fish pulling her slowly around in large circles. As the fish stripped off line, she shouted several times, "I'll never land him!" When the whitefish was finally in her net, she refused to release him. "I'll cook him for our supper," she declared.

I loved to watch Rosalynn fishing. Although her father was one of the noted fishermen around Plains when we were growing up, she had never done much fishing until after we were married and back home from the navy. Then, she and I spent many afternoons on local ponds and creeks. She had a knack for the sport and liked it, especially the solitude and beauty of the woodlands. She first tried fly-fishing in August 1978, on a raft trip down the Middle Fork of Idaho's River of No Return and then, on the same trip, took some casting lessons on the Snake River and the shore of Jackson Lake in Grand Teton National Park. Rosalynn soon developed a very delicate presentation which, on short casts, was especially effective with trout. Her skills developed even further during our presidential visits to Spruce Creek. Through it all, however, she relished being by herself, almost always within sight of me and others but far enough away to do her own thing. It was disturbing to me how many times she caught the largest or most trout, leaving me to equal her catches only by rising earlier and fishing longer!

When the wind picked up even more the next day, we decided to drive over to the Flat Rock Club on Henry's Fork, where we spent a few hours in this stream, well-known to all aficionados of fly-fishing literature. As there was no hatch on, we tried a broad range of both wet and dry flies. My best luck was on a small fore-and-aft Adams, which I often use, and on the Muddler Minnow until thunderstorms forced us back to our cabins. Rosalynn's large whitefish and a few other smaller ones made a delicious supper.

We were up early the following morning to drive into Yellowstone National Park with Charlie Brooks and Richard McIntyre, owner of Timberline, Inc., an outfit that specialized in refurbishing damaged and nonproductive trout streams. During the drive it became obvious that Charlie really loved this area, particularly the Madison and its watershed that he'd portrayed so beautifully in his book *The Living River*.

Now he described each tributary stream to us and commented on some of his more interesting experiences over long years of fishing here. Charlie had recently had a severe heart attack but was still active in trying to protect this river basin. He was especially concerned that since the earthquake of 1959, temperatures had been rising about one degree each year in the Firehole River, one of the world's most famous trout streams, into which the hot waters of Old Faithful and other geysers flow. The Firehole runs into the Madison River, the upper part of which is now becoming too warm for good fishing several months of each year.

We met George Harvey and his fishing partner, heart surgeon Paul Dougherty, at the park gate and drove our cars as far along the trail as they were permitted. All of us then hiked five miles up to Grebe Lake, at an elevation of about eight thousand feet. This crystal-clear body of water is one of the few places in the lower forty-eight states where native grayling have survived. The small lake is fed mostly by melting snow, but there are a few tiny streams around the periphery that seem to be spring-fed and flow permanently. From some of these, which we could step across, a federal hatchery had supplied grayling eggs and fry to reestablish these beautiful game fish in a number of other suitable places in the United States.

This lake, almost six hundred miles from the nearest ocean, had a large number of sea gulls. In the course of the day we also saw several osprey and a few otters. After walking halfway around the lake, we found a place where the water appeared to deepen quite rapidly near the shore. While we all rested after our strenuous hike, Charlie furnished us with multicolored wet flies, whose results he guaranteed.

This was the first time our family had ever used sinking lines; we handled them somewhat awkwardly while George and Dr. Dougherty were sending theirs far out over the lake. And yet Rosalynn, Chip, and I caught and released several dozen grayling, while the others were seldom catching a fish. We were casting out forty or fifty feet, letting the fly sink for about half a minute, and retrieving it very slowly. At times we had three fish on simultaneously. Somehow, we just lucked on to the right technique while much better fishermen were not doing as well, even when they took over our same spots. Chip caught the largest grayling of the day, a heavy specimen seventeen inches long, which Charlie said would come close to the state record.

On our last day before leaving for China, I had one of my most challenging and gratifying fishing experiences. I flew with George and Bucky to meet Rich McIntyre at Poindexter Slough, near Dillon, Montana, a spring creek that had been rescued from a cattle wallow by Rich and his crew and turned into a wonderful trout stream. The upper part was privately held, but the lower portion, where we entered, was a public fishing area now owned by the state. In most places there was a deep and strong flow of cold spring water, almost filled with moss and watercress. Although there were some narrow channels through the plants, we saw no fish in the crystalline water.

We all donned our chest waders and spread out along the bank to enter the stream, moving gingerly because the water was deeper than we had expected. It was lapping at the top of my waders, and at times I had to stand on my tiptoes. When I heard some commotion farther upstream, I went to investigate.

George, who is not very tall, had bogged up before he reached the fishable waters and was complaining: "I almost drowned and hadn't even got to the creek!" Once we were sure he was all right, we laughed uproariously at his predicament. George and some of the others left to fish in the nearby Beaverhead River, but I decided to stay in the slough because it would be a new kind of fishing for me.

It was classical dry-fly fishing of the most exciting kind: deep clear water, large and wary fish, small flies hatching, long and delicate leaders a necessity. I fished with a twelve-foot leader and #16 Adams and Caddis imitations, at first with a three-pound test tippet but soon with the next-larger size. Even then, I could not hold half the fish I hooked. The largest I landed was nineteen inches long and weighed over two pounds, and I succeeded in bringing several even larger ones within sight of my net.

Later, I congratulated Richard on his good work in refurbishing this stream. He had provided me with a fine ending to a wonderful week of western fishing.

~

The next day we left for Beijing, where my famly and I would be guests of the Chinese government. Ever since we normalized diplomatic relations with the People's Republic of China, I had intended to visit the country—or, rather, revisit it. As a young submarine officer I had spent several weeks operating out of the seaports along the coast, from Hong Kong up to Tsingtao. Then I was a lieutenant and now, more than thirty years later, I was returning as one who had only recently been Commander in Chief. As a gesture of friendship, the Chinese leaders asked me to bring several of my friends along on this trip. Three of them were people who were associated with me in my political career and the other was Wayne Harpster, whom we often visited at Spruce Creek.

To accommodate our Asian hosts, everyone had to have a proper designation on the diplomatic lists that described our traveling party, both in China and during our subsequent visit to Japan. I was "Former President of the United States," Rosalynn was "Former First Lady," and so on. Somehow, instead of describing Wayne as "Distinguished Pennsylvania Dairy Farmer," he had been given the title "World's Greatest Fisherman." As you can imagine, this was the subject of a lot of conversation during the trip.

Although we spent as much time as possible in the suburbs, small villages, and the countryside of China, we had only one opportunity to fish. We joined some farmers whom we saw alongside a lake near Xian and let them teach us how to catch carp. They had cane poles, silk lines, and small hooks without eyes, tied on with what fly-fishermen call a "nail knot" wrapped around the shank. Bait was tiny balls of sticky dough. Their technique was the same one we use on spotted suckers in the South Georgia creeks—fishing quite near the bottom, waiting for almost indiscernible nibbles, and then giving a strong and steady pull on the line. Some of the fish were so large that they just swam out toward the center of the lake, leaving the fisherman with a broken line. However, we caught several and kept a three-pounder for our supper, which the cooks served boiled in milk. It was delicious, reminding me of the oyster stew that my mother had prepared quite often when I was a child.

Later, on the last day of almost a week in Japan, our hosts arranged for us to fish in a creek at the base of Mount Fuji. The night before was spent in a mountain hotel, usually occupied only by Japanese guests. The toilets, sleeping mats, and other accommodations were, therefore, Eastern style. In our rooms we found straw sandals, kimonos, and other appropriate accoutrements laid out for us. Rosalynn and I were in a quandary about how to dress properly, but a geisha soon arrived and demonstrated how to put on the clothes.

Somewhat embarrassed by the prospect of being exposed to the female presence in his room, Wayne decided to dress himself. However, when he walked down the corridor to join us, the Japanese bystanders began to laugh loudly. Among other things, he had put on the costume for women. We were all in a festive mood by the time we sat around the knee-high banquet table for our multicourse meal. The conversation soon got around to the printed programs for the evening. Each person, American or Japanese, gave a brief explanation of his or her biographical note that appeared on the list of guests and hosts. While the *sake* flowed freely, the comments became increasingly hilarious in tone. Since Wayne's name was near the bottom, by the time it was his turn the "World's Greatest Fisherman" was not nearly so modest about his fly-fishing exploits as he would have been a couple of hours earlier.

Two of the Japanese were fly-fishermen, and they soon had a small bet with Wayne, challenging his claimed fishing prowess. Before we finally retired for the night, the wagers had been steadily escalated: Wayne would have to catch seven trout in his first forty-five minutes on the stream to keep from losing $40.

We had to start driving before daybreak to reach the stream, which was far down the mountain from where we'd spent the night. We found it to be both more beautiful and more challenging than we had anticipated. Formed by several large springs that boiled up out of the ground, the creek flowed freely for several miles and then was dammed up to form a small lake. From there the water was channeled in enormous pipes down the steep mountainside into turbines to generate electricity. We were to fish in the stream above the lake.

When we stepped out of our automobiles I was surrounded by an unbelievable number of news reporters. Once we agreed to a brief interview *after* fishing, I was free to assemble my fly rod, thread the line through the ferrules, and tie on a dry fly. There were at least ten television cameras focused on my fingers, from as short a distance as the Japanese security officers would permit. This was an impossible situation for fly-fishing, but eventually Rosalynn and I were able to negotiate an agreement whereby all the reporters would move upstream to a bridge, cross the stream, and stay on the opposite side while we cast. When we finally began to fish it was still uncomfortable, knowing that every move—particularly the inevitable bad casts and snarled lines—was being recorded for nationwide broadcast.

In the meantime, free of the press, Wayne Harpster had resorted to the more certain nymphs and wet flies to catch his first four trout in just a few minutes, then finished his quota on dry flies. It was obvious that the creek had been extremely well stocked to make sure that the Former President and First

Lady—and the Japanese television viewers—were not disappointed. Free of the crowd, Rosalynn and I enjoyed some fruitful hours of fishing, cheered on by the news reporters on the far bank and by local inhabitants, who filled the bridge to capacity to observe our piscatorial efforts. The valley reverberated with applause every time we landed a trout, and there was a chorus of equally heartfelt groans when we lost one.

All too soon it was time to pack our gear and begin the long drive back to the Tokyo airport for our return home. This was an extraordinary fly-fishing experience, and at least one of us Americans was $40 richer.

RUFFED GROUSE, FROM GEORGIA TO MICHIGAN

Plains, Georgia, is too far south for grouse, but I have had a few opportunities to hunt them. While I was governor, superb wood-cock hunting was available only thirty minutes from the mansion in Atlanta. Jack Crockford and I often reached the legal limit of five within an hour after arriving on the banks of the nearby Chattahoochee River. And just a half hour farther away there was grouse habitat in the more inaccessible areas of the North Georgia mountains.

These southern portions of the Appalachians are at the margin of grouse country, but in good years with moderate weather and plenty for the grouse to eat throughout the seasons, it is possible to flush a number of these fine birds. I, however, have found them extremely difficult to hunt successfully.

After shooting quail most of my life, it was not an entirely new experience for me when a surprisingly large ruffed grouse unexpectedly burst into flight from under a fallen tree or out of a mountain laurel, rhododendron, or pine and hemlock thicket along an abandoned and overgrown logging trail. Unlike quail, the grouse were almost impossible to approach closely, even when pointed. Most often they ran far in front of Jack's large Brittany spaniel and then took flight while still out of range of our guns. Even when Jack and I could get nearer to them, always in dense cover, the birds seemed to have an uncanny ability to keep trees or brush between themselves and us while they disappeared from sight.

On three successive hunts we had what seems to be typical luck in seeking grouse. The first time we found four birds and didn't get a shot. On our next foray we flushed eleven of the birds, fired four times, and Jack bagged one. Later, we hunted all day without flushing a grouse. Although each time we were hunting with a Brittany who was well trained to approach the birds very gingerly, none of the grouse held long enough for us to shoot over a point.

Grouse hunting is most difficult when climbing or descending the precipitous mountainsides—over the ridges from one hollow to another. On our first hunting trip we didn't follow many trails; I told Jack it was the only time I ever walked all day with at least one hand on the ground!

For many years I have run from fifteen to forty miles a week. When my dogs, Sport and Sadie, and I seek quail on my own land, I walk for several hours, sometimes morning and afternoon, through soft fields, swamps, and dense underbrush. On the large quail plantations, however, we hunters spend most of the day on horseback—something I don't do very frequently. Some of the woodcock habitat in the river bottom lands is almost impenetrable, and most of the time I bear the telltale bramble scratches on my hands and face for a week or two afterwards. In contrast, turkey hunting is not particularly strenuous once the hunting site is reached, even though it requires the most intense concentration, almost perfect stillness, and excellent cover and camouflage.

In none of these cases, usually in the South Georgia flatlands, do I ever feel particularly weary or inclined to interrupt the hunt for a rest. And yet I find several hours of North Georgia grouse hunting exhausting. The sustained physical exertion and the elusiveness of these game birds help to make this sport the most difficult of all the hunting and fishing I have ever done—but it is certainly worth the effort in spite of its frustrations.

One of the benefits of our building a small log cabin in Northwest Georgia was to be nearer to good grouse hunting, but I still knew very little about the sport. In the winter, grouse feed on buds and green leaves from mountain laurel, galax, clover, wild strawberry leaves, and Christmas fern. Around our cabin and along the hunting trails Rosalynn and I often saw the signs of the birds: droppings like white and gray caterpillars, and leaflets piled up neatly where grouse had consumed the main stems of the fern leaf. On one December day in 1985, we decided to get some exercise by walking down the frozen banks of Turniptown Creek. Within a quarter of a mile of our mountain home we flushed three grouse. I hadn't brought a gun with me, but I decided then that on our next trip up from Plains, I would be better prepared for some hunting.

Since I knew so little about the territory, I asked several people about the known grouse hunters around the neighborhood. It wasn't long before I met Georgia game biologist Monte Seehorn, who has analyzed the craws and gizzards of hundreds of grouse in Virginia, North Carolina, and Georgia to compare feeding habits in the three states and to improve habitat. He is an expert on ruffed grouse, and it was a special pleasure to hunt with him because I was also able to get a good biology lesson during the hours we spent in the woods together.

On our first hunt it was bitterly cold. A light snow or sleet was falling all day, but we were in beautiful, almost virgin territory and the dog performed superbly. Although we flushed eight grouse, we got only one shot and came home empty-handed. That's grouse hunting!

After several long hunts in the nearby mountains with only one fruitless shot across a valley at a disappearing bird, I decided to relegate grouse hunting to a much lower priority on a long list of things to do in my leisure hours. But a call late the next summer from Jack Crockford almost changed my mind. "I'm planning a trip to my old stomping grounds in northern Michigan in October, and the grouse hunting up there ought to be pretty good this year. Can you get away for a few days?"

I glanced at my calendar and saw that I couldn't—I had to be in Japan on business for that entire week. "Maybe another time," I told him.

I confess that I wasn't overly disappointed, but the next day fate took a hand. I was informed that my host in Japan would be having some minor surgery early in October; he was canceling all his appointments for that month. And so I called Jack with a careful question, keeping my options open: "If it were possible for me to get away, what could we expect on the trip?"

"The weather is unpredictable in northern Michigan," Jack said. "It can go below freezing every month of the year, and there is often snow before the time of our trip. Even if it's not snowing, there will probably be a heavy fog or drizzling rain most of the time. But a few days in October are as hot as South Georgia, and then just a T-shirt and jeans is enough. We would be hunting in heavy cover, with some briers and a lot of fallen logs. Some of the time we'd be in wet areas, particularly if the migrating woodcock are there. Our lodging is at a remote state forestry station, quite comfortable. Bring your Ruger and those shells with the seven-and-a-half chilled shot you've been using. I guess you have a sleeping bag," he concluded.

I thought for a few seconds about the tales I had heard Jack tell about how many grouse there were around his boyhood home in Michigan and made up my mind. "Yes, of course. I'll be with you, but I can be away from home for only about three days." Why prolong the possible agony?

When the time came, Jack, Don Carter (a North Georgia friend who always disclaims any kinship with me), and I flew into Detroit and then drove 250 miles up to our destination. Along the interstate we saw a number of pickup trucks loaded with carrots, apples, ear corn, and sugar beets. I wondered aloud why they were taking such a small amount of farm produce to what I assumed was some central market up north. Jack explained: "Unbelievably, Michigan permits baiting of game, including deer. Although right now hunting is restricted to the use of bows and arrows, firearms will be allowed in a few weeks. These hunters are going up to place favorite food items in the best hunting spots to entice deer and then shoot them under these artificial circumstances when the season opens."

To us Georgians this seemed a strange custom; it obviously gave the hunters a significant advantage over the game.

Forester Ned Caveney met us at the rustic and isolated lodge shortly after sundown. He immediately suggested that we try to locate some elk that might be feeding in grassy areas near the woods. We soon sighted nine of the beautiful animals on a nearby hillside and watched them for a few minutes with binoculars. Suddenly we heard what sounded to me like a shrill whistle coming from the more distant forest. "That's the mating call of a bull elk," Ned explained. We tried to locate the bull by walking up some of the trails in his area, but the gathering darkness forced us to give up the search. Ned's attempts to simulate the call on a long whistle brought no response.

"We have too many deer to count, but there are about twelve hundred elk here in a one hundred and twenty thousand-acre area, and the nearby farmers sometimes complain about damage to their crops," Ned told us. "Also, we don't want the elk to overgraze their favorite regions. To restrict the size of the growing herd, we've been issuing a few hunting permits for the last few years—roughly equal to ten percent of the elk population. There is not much sport to it, since the elk aren't very afraid of humans, but thousands of people compete for the few chances.

Back at the lodge, our conversation shifted to grouse. The other more experienced hunters explained to me the special Michigan habitat that provides a good home for these most elusive birds. The surrounding forests include white and red pine, balsam fir, white and black spruce, northern white cedar, maple, red oaks, alder and other smaller trees in the marshy places, and—most important of all—aspen. In many parts of our country there are grouse where aspen thrive, and for good reason. In the spring the birds consume young aspen leaves as a major part of their diet and then eat the buds in the fall and winter when the ground is covered with snow. The grouse relish the overhead cover provided by the thick stands of young trees, which make it very difficult for hawks or owls to swoop down on them. Also, the relatively open ground under the trees protects the birds from the concealed approach of foxes, skunks, and other preying animals. (The best combination of these advantages is when the trees are from twelve to twenty-five years old.)

In these same areas, grouse find clover and wild strawberry leaves on the ground, thorn apple, high-bush cranberries, other fruit on low bushes, and the buds and catkins of various trees. Sportsmen, increasingly knowledgeable about grouse habits, have helped to make sure that forestry and game management practices enhance the habitat in natural grouse territory. As a result, our nation's grouse population far exceeds what it was when the first white settlers arrived on our shores.

This north central part of the lower peninsula of Michigan is greatly affected by its peculiar climate. Despite adequate rainfall, the cold winds blowing in from east, north, and west limit the growing season to only about seventy days a year— not much more than half what it is just a few miles nearer the coasts of Lake Huron or Lake Michigan. Trees grow slowly, and land cleared and cultivated for a few years will remain open for several decades. Some areas around old homesites, abandoned more than sixty years ago, are still devoid of native bushes or trees. Only one or two gnarled apple trees—which we would partially harvest for a quick snack—live in the thin soil, which had proved inadequate to support a farming family.

The first morning we followed either Jack's small German shorthair or Ned's female Brittany through choice grouse territory and had good luck finding the birds. However, hunting conditions were not as easy as they had been described the night before. The aspen were there as expected, but so were swamps, scattered stands of dense conifers, steep hills and valleys, and numerous small logs on the ground, left behind from previous timber cuttings. Some of these were as slick as glass in the constantly drizzling rain, and at least once a day I fell flat while watching for game and at the same time trying unsuccessfully to feel for adequate footing on the uneven ground. The worst problem of all, however, was in aspen stands that covered downed spruce trees.

Spruce budworm attacks had killed many acres of trees. Eventually these had toppled over and were now lying horizontally about three feet off the ground, each main stem surrounded by dozens of small limbs that had grown almost perpendicular from the trunk. Seemingly impervious to decay, they formed a bristling barrier as we tried to move through the woods—something like attempting to penetrate an eight-foot-high network of interwoven porcupine quills.

Every now and then we came across one of the thirty free-flowing oil wells that provide more than $10 million annually to the state of Michigan. These funds are earmarked by the legislature for the acquisition of land for parks, recreation, and forest and game management. The cleared areas around the oil wells made good pastures for wildlife. Once we were suddenly confronted by four enormous bull elk grazing in one of these openings. They looked at us calmly for a few minutes and then moved majestically off into the surrounding woods.

During this time of year, in October, the woodcock were migrating from farther north in Canada down toward their winter nesting areas around northern Louisiana. Now, in the wetter areas and among smaller aspen, at least two thirds of the flushes were woodcock. The shrill whistle of their wingtips and rapid flight upward were both exciting and somewhat disappointing when we realized they were not the larger and more desirable grouse.

Usually we were able to move abreast, slowly, about thirty yards apart, listening carefully for the bell or electronic beeper on the dog's collar that indicated its location, and always watching carefully for a grouse to flush. Without the beeper it would have been very difficult to keep track of a bird dog in the dense forest. The electronic tone sounded about every five seconds, the frequency increasing when the dog was pointing. I had often used a small bell at home, but when a dog is immobile on a point, it can be hard to find. Now I decided I would order one of these electronic signals for use on my own farm. Especially when training a young dog, I'd have less fear of losing the puppy in woods unfamiliar to him.

Unlike quail dogs, these were trained to point at the slightest whiff of scent, so there were a lot of what we in South Georgia would have considered false points. Even with this extremely careful approach, we never saw half the grouse that flushed. We could hear the thunder of the wings, often originating in the top of a nearby tree, but then could only guess where they were or the direction of their flight. Sometimes the grouse would run on the ground for a hundred yards or more while we and the dogs attempted to follow their trail. The birds would then take off through the trees, leaving us only the distant sound of throbbing wings. At other times the birds would explode almost at our feet or several yards behind us, disappearing before we could whirl around and see them or get our guns to our shoulders. One large cock rose forty yards ahead of me and flew low into an area of fallen spruce. Trying to get within gun range, I followed to see him running on the ground, but he quickly left me behind and disappeared into a low swamp area, where we never saw or heard him again.

We found that a favorite place for grouse to congregate in the late afternoon was under the isolated thorn apple trees growing around small hills underneath the larger hardwoods. The bright-red morsels, some still on the limbs and the rest scattered on the ground, were very similar to our South Georgia mayhaws in both size and taste.

Despite all my previous efforts, I had never killed a ruffed grouse. Still, my hopes were high because we were hunting in some of the most desirable territory in our land. It was cold and drizzling rain at the beginning of the week, but we hardly noticed the weather—we were remarkably successful in finding birds. My first chance for a good shot came as I was approaching a low mound of earth, about fifty yards in diameter and eight feet high. As I started up the steep grade, I stepped on the rotting trunk of a dead tree, slipped, and fell flat on my stomach. Embarrassed, I stood up and looked around to see who was watching. Abruptly, two grouse flushed off to my right, twenty yards away. I was quite startled but brought my 20-gauge over-under to my shoulder, swung with the leading bird, and squeezed the trigger. I wasn't doubtful about that one; it would be my first success. The other circled left and began to disappear over the top of some small aspens. I snapped off my other shot and saw the bird swoop down toward the ground, beyond the knoll. Before I could get there to see whether or not I had missed, our dog came trotting up with the second grouse in his mouth.

In all, we found sixty grouse and bagged fifteen of them during the first two days, which was a very high percentage. Even the best hunters can normally expect to get only about one out of ten they flush. We were quite proud of this early success and confident about the coming days, particularly when Ned informed us that he had saved the best hunting areas for the last day and a half that I could be with them.

As we hunted together, I noticed that the experienced hunters were much more aggressive with their shooting, often firing three or four times more than I would during a day in the woods. They had learned to take maximum advantage of the few opportunities. I was too accustomed to quail hunting, where most birds flush just under one's feet or in front of a pointing dog. It was quite different with ruffed grouse. As we discussed the result of our hunt, we realized that we had taken only two grouse over a pointing dog. All the others had been flushed as we carefully walked forward abreast through the heavy cover. And yet I would not want to hunt without the bird dogs. They focused our attention, performed well, and their actions most often alerted us to the proximity of game.

On the third day, despite Ned's promises, we flushed only nine birds, had long shots at two, and downed none. He was apologetic and said we would just have to get up earlier and try harder. And so, on the last morning, we started shortly after sunrise to help guarantee a successful hunt. That day we heard six grouse, four of which flew from distant trees, and again came back to the lodge empty-handed. This experience was more typical of the grouse hunting I had known in North Georgia and what most hunters can expect when they attempt to outwit ruffed grouse, *Bonasa umbellus*.

Despite the often meager results, severe weather conditions, and strenuous physical exertion, the beauty of the for-

est, companionship of other sportsmen, incredible performance
of highly trained hunting dogs, encounters with many kinds of
wild game, and the contest of wits with this elusive bird all
make me determined to try again—as often as I can.

THE FORTY-NINTH STATE, BUT FIRST IN FISHING

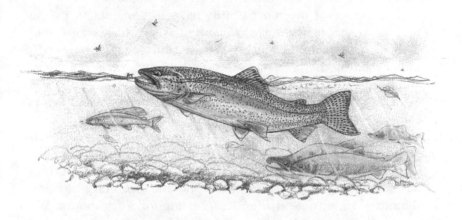

One of my major legislative battles as President was over the resolution of a longstanding controversy concerning the disposition of tens of millions of acres of Alaska lands. When Alaska became the forty-ninth state in 1959, a serious question arose as to how much of the enormous area would be in private hands and how much owned by the state; retained by the native Eskimos, Indians, and Aleuts; opened for mining and oil and gas exploration; or set aside for public use as monuments, parks, scenic and wilderness areas.

For more than twenty years a bitter debate had raged in

Alaska and in the Congress. I was determined to settle the issue. With Secretary of the Interior Cecil Andrus and key members of the House and Senate, I pored over the detailed maps of the region, trying to decide how much of Alaska's natural beauty could be preserved without interfering too much with the state's economic development. Slowly we forged compromises that resulted in a landmark bill, which I signed into law on December 2, 1980, one of my last legislative decisions as President. We set aside for conservation an area larger than the state of California, doubled the size of our National Park and Wildlife Refuge System, designated twenty-five free-flowing Alaskan streams as wild and scenic rivers—and, as a result, instantly tripled our nation's Wilderness System. At the same time, we were able to open up all the potentially productive offshore areas and 95 percent of the land areas where exploratory drilling for oil and mineral resources might be fruitful.

It was one of my most gratifying achievements in public life. I knew that for centuries to come, visitors to Alaska would be thrilled by some of the most beautiful scenery on earth, undisturbed by the ugly scars of an advancing industrial civilization. This final victory was especially pleasing because it was also a triumph over a mighty phalanx of greedy special interests who had made a last-minute effort to kill the bill.

In July 1980, when I stopped briefly in Alaska on a return trip from Japan, Governor Jay Hammond, Rupert Andrews, Director of Sport Fishing, and Chris Goll, outfitter and hunting and fishing guide, had arranged for me and Secretary of State Edmund Muskie to go fishing for grayling for a few hours. We flew northward from Anchorage, circled Mount McKinley, landed on one of the glaciers to see the slowly flowing ice at first hand, and flew close to some cliffs to observe a number of Dall sheep on the steep mountainsides. I was thrilled by the stark, spectacular beauty. During this summer, passage of the Alaska lands legislation was still in doubt, but this brief trip renewed my determination to succeed, at the same time giving me some new arguments to present to doubtful members of Congress whose votes I would be seeking back in Washington.

We finally landed on a small body of water known as Clarence Lake. Wading out into the extremely cold water for a few yards, we placed our flies as far out as possible, let them sink for twenty or thirty seconds, and then reeled in slowly as the fly conformed to the steep underwater slope. Although I was relatively inexperienced at fly-fishing with sinking tip lines and my casts were shorter than most of the others, I had one small fly I'd created that seemed to be exceptionally attractive to the grayling. It was an imitation of a small yellow caterpillar, tied with a chenille body and peacock herl strips down the back, and it worked when nothing else would. That was a proud moment for me, as a novice fly-tyer, when I shared my creation with the other more experienced anglers.

We kept enough fish for a noon lunch, which we cooked on the lake bank, and then moved to the narrow but deep stream draining the lake. Since the water was crystal-clear and quite swift, wading was difficult. I spotted fish rising on a curve in the stream, but after wading out chest-deep was barely able to reach the feeding grayling. Unable to see any edible insects on the water, I tried several small Alaska patterns without success. Then I tied on my smallest Irresistible, a fuzzy-looking deer-hair pattern that floated like a tiny cork, and began to catch fish regularly. Again, I could share my flies with the other fishermen.

On the way back to Elmendorf Air Force Base, flying low over small streams, we saw hundreds of Chinook salmon on their spawning run. Their red bodies were packed together in the larger pools, and a number of bald eagles and grizzlies were feeding on them. This scene typified the savage beauty of the region.

Although the entire trip had lasted only about six hours, it was a pleasant respite from the duties of my office, compounded at that time by the Iranian hostage crisis. I resolved to return to Alaska as soon as possible for a more extensive visit, with enough time to see the natural beauty and wildlife and to fish for some of the trophy rainbow trout that dwell in the remote streams.

While I was in the state, opponents of the pending Alaska lands legislation had made their feelings obvious. Led by land developers, professional hunters, and leaders from the mining and oil companies, organized demonstrators expressed their disapproval of my well-known position. There were strong feelings on both sides. On my arrival I had met several hundred of the citizens at an airport reception, and both the supportive and the critical comments were delivered to me with little restraint. Later I heard that at the state fair in Fairbanks the Junior Chamber of Commerce had accumulated a large pile of empty bottles. For a fee the fairgoers could throw them at photographs of me, Secretary Andrus, Congressman Mo Udall (a key sponsor of the legislation), and the Ayatollah Khomeini. I never did know for sure who won this "popularity" contest, but I was told that my pile of broken bottles was a little larger than that of the Ayatollah.

After leaving office, I looked for a chance to go to Alaska again, this time for a visit devoted primarily to fishing. Then, early in 1985, Chris Goll called to invite Rosalynn and me to come to his isolated Rainbow River Lodge on the Copper River, about two hundred miles southwest of Anchorage. We accepted immediately, planning our trip for late June, after the ice melted and before the enormous runs of sockeye salmon began. We wanted to fish for rainbow trout, not Pacific salmon, because we thought the trout would be more elusive and challenging in their permanent habitat than the salmon, who were crowding into the stream of their birth for a final spawning run.

A couple of weeks before our departure, Rosalynn found that business obligations would prevent her going. As I thought about the perfect companion to replace her, I recalled the good times my father and I had had fishing together when I was a child. All my sons were grown men, and so I decided to call Chicago to invite my oldest grandson, Jason, who was nine years old, to join me. He was overjoyed, even after I cross-examined him.

"How about the bears?"

"I'm not afraid," he said.

"Big black moose?"

"They won't attack us."

"Bald eagles? Mammoth ice floes, frozen hands, big mosquitoes, perpetual daylight and no dark hours for sleeping, a long time away from your parents?"

"You can't talk me out of it."

"Can you cast with a fly rod?"

116

"Not good enough, but I'll practice now and learn more in Alaska."

Although Rosalynn and I had had all our grandchildren with us on several occasions, including fishing at Spruce Creek, this would be the first time I would be off alone with just one of them. I was as excited as Jason, eager to please him and to be a special friend. Before the trip we talked often on the phone, every time either of us could think of a new idea about fishing tackle, books to read, travel arrangements, or just an old subject that was good enough to be revived. Jason had never made a journey so distant or different before, but he didn't seem concerned about being away from home. His dad, Jack, added to the excitement by pretending to be jealous and wanting to replace Jason on the trip.

When we met in the Atlanta airport, Jason was proudly and ostentatiously carrying his oversized hip boots (there were no chest waders available for his small size) and his dad's fly rod. As we waited for our flight, he told me that he and his father had been practicing every day.

"Can you throw a fly to that wall?" I asked him, pointing to a partition about forty feet away.

"No, sir, but I wouldn't have any trouble reaching those chairs."

"Could you hit the one in the middle?"

"I could come close to it on the first cast and hit it on the second."

"That's good enough to catch fish," I informed him, laughing.

During the long flight Jason read a simple book I had brought him on casting and fly-fishing techniques. As I questioned him, I was surprised at how much he remembered from the few times he had fished with me in Pennsylvania.

When we stepped off the plane in Anchorage, Chris was there to meet us. Soon we had loaded our gear into his single-engine float plane and were on our way to the Copper River. Jason and I plied Chris with questions about the camp, fishing, distances, mountains, tackle, boats, wildlife, and other important subjects. It happened to be the first day of summer, and Chris reported that he had observed a large caddis hatch the previous week. He interrupted our questions about fishing long enough to express a hope that we might see some whales as we flew southwestward from Anchorage over the Cook Inlet. Looking down at the shoreline, we noticed that the thirty-two-foot tide seemed to be at maximum ebb; in some places the milky glacier water lapped miles from the nearest bluffs, where the shacks of duck hunters were erected.

Jason, sitting in the back, had his nose pressed against the window. Suddenly, Chris pointed ahead and exclaimed, "There's a whale!" Jason and I finally sighted the white shape maneuvering on and near the surface. Soon we could see several hundred, their rolling white bodies easy to spot. "They're belugas, mostly twelve to fifteen feet long, feeding on king salmon," Chris explained. "We usually find them when the salmon are approaching the streams for their spawning run, but this is the most I've ever seen at one time."

When we reached land we flew at minimum safe altitude, at times just a few hundred feet above the surface, all of us on the lookout for wildlife. We saw nesting trumpeter swans on the small lakes, several bald eagles, an occasional moose along the riverbanks, two grizzlies, and a black bear. Finally we crossed Lake Iliamna. Almost halfway down its ninety-mile length we sighted the Copper River and then landed alongside it on a small lake, just large enough for a heavily loaded float plane to take off safely.

Being in this secluded lake was a special thrill for me as I recalled the political battle we had waged to protect this and other wild regions, many of them equally beautiful. As we taxied to the shore, Chris said to Jason, "This is called Pike Lake; it drains directly into the river. Maybe later this week you can learn firsthand where it got its name. Mostly, though, we're going to be fishing for rainbows. The ice has recently cleared out of the river, and the sockeye salmon haven't yet moved this far inland from the sea, so it's a good time to concentrate on the trout. We'll be seeing some trophy-size fish, whether we catch them or not. Because we would like fishing in the Copper to stay as good as it is, we'll be fly-fishing only—it is an Alaskan policy that in the Lake Iliamna drainage basin we release all the rainbows we catch."

This was exactly what we had planned, but Jason asked if there would be any fish to eat during the week. "You might catch some grayling, Arctic char, and northern pike—if you're lucky," came the wry reply.

After Chris beached the plane we quickly unloaded our gear. Rainbow River Lodge was a beautiful spot, almost completely in its natural state. The manmade structures that made up the camp had been placed with great care to disturb the hillside as little as possible—just a few small cottages along the wooded shore, connected by narrow paths. The only surrounding trails leading up the steep hills and around the lakeside were made by bears and other wild animals, each path only six or eight inches wide and at least a foot deep in the tundra. There were no open or flat places; I would not need my jogging shoes and Frisbee this week.

In the center of the camp was a shallow open pit lined with stones for a campfire and outdoor cooking, surrounded by a few small cabins, a mess hall, two outdoor toilets, a shed within which the diesel generator ran during the necessary hours, and a storage room submerged in the tundra that served as a natural icebox. Aside from the wonderful food, one of the most enjoyable features of the lodge was the shower, which provided unlimited hot water, instantly heated by propane gas when the water was turned on. The June weather was chilly but not uncomfortable.

Tired from the long trip, we went to bed right after supper. In this far north country it was light enough to read a newspaper all night, except for an hour or two after midnight. Although the long hours of dusk and predawn light conjured up eerie feelings for us southerners, I never had any trouble sleeping. But Jason must have been too excited to stay in bed. I heard his voice out by the campfire, asking trivia questions about baseball. An avid Chicago Cubs fan, he easily dominated this and many other conversations during the week with his encyclopedic knowledge of the sport.

The temperature was a little above forty degrees Fahrenheit the next morning as we moved through Pike Lake and entered the Copper River. We had rain gear in the boat, but a light sweater was enough to keep warm. This is a beautiful stream, whose ample flow of water is so powerful as to be frightening. With a gravel or rock bed and little if any runoff from glaciers, the water is almost perfectly clear. Although there are deep holes where very large fish can be seen, wading is quite safe in the tail ends of pools and alongside gravel bars if normal precautions are observed. I warned Jason that he had to be careful when he stepped off the bank, because the water's clarity caused us to underestimate its depth. Jason usually stayed in the boat or quite near the shore. With the help of a wading staff in the deeper water, I had a close call for a bad spill only once during our stay.

The first morning we traveled upstream about five miles. Since no trout were feeding on the surface, we decided to fish each pool as near the bottom as possible, using sinking tip lines. We tried nymphs, streamers of different kinds, and imitation salmon eggs, but neither Jason nor I had any luck for the first few hours. I watched Chris carefully as he took three or four nice trout and finally sought his advice.

"You're waiting for a heavy strike, which will rarely come," he said. "The extremely delicate 'takes' are almost impossible to detect, so you almost have to sense the proper time to tighten your line. If I feel the slightest tug or observe just a fleeting hesitation of the line, I assume it's a fish and respond instantly. This happens several times on almost every long drift downstream. There are a lot of false alarms, but every now and then you land one."

Using his technique, I soon had a heavy fish on my line, but after a few minutes he broke off.

"What tippet are you using?" Chris shouted across the stream.

"Three-X, about five-pound test," I replied.

"Go to two-X or bigger when fishing deep," he instructed. Naturally, I complied.

Jason practiced for a long time, standing in the relatively shallow water or in the boat, and his ability quickly improved. Chris and I taught him a few of the standard knots that are necessary for fishermen. Nevertheless, the length of casts and the patience required were a little more than a nine-year-old could handle. Soon Jason was spending more time with the binoculars and exploration of bear trails than with the rod. Since Chris's daughter, Betsy, who was the same age as Jason, had come along for the day, they had a good time rambling along the shore.

By noon, after four hours of steady fishing, I had not landed a single fish and was somewhat discouraged. My limited skills did not rest in the use of heavy tackle, deep water, long casts, and subtle takes. I'd spent most of my time fishing on the surface with dry flies, or with small wet flies across and downstream. I knew the fishing in farm ponds and small creeks very well, but had been in large rivers like this one for only a few hours.

In the early afternoon came a sign of a possible turn in my future: I was delighted to observe the beginnings of a caddis hatch. Soon a few trout began to rise in one of the deep pools. They were quite distant, under an overhanging cliff, and I could reach them only by fishing downstream. Every now and then I managed a good float, but the fish ignored my best caddis patterns. Finally I tied on a very small Adams and caught a couple of rainbows, the smallest about thirteen inches. Even though the hatch was short-lived, this fisherman's spirits rose.

Chris commented, "The hatches will be much better later this week if we have some warmer days."

In midafternoon, while Jason was playing around the boat with Betsy, she fell in the river. After a great deal of laughter from the two, Jason "accidentally" fell in also, and now both of them had fun splashing around near the boat. Although the water was very cold, they assured everyone that they were all right and would prefer to let the warm sun dry them out rather than go back to camp. I kept quiet, figuring that forty-five years ago my daddy would have let me swim too.

Shortly afterward, Chris and I spotted several large trout feeding in the tail end of a long pool, their heads softly breaking the surface every now and then as a choice morsel drifted overhead. Although the surface riffles made it difficult for me and the fish to see one another, I decided to stay well away from them to avoid detection. While Chris and Jason watched, I waded out waist-deep and tried all my tricks and a wide variety of flies in vain attempts to coax a trout to strike. One of the fish, well over three pounds, attacked a multicolored Sculpin, but after a few seconds of furious rushing he was able to dislodge the hook.

In the aftermath of this encounter, I moved downstream a few yards and took a position on a submerged gravel bar, with the water chest-deep and a deeper channel on either side of me. Now I could cast somewhat upstream, have a better and more natural float, but could not see as well the location of the fish. During this time Jason's teeth began to chatter, and Chris volunteered to take the two children the three miles or so back to the camp for a hot shower and a change into dry clothes.

After the boat's motor sounds faded down the river, I waited about ten more minutes and began to cast again, trying a series of wet and dry flies. I got an occasional rise, and once I was startled to see a huge head come gently out of the water and then sink quietly back. This was truly a monster rainbow! As I looked through my box of flies, I noticed a yellow stonefly nymph that George Harvey had sent me as a gift, one of his skillfully woven patterns on a #10 hook.

I tied it on and placed it far above where the fish seemed to be, stripping in line as the fly slowly sank and drifted back downstream. Suddenly there was a tremendous whirl in the water, and the rod was almost pulled from my hands. At first the trout moved upstream, near the bottom; through the vibrating line I could feel its head shaking. As I carefully shifted my feet around to move toward the fish and into shallower water, he leaped into the air—the biggest trout I had ever seen.

The fish headed resolutely downstream. I put maximum pressure on the tackle, keeping the #8 rod bent as much as it and I could bear. With majestic inexorability, the great trout continued on its course. In a few minutes my fly line was gone and the twenty-pound backing was disappearing at a steady rate. From time to time the fish would pause, and I would attempt to regain some line and turn him my way, but this aggravating pressure always precipitated an additional run downstream. The water was already lapping over the top of my chest waders and, because of the much deeper water on three sides, it was impossible for me to move in any direction except upstream, away from the fish. I could think of no way to shorten the distance between us. I had mixed emotions about being alone; it heightened the drama of an epic struggle between man and fish, but I could have used Chris's advice—and I knew that the distance was rapidly increasing between my adversary and me.

The fish and I struggled for every foot of line as I tried to keep the pressure strong but steady. Once, when I gave the rod an extra tug, way down the river a big fish leaped. I could hardly believe that this was my fish, so far away, almost out of sight. Practically all of my 150 yards of backing was gone and the outcome of this angling saga was becoming quite clear, but my dwindling hopes were revived when I heard the distant sound of a motor and saw Chris and his boat rounding the bend. He instantly saw what was happening and proceeded toward me cautiously, going around the other side of an island just below me and keeping the boat in shallow water, as near the shore as possible.

"He's really a big one," I shouted as he approached. "I've had him on about twenty minutes, but my line is almost gone."

Chris brought the boat close to me. With his help, I managed to hang over the side and then fall in, holding my rod as best I could so it wouldn't break. I didn't let Chris touch it; this had to be my struggle alone. As the boat drifted downstream I reeled in some line. The trout had by then gone around a sharp curve below the island, and the line was running through grass and tree roots against the bank. When it was clear again we moved closer to the fish, into shallower water. I stepped out of the boat, got a firm footing, and managed to bring in enough line to return all the backing to the reel.

Chris was giving me a constant stream of advice. "There's a gravel bar ahead. Maybe you could beach him there. But watch out for that big cluster of submerged roots in the deep water under the bank."

I couldn't stop the fish's progress toward the roots, and soon my heart sank as the vibrant motions of the trout were replaced by the sickening, steady pull of a fouled line. Following a brief expletive, I added, "I've lost him!"

I waded as close to the roots as possible, stuck the rod tip into the water, and the line came clear. Again the rod came alive in my hands.

"He's still on," I told Chris in excitement, "and not ready to give up!"

As I brought the big rainbow closer, Chris beached the boat and walked down the bar to help me land him. Finally, the fish was in shallow water, still wanting to fight but subdued now by the tight line. Chris prepared his camera while I protected the trout from any injury. I supported the fish gently upright as its body eased up on the sand bar. My fish, as I thought of him, was a brilliantly colored male, deep-bodied and heavy, with his lower jaw hooked slightly upward. He measured thirty inches long and nineteen inches around his midsection; Chris estimated his weight at twelve pounds.

I eased the tiny hook out of the corner of his mouth, supported his body with both hands under the stomach, and slowly moved the fish forward into the current as he faced upstream. After a few minutes, the trophy rainbow moved his tail strongly and eased off into the deeper water. As I watched him swim away I knew he was probably the largest trout I would ever catch in a lifetime of fishing.

"How would you like to have him mounted?" Chris asked.

I was a bit surprised by such a foolish question. "I'd rather the fish were alive in the Copper River," I told him.

Chris explained that I could have it both ways. "We've taken a representative number of Alaska rainbows to a superb taxidermist, along with photographs of the fish taken just as they came out of the water. Now we measure and photograph each trophy fish, and the taxidermist then creates a mounted trophy identical in color and size to the fish you caught and released. Along with it you get a plaque certified by an official guide, describing the circumstances of the event."

"Sounds good to me," I said. I certainly wouldn't mind having proof of my catch, as long as it wasn't at the fish's expense.

Inspired, we prepared to resume fishing, but before long I realized I had a chill; I couldn't get warm. Perhaps the excitement plus the long time in the deep and cold water had sapped my strength and taken away my inclination to fish any more just then. Or perhaps I felt that the great fish deserved to be honored in some fashion—if only by an hour or two of quiet contemplation of the event. In any case, we were soon on the way back downriver to Rainbow River Lodge. Our arrival was somewhat anticlimactic; there was just no way to recount to Jason and the others the excitement of my adventure.

That night Chris explained that the sockeye salmon was the foundation for the rainbow-trout life cycle in the Copper River. About 500,000 of the salmon enter the river each year to spawn, dying after their eggs are laid and fertilized. The decaying bodies, eggs, spawn, fingerlings, and growing salmon then support the indigenous rainbows. In this particular Alaskan stream, there are good hatches of mayflies, stoneflies, and caddis flies; they and their larvae and nymphs supplement the diet of this native strain of trout and help to explain their large numbers and exceptional size. Furthermore, in less-remote areas, long years of hatchery breeding for fast growth have reduced the life span of trout, but these wild rainbows have not been affected. They live much longer than stocked trout and grow larger when fully mature.

Although Jason and I fished hard, we didn't land a fish the next morning. However, about 2:00 P.M. there was a good caddis hatch, and our dry flies began to pay rich dividends. Since we couldn't reach the rising fish from wadeable water, we anchored the boat near enough to make successful casts. With a little help Jason landed two large rainbows. I caught several larger than seventeen inches and brought a twenty-four-inch fish in close enough to net, if we had been using a net. Demonstrating a final explosion of power, this fish broke my leader and swam off with a Royal Wulff in its mouth.

When not exclusively preoccupied with fishing, we also observed some of the wildlife in the valley and on the hillsides near the Copper. Both mature and immature bald eagles soared overhead or perched on rocky crags or in the tops of the spruce and cedar trees. Brown bear and moose could also be seen every now and then, watching our boat go by or cautiously observing us from a distant vantage point. Once, while eating lunch on a bluff above the river, we thought we glimpsed an enormous trout moving downstream. It turned out to be an otter, underwater, looking for his lunch too. An occasional marten or other small animal scurried up and down the riverbank. Although there were also a lot of beaver dens, one recently destroyed by a grizzly, we never saw a single beaver during our fishing excursions.

One day we flew about seventy miles southwestward to the Brooks River and Nanuktuk Creek, but the drizzling rain and strong winds made fishing difficult. After flying about half way back home, we landed on Lake Kukaklek to take a look around. As we walked back toward the float plane, we suddenly confronted a large grizzly, less than a hundred yards away. He was proceeding toward us, rising up periodically to feed on the tender leaves growing near the stream. I looked around quickly to find Jason. He was between me and the plane, also watching the bear and wondering what he and the bear were going to do next. We and the grizzly examined each other carefully, our side snapped a few photographs, and we moved quietly out of his way. Unmolested, the bear pretended to ignore our presence and soon disappeared over a small hill.

We then flew over to the Battle River, spotting two more single bears on the way. They seemed to be gathering around the streams in anticipation of the forthcoming salmon runs, when they and the eagles would feed voraciously on the spawning fish. Leaving the planes at the mouth of the river, we began a long hike parallel to the water, visiting the bank every now and then to see if we could find a fordable place or spot any fish rising. A bull moose watched us calmly from just across the stream. I thought its four-foot antler span magnificent, but Chris told me that was about average in these parts.

Walking several miles on this particular tundra was extremely difficult for all of us, especially for Jason and Betsy. Although covered with beautiful tiny flowers of many kinds, the springy surface was pockmocked like a moonscape. Each round hole was from two to six feet in diameter, sometimes three feet deep, and most often filled with water. To make things even more difficult, the holes were too close together to walk between them. In addition, large areas of the terrain were covered with low bushes whose branches were frequently intertwined. A careless step put us in the bottom of a hole, ankle-deep or waist-deep in water. Then again, getting wet was not much of a concern, because after just a few minutes we were all soaked with sweat. Later, when I asked Jason to tell me his greatest achievement of the entire trip, he replied, "Walking up and down the Battle River without crying."

His greatest fishing achievement came two days later, when we flew over to the north side of Lake Iliamna to scout for grayling and Arctic char in some small, unnamed lakes. On the way over we saw our first caribou herd, about a dozen moving eastward through the tundra. We had no luck in the lakes, but the connecting streams were small and wadeable—just right for Jason. He had been at a decided disadvantage in the large Copper River and so far had landed only two or three trout. Here, the water never lapped over his wading boots. I stayed with him and gave him a few pointers while he fished upstream with dry flies in the riffles, using a classical approach and a surprisingly delicate presentation. The strikes were swift and immediate. I was very proud to see him catch more than two dozen trout during the afternoon. Again, we released all the rainbows but kept enough of the larger grayling for our supper that evening.

The abundant wildlife provided almost constant excitement during the trip. Bear, caribou, otter, moose, and eagles were plentiful, and once, while I was fishing under an overhanging bluff, a light-gray wolf came across the tundra, lay down on the cliff above me to watch for a while, and then quietly loped away. I spent several hours watching two common loons who were nesting near the lodge on a small island. While one stayed on the nest, the other was usually on the lake fishing. They are anything but common—among the most beautiful of birds, with their intricate black-and-white summer markings. Only once or twice did we hear their strange cry, like a maniac laughing.

When we arrived back at the lodge that afternoon, some of Chris's neighbors were there as additional guests. While the children played up on the tundra, the rest of us sat on rocks and logs along the shore and discussed how the permanent residents were trying to prevent too many changes in their Alaskan way of life while still welcoming tourists and new jobs. It seemed like a hopeless task, but at least this group agreed that the new Alaska Lands Bill offered the best guidelines for protecting the places that were especially lovely.

Chris thought we might need a few more fish for supper, so he and I decided to try the northern pike just around the bend from our camp. On my first cast with a small silver spoon I landed a twenty-four-inch pike—a ferocious prehistoric-looking monster. Two casts later, a larger one nearly came into the boat with us when he attacked the lure just as I prepared to lift it from the water. It was almost frightening. We moved a hundred yards and began casting again in the gathering dusk. As the lure hit the surface in one small cove, we could see waves from several pike converging on the splash point. Each racing to see which could reach the lure first, they looked like crocodiles in an old Tarzan movie. In anticipation of a strike—or perhaps subconsciously to avoid one—I snatched the spoon out of the water! On the next cast, I took a thirty-four-inch pike, enough for a fine meal. Later, cooked in foil, the pike fillets proved to be the favorite fish of all the diners.

The weather had warmed rapidly since our arrival. The morning temperature was now up above fifty degrees Fahrenheit and the afternoons fifteen degrees warmer. We could tell within the week that much of the snow on the nearby mountaintops had melted. More important for us, the caddis and stonefly hatches multiplied. After lunch on the last few days of the trip it was not hard to spot rising trout. Usually we would catch a few fish during the early morning on wet flies and heavier tackle, and then shift to dry flies, a #5 rod, and fine leaders to fish the hatches. While Jason cast in the shallow pools and around the edges, I braved the deeper waters where we could see the larger rainbows.

Despite the plentiful feeding trout, it wasn't easy to match the tiny caddis flies the trout seemed to be taking. Sometimes, after trying small flies of all sizes, we had success with a #12 Royal Wulff. On only one occasion did the trout rise regularly to a #16 or #18 elk-hair Caddis, but this was to be the preeminent dry-fly fishing of my life. In midafternoon, large fish began feeding near the deeper bank on a wide stretch of the river. Even when I waded out the maximum safe distance, standing on my tiptoes, I could barely reach them with my longest cast using a double haul. The strong center current between me and the trout began dragging the line as soon as it landed; at best I was able to give the fly four or five feet of natural float. However, with almost every "perfect" cast, a big rainbow would take the tiny fly with a determined, rolling strike. Then I would have to keep a tight line and at the same time ease back out of the deep water until I found a firm enough foothold in the loose bottom gravel to let me put tension on the line.

It took me twenty-five minutes to land my first fish, a twenty-one incher, using a three-pound test tippet. After that I changed to a stronger leader, so that neither the trout nor I would be too exhausted when the battle was over. Despite a careful retrieve I still broke two leaders but landed a dozen rainbows, the smallest one fourteen inches. When the hatch was over I could hardly raise my arm. Fishing from a sand bar farther downstream, Jason had had an equally thrilling time.

He and I were both saddened as our week drew to a close, a feeling tempered only by the prospect of a reunion with my wife and Jason's parents. We knew it would be impossible for us ever to recount our experiences to them. They were truly indescribable: our immersion in the beauty and grandeur of Alaska's mountains, tundra, and waterways; our close encounters with the bears, moose, eagles, and other wildlife; and the testing of our wits and skills against some of the greatest fighting fish on earth. Most important, at least for me, was my companionship with Jason. Repeatedly during these few days I was flooded with memories of outings with my father. Sometimes I watched my grandson react to a thrilling spectacle—or an unexpected challenge—and imagined that I was seeing myself two generations ago.

From Rainbow River Lodge we flew up the Copper River, west across Cook Inlet, and then northward up the Kenai Peninsula back to Anchorage. It had been an exhausting week, but Jason still had his face pressed against the window as we looked down at just a few more of Alaska's wonders. We didn't talk much, except to speculate on when we might return. Jason and I had developed an undying appreciation for our forty-ninth state.

HOME-GROWN

THE NOBLE TURKEY

Between 1966 and 1970, I was campaigning all over the state of Georgia, running for governor. Whenever I could take time off from our farm and warehouse I would drive my own car to various communities, usually returning late at night with a list of people to add to our roster of prospective supporters. On a few of the longer trips I had to spend the night and return to Plains as early as possible the following morning.

It was the time of the early environmental law debates, in which I had been actively involved as a state senator and as one of the founders of the Georgia Conservancy. In my campaign speeches I frequently emphasized my concerns about pollution damage to Georgia's air, water, forests, marshlands, and other natural areas.

On a trip to Savannah, on the East Coast, I had strongly condemned the serious air and water pollution there from the large paper mills and other industries—and was just as strongly denounced by some of the city fathers, executives of the companies, and leaders of the local Chamber of Commerce. They stated to the news media that I was unfit to lead the state with my radical protectionist views, which would only bring destruction to Georgia's industry, resulting in massive unemployment.

Leaving the city before sunrise, I was driving westward along an interstate highway, contemplating the previous day's events and looking every now and then in my rearview mirror at the smoke and smog that covered the horizon.

Suddenly there burst from the woods on my left an enormous black bird. As he set his wings and sailed in front of my car I recognized a wild turkey gobbler, his neck stretched forward and a long beard hanging from it. The thrilling sight restored my lagging spirits. It was the first wild gobbler I had seen in more than fifteen years. There were just a few left, mostly along the Georgia coast. I wondered then if my baby daughter, Amy, would ever have a chance to witness such a sight before the noble creatures were all gone from our area of the world.

Benjamin Franklin wanted the turkey to be the official American bird instead of the eagle, which he characterized as a scavenger and "a bird of bad moral character." He must have been a good woodsman, because those of us who have gotten to know the wild turkey would certainly agree that its character, clean feeding habits, intelligence, nobility of bearing, uniqueness to America, strong role in our lives since Colonial times, and its inducement for us to preserve some of our most precious habitat, all warrant recognition in a special way.

During the early part of this century wild turkeys became almost extinct in many parts of the United States; even in Georgia they were hard to find. When I was a child they were still more plentiful than deer, mostly in the isolated swamp areas along the larger creeks and rivers. We would see turkey tracks around the edges of our most remote fields adjacent to big woods, and even glimpse a bird every now and then. However, during the Depression years, when the game laws were not well enforced, we knew that some of our neighbors would bait turkeys in a trench aligned with a blind and slaughter every bird they saw in order to put meat on the table, even including hens during nesting season.

Later, game and fish biologists tried to reestablish turkeys in their original habitat by hatching wild turkey eggs, raising the young poults, and releasing the adults. But few if any of these sheltered and disease-prone birds survived in the wild. Trapping or netting grown birds along the coastal areas and transferring them to the inland regions of our state had a much greater possibility of success. Unfortunately, this program was also doomed, at least in Georgia, because of politics. While I was in the State Senate, it was common knowledge that members of the Game and Fish Commission, the governor, speaker of the House of Representatives, and a few other powerful people received the turkeys. The birds found their way either directly into ovens as a rare and special culinary delicacy, became semidomesticated, or were released in unsuitable habitat and soon perished.

When I became governor of Georgia, I was determined to bring an end to these kinds of practices. Under the supervision of Jack Crockford, a survey was made of the entire state, determining the most promising locations for the rehabilitation of wild turkeys. Thereafter, when any of the birds were captured they were transported to these communities and released without notification, even to the landowners. After a year or two, when the turkeys had established themselves in the new habitat, the farmers were informed about the presence of the flock and urged to provide maximum protection for them.

After a few years of observation by game and fish biologists, it was clear that the flocks had become large enough to be self-supporting, and turkey seasons were opened in individual counties. This was a slow process, but it proved to be successful. Now, in many areas of our state the turkey population is adequate to perpetuate the species—provided strict game laws are observed. This conservation effort has been followed throughout the country, and as a result there is a turkey hunting season in thirty-six states. For about six weeks, late in the spring, it is legal in some Georgia counties to hunt gobblers only. Rifles are prohibited, and the season is delayed until after the gobblers and hens have completed their necessary mating so that nesting eggs will be fertilized.

Hunting gobblers during the springtime is a highly specialized and very difficult pastime. Turkeys range in a wide area, change their roosting places frequently, unpredictably, and prefer the deeper and more isolated regions for their habitat. Among the wariest of birds, they favor isolated woodlands with adequate water and enough broad-leaved trees to provide shade and cover. The shade minimizes dense growth of weeds and smaller bushes, ensuring that the ground area is open enough so that the large birds can fly down from their roosting sites and land in clear areas. It also allows them to scratch and feed without being surprised and killed by predators who might otherwise creep up on them undetected. These same trees, mostly oaks, provide nuts that remain edible throughout the winter.

Even mature turkeys are the potential prey of great horned owls, bobcats, and coyotes, and their nests and eggs are eagerly sought by snakes, raccoons, weasels, skunks, and other small animals. Although not able to detect their potential enemies by smell, turkeys are known to have superb sight and hearing. Fast runners, they can move quickly and almost silently from danger. Ever alert, turkeys can launch themselves from the ground almost instantly, their strong wings thrusting them swiftly through the forest for more than a quarter of a mile. Turkeys are protected from predators by being so elusive. An experienced hunter can go for an entire hunting season and succeed only in enjoying the solitude of the woods and perhaps learning from his mistakes.

In the mid-seventies two pairs of turkeys were released on our own family farms. For more than ten years we have watched them thrive. Every now and then turkeys flush near us while we're quail hunting. The large and heavy birds always thrill us with their beautiful flight. Most of the time we would find them on the ground feeding or dusting themselves, but sometimes they fly from high up in the trees, even late in the morning after most other turkeys have come down from their roosts to feed.

Using binoculars from several hundred yards away, I have often watched wild turkeys feed on the edge of one of our fields. Experimenting, I found that an amazingly slight sound will send them scurrying for cover; when a gobbler's head is raised to scan the horizon, even the tiniest movement will cause him to sound an alarm for the entire flock. In the deep woods the birds are equally alert, especially when anything makes them suspicious—such as the off-tune and unrhythmical hen calls made by a novice hunter.

I began my turkey hunting a number of years ago, in partnership with more experienced hunters who were skilled in imitating turkey calls and would attempt to take a turkey only from areas where they were plentiful. I have never done anything except springtime hunting, when the goal is to convince an amorous tom that a lonely hen is calling him to respond to her love call. There are many kinds of callers, including diaphragms that fit into the roof of one's mouth, turkey wing-bones that can be sucked with a kissing motion, flat pieces of slate that are stroked with the end of a charred stick, and wooden boxes of various shapes and sizes, the edges of which resonate when rubbed and give forth the appropriate sound. I understand that some people can imitate turkeys using their own lips and vocal cords without any accessories, but I've never hunted with anyone who had this gift.

Since my own efforts to get an appropriate sound from diaphragms and turkey wing-bones proved embarrassing failures, for several years I was reluctant to try calling. I was lucky enough to hunt with partners who could call and were willing to let me stay up front and share the shooting. Despite a number of attempts in some of the best turkey-hunting territory along the Georgia coast, we had a lot more failures than successes; in my early years I was able to come home with only two gobblers. Once after an hour and a half of classical maneuvering and calling, I bagged a very large old tom that weighed twenty-one pounds.

I know of no other kind of hunting that requires more skill, patience, practice, knowledge of woodsmanship—and luck—

than seeking the wily gobbler in his own territory. When two or more are scratching or feeding together, at least one of them will have its neck extended, carefully looking and listening for any sign of danger. If an observer is well camouflaged and completely immobile, however, wild turkeys can be seen at close range.

One morning I was sitting under a scrubby pine tree on the edge of a clearing when a lone turkey hen emerged from the thick underbrush less than twenty yards away. She must have sensed my presence, because she was very cautious as she moved forward and began to scratch in the leaves and grass. Her head was erect 90 percent of the time, constantly turning back and forth to give a complete circumferential view of the surrounding area. With 270-degree vision, only slight movements of her head were necessary. At one time she and I were only fifteen yards apart. As we looked directly at each other for quite a while, I neither blinked nor moved a muscle. Although I had no blind to conceal my body, I was clothed in camouflage trousers, shirt, gloves, head cover, and mask, with my gun covered in camouflage tape, and she was not alarmed enough to stop feeding.

Even after turkeys became plentiful in Southwest Georgia, I was reluctant to hunt them in the vicinity of Plains. I wanted to be sure they were really well established. That was before I met our local game and fish ranger on a country road through my farm and he asked me when I was going to harvest some of my turkeys. When I said that it might be better to let them multiply for a few more years, he told me: "There are enough of them here now. In fact, on the farms joining yours we've been trapping some of the excess turkeys and transplanting them to other parts of the state. There may be too many toms around here already."

He had me convinced. In preparation for the next season, I began to learn more about the necessary techniques. I talked to experienced hunters, read their books, listened to audio tapes of calls, practiced with various calling devices, and began to scout the more inaccessible forest and swamp areas for signs of turkey habitation. Droppings, V-shaped scratched areas, and tracks in soft sand or muddy places were good signs of where turkeys had chosen to reside. On occasion I would sight one or more of the birds feeding in some of the open woods or around the edges of fields.

Finally, late in April 1987, I decided to try my luck. Completely camouflaged, I entered the woods at what I believed to be the most likely spot for turkeys. It was still quite dark, at least an hour and a half before sunrise. Making as little noise as possible and using the shielded beam of a small flashlight, I moved silently through the underbrush to an opening and sat down under a large bay tree near a small stream, about a half mile from Choctawhatchee Creek.

Within three quarters of an hour the forest began to come alive with the increasingly frequent whippoorwill calls, the unmistakable cry of a mourning dove, an occasional "Who cooks for you? Who cooks for you-all?" of the barred owl, and once the "Hoo, hoo-hoo" of the great horned owl. As day began to break, song birds flitted from one limb to another and crows began to call. I could hear the distant crowing of a rooster at the nearest house, at least a mile away. A fox squirrel startled me by rattling across the dry leaves; out of the corner of my eye I saw him climb a nearby tree. Even this early, when no turkeys were moving around, I was reluctant to turn my head.

The minutes ticked away, and the eastern sky grew steadily brighter. As the forest noises became more routine, I began to feel a little drowsy. All of a sudden I was electrified. Was that a gobble in the distance toward the creek? With every muscle and nerve focused ahead, I listened with breathless intensity. The peculiar noise came again. I recognized it this time as the hammering of a pileated woodpecker. I gobbled with my largest box caller and yelped a time or two, without response. By sunrise, it seemed increasingly unlikely that any gobblers were going to sound in my vicinity.

I waited another half hour, giving an amateurish call every now and then, before deciding to explore the deeper woods more thoroughly. I then began to move slowly and carefully through the trees, picking out paths where my footsteps made the least noise. Some people say not to worry about that too much because a turkey walking through the woods sounds just like a man, but I knew that turkeys couldn't break dry limbs. I was looking closely at the ground for turkey signs and pausing every couple of hundred yards to give a call. Each time I waited a few minutes, perfectly still, to listen for a possible gobbler response.

For two and a half hours I explored the woods, observing them more carefully than ever before. No turkeys, but I learned a lot about my own place that I had never noticed. Almost perfectly camouflaged and moving or standing as quietly as possible, I could often observe wild creatures at close range. Common birds and small animals of many kinds showed little timidity, and occasionally I saw deer moving through the forest. At one time, while standing quite still, I saw a shadowy shape approaching, and a lean and mangy coyote passed not more than fifteen yards away; he never even knew I was there.

His presence did explain the death of a hen turkey whose remains we had found in these woods a couple of weeks before. Coyotes had only recently been seen in our part of Georgia, having migrated in from the Southwest. I was tempted to shoot this one, but the birdshot would not have been fatal—and the sound of the gunshot would have frightened all the turkeys within half a mile.

Later, while I was walking in a different part of our farm, I heard some loud taps near the top of a large short-leaf pine. Slowly I moved my head upward to see what was there. Soon a large and beautiful bird came swooping down to light on a limb just a few yards from me. It was a pileated woodpecker, one of the most spectacular creatures of our southeastern forests. I had never seen one so close before. About the size of a crow, the bird had a brilliant red crest that glistened in the early morning sun. It hopped midway out on a two-inch dead limb and pecked several times on top, then bent around and pecked on each side, almost as far as the bottom of the limb. After digesting or contemplating the results, the great woodpecker departed, undulating through the air on its powerful wingbeats.

Deer, coyotes, and woodpeckers, but no turkeys. I was discouraged by my failures on this and other mornings, but during my spare time I continued to practice my turkey-hen imitations, and eventually two or three of the calls began to sound similar to those of experts coming from the tape player. One afternoon, walking toward a small and remote field surrounded by standing timber, I surprised a young gobbler ahead of me on the path. The field was almost covered with turkey

tracks, and I was quite excited about the prospect of a successful hunt in an area that I had not previously considered. I
located a good place in the woods, marked the path so that I
could find it in the dark, and prepared for another excursion
the next morning.

A light rain fell through most of the night, but it was fair
and cool when I returned to take my position. After a fruitless
hour of calling and listening I decided to move deeper into the
still-dripping woods. With both a box and a slate caller I was
well prepared to give my best imitations, but the farther I went,
the less sound I could get from my box caller. Finally it did not
sound at all, and I was distressed to discover that the slate had
also lost its voice because dampness prevented the necessary
vibrations. I had not brought along a supply of chalk with
which to dry the surfaces of the callers, and my other efforts to
dry them were fruitless. My only choice was to give up hunting
for the day and walk the mile back to my vehicle, having
learned one more lesson the hard way.

One day, checking on some timber we had sold, Rosalynn and I
walked to the top of a small rise where we had a clear view of a
thirty-acre field. Although alfalfa had been planted in most of
the area, there were some volunteer peanuts in the lower
section near the thick woods. I immediately saw three black
dots in the distance. My binoculars revealed that they were all
gobblers; their white heads were obvious as they lifted them
frequently to take a careful look around. We enjoyed watching
the turkeys scratch and feed. Two of them apparently became
alarmed and moved into the woods, but the other was undisturbed. Looking closely, I saw another white head come up
above the weed level and realized that a fourth bird was scratching in a shallow ditch. We eased away, but I knew where I
would be heading early the next morning.

I presumed the turkeys would be roosting fairly deep in
the woods, and so I found a spot under a pine tree about fifty
yards from the open field. There were few oak or hickory trees
in the area, but thick young stands of pine were growing in
spots under their parent trees. I had a fairly unobstructed view
of a small clearing ahead and to my left. Still, it was difficult for
me to see much in the other directions. I made a small blind of

broken limbs and bush tops, scraped up enough pine straw to form a comfortable seat, and settled down to listen.

Shortly after daybreak I heard the unmistakable gobble of a tom turkey far off to my left, too faint for me to pursue from my location. Nevertheless, I gave a "tree" call just in case. Soon a flock of crows flew past me, their caws reverberating through the woods. A gobbler answered the crows off to my right, much closer. I glanced at my watch: 6:43 A.M. I was using a box caller and responded with a hen's yelp, just a couple of them. Eight minutes after the first gobble came another, apparently from the same location. After a while I gave two or three yelps. Waiting almost the same interval, the tom announced his presence again. He still had not moved.

I gave another call, but the small and bushy pines blocked my vision in the gobbler's direction. I had about decided to move toward him when I heard a slight sound of feet on leaves. I froze, shifting my eyes as far as possible to the right. A turkey went by, slipping quietly with its neck stretched forward. The head was a bluish color—a hen, not to be hunted. A few minutes later I thought I heard the leaves rustle on my other side; obviously, changing my location was not a good idea right now. I yelped about every ten minutes, but there was no further response.

My confidence was gone. Clearly, I had forgotten all I had learned from my practice while listening to the tapes of champion turkey callers.

Then, not more than a hundred yards away, there was an explosive gobble. I was electrified with excitement but alarmed, because the turkey was to my right and behind me, apparently near the edge of the open field. Leaving my blind, I crept around toward the turkey's position. I gave a call. There came another gobble, quite close, and I dared not move again. With no tree nearby, I just squatted in some grass and peered through the underbrush. Through a small opening, I glimpsed the amorous gobbler, moving toward me with his feathers spread wide in his proudest strut. I had moved closer than intended.

For a while there was only silence. If I had seen him, surely he could have spotted me. Turkey hunters had told me many times that a gobbler could see all around. He could have detected me for sure if his head hadn't been buried in his

142

feathers. I dropped back on the ground out of sight, but every now and then I could hear the tips of his wings scraping the ground. He seemed to be walking away. With shaking hands, I gave two short yelps, laid my box caller on the ground, and fixed my gun barrel in line with a small opening to the field.

Trying to quiet my labored breathing, I peered intently at the edge of a small space between some plum bushes and a dogwood tree. For a long time there was total silence. Then I began to hear the slight scraping sound again, drawing nearer. The gobbler, in his passionate abandon, had lost some of his usual caution.

His dark bulk blurred the tiny openings among the thick leaves, but there was no chance for a successful shot. The #4 pellets would not penetrate the underbrush and the ruffled feathers of the big bird. Then he stopped, folded his chest feathers, and raised his head above the weeds to take his last look around.

A few minutes later I was on the way home from my first successful effort as a solitary hunter. My tom had the pink legs, fully developed tail feathers, the beard of a two-year-old, and weighed a heavy eighteen pounds. Surprisingly, at this time of year, late April, his crop was full of last year's peanuts that were beginning to sprout, along with some unidentified green foliage. He would make a fine Thanksgiving dinner for our entire family.

Turkey hens are protected at all times in Georgia, although in some states they are plentiful enough to be hunted for a few days each year. The gobbler season is nesting time, and the hens I had seen recently were probably setting on a clutch of a dozen or so eggs, waiting for the poults to hatch.

A couple of weeks after I got my tom, Rosalynn and I were walking around the edge of a swamp, looking for Indian arrowheads and checking the survival of newly planted pine seedlings in an area where the mature trees had been recently harvested and the bare ground exposed. As we approached a thick stand of wild plum bushes partially covered with blooming honeysuckle, we were startled by a wild commotion of flopping wings and shrill cries of something like "cut-cut-cut."

Then a turkey hen flopped into view, struggling along the ground as though one of her wings were broken.

She came deliberately close to us, moving past to attract our attention away from where she had been. I understood her tactics and observed a small flock of newly hatched turkey chicks, mostly squatting immobile on the ground, but two or three still moving to find concealment. The hen made a semi-circle around us, then ran to the edge of the swamp area and soared off through the trees. We watched her as we left the site, careful not to disturb the chicks. Her flight was circular. She landed about thirty yards from her starting point, heading directly for her brood.

It happened to be May 9, the day before Mother's Day. Rosalynn and I, walking away quietly, agreed that, with good weather, careful observance of conservation laws, protection of native habitat, and courage and survival instincts like those of this mother bird, the noble turkey would have a bright future in America.

CATCHING
BASS ON
TELEVISION

When I was governor of Georgia, I fished a few times in the
Walter F. George Reservoir—or Lake Eufaula, as it is known by
all Alabamians and most Georgians from the western part of the
state. After one of these trips, some of the news stories
reported—accurately—that my catch had been very small.

Within a few days I received in the mail a small box of
lures and a book entitled *Tom Mann's Methods for Catching
Bass*. The gift was from the book's author and recent winner of
the national B.A.S.S. tournament at Lake Kissimmee, Florida.
At that time, in 1972, the Bass Anglers Sportsman Society was

a well-established and widely known organization among all warm-water fishermen. A few years later, I was to welcome Tom Mann to the Oval Office to receive a presidential award as the outstanding small businessman of the nation.

Tom had grown up as a farm boy with a life very similar to mine. He'd plowed a mule, fished for "horney heads" and small bream in the tiny branches, for catfish and eels in muddy and rising creeks when it was too wet to work in the fields, gigged suckers during their spawning runs, and then graduated to plug fishing for bass in nearby ponds.

Fishing became his greatest passion. As a schoolboy his goal was to be a conservation officer, a professional guide, or to get a job with a fishing lure manufacturer. After high school he worked for a time in a cotton mill, deliberately choosing the night and early-morning shifts so that he would have plenty of time to fish in the afternoons. After serving in the Korean War, he came home to a job as an Alabama game and fish biologist. Then, in 1958, he and his wife, Ann, bought five dollars' worth of lead and some polar-bear hair and began to make lures on the kitchen table. Tom carved and molded the jig bodies, Ann painted them, and then he tied the white tails.

Tom caught so many fish on his innovative designs that he began to sell them to some of the neighbors. The business grew, and soon the Manns were making more income from the lures than from his state job. They bought an entire polar-bear hide for $800, used it all, and shifted to other more readily available materials. Within a few years, more than a hundred employees were producing the various lures that Tom devised, and his prowess as a successful fisherman became known through competitions, from numerous articles in outdoor magazines, and an aggressive public relations campaign. Among bass fishermen, he was preeminent.

He won a number of fishing tournaments and continued to expand his various business enterprises, all centered around fishing. In 1969, using Heathkit circuits, he began to produce a sonic depth-finder that was relatively inexpensive and able to operate in a fast-moving boat with a minimum of interference from the motor or water noises. Under the Humminbird brand, many thousands of these devices were sold to the rapidly expanding number of fishermen who knew that the bottom configuration of lakes was a vital clue to the most likely spots for fish. Thanks to this device, they could at times actually see schools of fish on the electronic screen.

I watched Tom Mann catch fish on many television programs and tried to put his fishing techniques into practice on my own excursions in the warm waters of Georgia. By the time he came to the White House to be recognized for his success in business, I was eager to ply him with questions. However, we had no chance to talk during our busy schedules that day. Later, when my term as President was over, I was delighted to receive an invitation from him for a day's fishing.

On the day before my visit I called him just to make sure that all the arrangements were understood, ending our conversation by saying eagerly, "Okay, I'll be leaving here at six o'clock in the morning."

There was some hesitation, and then Tom said gently, "Mr. President, you'll get here too early. It's only a fifty-mile drive, and don't forget we're an hour behind you across the river in Alabama. The older I get the more I realize that the fish will still be biting after sunup."

The next morning, an hour later than originally planned, I traveled westward from Plains through a heavy fog, crossed the Chattahoochee River, followed the signs north of Eufaula directing me to Fish World, and drove up in front of a beautiful mansion just a few yards from Tom's large freshwater aquarium. Tom and Ann welcomed me with a big breakfast of cheese grits, country ham and sausage, scrambled eggs, fresh-baked buttermilk biscuits, mayhaw jelly and pear preserves, and hot coffee. When I complimented Ann on their lovely home, she said, "We were very proud when we built it, but we don't live here. A few years ago we went up the road to spend one night at the old house on our farm and never moved back. Now we just use this big house for office space and for special occasions like this."

The Manns, obviously full partners, brought me up-to-date on the latest developments in their business enterprises. They had sold both Mann Lures and the electronics company, but they and their children were still inventing new lures, manufacturing plastic worms, and publishing an outdoor magazine for children. The Manns were especially excited about expanding Fish World to include an eighteen-hole fishing course for young people which Tom was building in the lake just behind the house. Tom still entered some of the major bass tournaments just to keep his name before the public, but claimed he lacked the time and was not in good enough physical shape to be a top competitor. Nevertheless, he had just signed a contract for a new television series, for which he would begin filming twenty-six segments early in the summer.

After breakfast the fog was still too thick to move safely on the big lake, so Tom suggested that we try out some of his experimental lures on the pond across the road. "I've got a new plastic worm with a tail copied from the design of a common Indian arrowhead we find around here, and it is a lot simpler to use, has great action, and really catches fish. Because it wiggles so much, I'll probably call it the Hawaii Worm," he told me.

In the twenty-acre reservoir Tom had used his own bulldozer to scoop out deep holes, piling up the dirt to create many small islands. He suggested that I use one of my favorite lures while he tied on one of his new ones, a "walker" that he had named Hard Worm.

I fished hard with a five-inch Rapala, and *he* began to catch bass regularly. With a grin, he finally threw me one of his lures. My fishing improved immediately. After a half hour or so, we shifted to his new plastic worm. When pulled steadily through the water, the tail wiggled vigorously. "You don't have to know any tricks," said Tom. "Just throw it out, let it sink to the depth you want it, and crank it back in slowly."

I had as many strikes as he, but he caught two or three times as many bass. Tom held his rod almost vertical, was extremely sensitive to any nibble, and, with a quick flick of his powerful wrist and a half turn on the reel handle, could almost instantly set the hook firmly in the fish's mouth. I have noticed that most fishermen, including me, use a much slower movement of the entire arm to get as much leverage. Some have to use so much body movement that they almost fall out of the boat when they set the hook.

Within an hour the fog lifted enough to move to Lake Eufaula. We had caught about thirty nice bass. I kept only one;

after a photograph I carried it to the water's edge and released it too.

At the boat landing on the lake we talked to several fishermen, all of whom reported that the fish had just not been biting that morning or for the last few days. None of them had caught a fish. Tom was not discouraged, saying quietly, "We may be able to find a few."

As we moved away from the pier, my fishing partner commented that now, in the middle of May, most bass away from the immediate shoreline would likely be found at a depth of around ten feet, moving an average of five feet deeper each month as the water warmed up through the late spring and summer. We would first stay out in the lake and try plastic worms, tied twelve to sixteen inches below about half an ounce of lead weight, fishing the relatively shallow submerged banks around the old riverbed (the bottom of which at that time was about seventy feet deep).

A large flock of Canada geese was flying around the islands in the lake, some of the birds on the water with several goslings. "A lot of them over-winter here now," Tom said, "and one of their favorite nesting places is on the small islands in my ponds. They're protected from most of the foxes and raccoons, and the survival rate seems to be pretty high." We also watched several osprey that circled overhead, surveying the lake for fish from the tops of the dead trees. This beautiful bird, as big as some eagles with its five-foot wingspan, had almost been eradicated by the extensive use of the pesticide DDT, now banned in our country. We were delighted to see that now it was coming back. At one point, fishing near a steel tower supporting a shallow metal saucer, we saw an osprey nest with two adults perched on its edge. The game and fish rangers were trying the tower as an experimental nesting place, and it seemed to be working well.

Tom and I fished all the rest of the day except for a brief stop in a shady place for lunch. I learned a lot that I had never known before. It seemed that the key to Tom's success was an intimate knowledge of the lake bottom and an uncanny ability to read the depth-finder results. In the middle of the lake it all looked the same to me, but as he explained from his own memory, using the depth-finder on occasion to illustrate a point, each of his casts was placed to take advantage of the configuration of the bottom. We threaded our lures along old ditches, through and across standing and fallen timber, across grass flats that would be exposed if the lake level had dropped a few feet, and up and down the steep slopes of the original riverbank.

Although our rig was relatively weedless without any hook exposed, we lost a lot of plastic worms in the thick underwater brush. "This is why we sell about four million dollars' worth of these a year," Tom said. "You have to put the worms in the rough places to catch fish. They're still the cheapest and best lure to use. Eighty-five percent of tournament bass are caught on plastic worms."

Each time we caught a fish in a new location away from the shore we threw a small marker buoy over the side, then circled it and fished the area thoroughly. Tom caught his fourth fish before I ever landed one. He was very gentle with his advice, but I watched him closely and tried to copy what he did. Since a few bass were taking shad near the surface, we tried some spinner bait and the Hard Worm, but the plastic worm on the bottom was what the fish wanted.

We also fished some in the coves. I caught a few, and again the plastic worm was the most effective lure. The only strike we had on spinner bait was from a ten-foot alligator, when Tom pulled the lure too close in front of its nose.

I asked Tom a lot of questions about the fishing tournaments. Even he was amazed at how large and lucrative they had become. "I'll be fishing in a 'megabucks' tournament later this year. There will be two hundred contestants, and the entrance fee for each of us is five thousand dollars. First prize will be two hundred and fifty thousand dollars, with sixty prizes in all." When I asked him what chances he would have of at least winning his $5,000 back, he thought a while before answering: "About ninety percent."

Then he added, "Next month I'll be in the Lake Okeechobee tournament, one of my favorites because it's managed well and there are more bass per acre there than anywhere else I know. It's a lot better to compete when everyone can catch some fish.

"I remember one year we had a tournament at the West Point reservoir farther up the Chattahoochee, which is usually a fine place to fish. The temperature dropped overnight to thirty-nine degrees, and the fish just wouldn't bite. There were two hundred contestants, and only one fish was caught in three days. On the other hand, I've seen a hundred and thirty-nine pounds of bass caught by one fisherman here in Lake Eufaula. My top in a tournament is ninety-six pounds, but fishing with a friend in 1972, we took a hundred and fifty-five pounds of bass in one day. The top seventeen averaged over seven pounds, with the biggest one a little over thirteen pounds."

"With all the tournament fishermen, it seems that the bass population would soon be depleted on the more popular reservoirs," I commented.

"We used to kill most of the fish, but now there is a two-ounce penalty if a dead one is brought in to be weighed. We're very careful to keep them alive, because a dead fish might cost you the big prize. I would estimate that ninety-five percent of the bass we catch in tournaments are released and survive. It's a big improvement, and we all feel better about it."

Around sunset, clouds began rolling in from the west and we could see lightning in the distance. It was time to return to the landing—the end of a fine day with one of America's greatest fishermen.

On the way in he asked me, "Would you be willing to come back next year and join me in making one of my television programs?"

I thought about it. "I wouldn't want millions of people to see how many more bass you catch!" I concluded.

Tom was ready for me. "You bring your fly rod, I'll fish with my spinning outfit, and if there is any difference we can blame it on the tackle." I agreed to work out a mutually convenient date.

This is the kind of invitation I never forget, and so the next summer I was back with Tom Mann again. Along with my bait-casting outfit I had my #5 fly rod, a floating line, and a good selection of flies that had proven effective with bass. We first had a few words with the television crews, who would have their cameras at strategic places on the shore and in a boat that would stay as close as possible to Tom and me. He and I were outfitted with microphones on our shirt fronts and a small transmitter in our pockets so that our comments could be recorded by the technicians.

By noon the temperature was 105 degrees in the shade, and all of us were soaked with sweat. Some of the television camera batteries were damaged by the heat and there were a number of interruptions in their recording of our activities, but we didn't let this interefere with either our conversation or our fishing. Using a small deer-hair fly on the surface, I was catching more bass than Tom with his spinning tackle, although his were somewhat bigger. In the meantime we talked about our early boyhood days, fishing tournaments, and my fly-fishing experiences in different streams around the world. For lunch we ate beenie-weenies, Vienna sausage, cheese, and crackers in the boat under the shade of a large pine tree, continuing our conversation for the benefit of the television crew.

Almost nine months later the program was telecast, and Tom sent me a videotape for my library. The size of the audience was amazing. Everywhere I went, people would let me know they had seen Tom Mann and me fishing together. And all the comments were friendly. In more ways than one this was a media experience quite different from those of my life in the political world.

THE
PRINCE OF
GAME BIRDS

When I was selling boiled peanuts around Mr. Woodruff's livery stable, the automobile garage of Rosalynn's father, the service stations of Mr. Kitty Timmerman and Mill Jennings, Bud Walters's cobbler shop, and the barbershop of Mr. Broadus Wellons, the most prevalent subject of discussion was the common bob-white quail *(Colinus virginianus).* There was no facet of their existence that was not thoroughly analyzed; no Plains citizen came back from a hunt without his own vivid stories about the birds, his dogs, or how he or his hunting companions had reacted to the always unpredictable circumstances in the fields.

I listened to those oft-repeated tales for hours, hearing them in snatches but knowing that over a week's time the interesting parts would all be told—and retold—in my presence.

There were the apocryphal hunting jokes, usually at the expense of ignorant big-city hunters who came in to try the sport with a local farmer. On one such occasion, the hunters were riding horses, observing the dogs working back and forth ahead of them. At the first point, the visitor asked, "Is it all right to shoot from off this horse?"

The farmer replied, "Of course it is."

When the birds flushed, the city slicker fired at them from the saddle, and the horse pitched him head over heels into a thicket of blackberry briers. He stood up and confronted the farmer: "I thought you said it was okay to shoot off this horse."

The reply: "You can shoot off him, but not on him."

In those days it took a long time to plant or cultivate an acre, because farming was done with mules (and a few horses). The fields were small, divided by a latticework of fences, terraces, and hedgerows. Except for the most industrious farmers, few made much effort to clean the briers and small bushes off these linear plots, so that quail had an almost perfect habitat for breeding, nesting, raising their young, and finding refuge from the hawks and other predators who sought them. Fire ants, a scourge among baby quail chicks, were not yet prevalent around Plains. (We didn't know then that they were farther south, moving up at a rate that would bring them to our farms after another twenty-five years.) The deadly herbicides and insecticides of all kinds that were later to threaten the existence of some bird species were unknown. And so bobwhite quail flourished during the Depression years, offering prime sport and many wonderful meals to the people of our community.

It was inevitable that I would become an avid quail hunter, looking for every opportunity to roam the fields with my father or any of his close friends who were permitted to hunt on our farm. Later, of course, I could go by myself if necessary, often accompanied only by one of our bird dogs. The hunting season was always between November 20 and February 20, when field-work was least demanding. Although there were still fences and buildings to be repaired, livestock to be tended, wood to be cut, and some land to be turned, many days were still available for bird hunting to those who, like my father and me, elevated the sport to a high priority in life. The nearest coverts were within a stone's throw of our house, so that a circular walk of almost any desired length could be planned around the farm, to begin and end in our yard. Furthermore, even the most industrious of farmers had no sense of guilt about not working; while hunting, they could also examine livestock, make plans for each field for the coming season, and assess timber for possible harvest.

Another advantage that some quail hunters consider important is convenience. To pursue foxes, coons, possums, doves, grouse, ducks, and turkeys, it is necessary either to hunt during the night or rise long before dawn, to walk mostly through swamps and thick underbrush, to stand for hours in cold water or in windswept blinds, or, perfectly camouflaged, to crouch or sit uncomfortably while a gobbler makes up his mind whether you are an enemy or a potential lover.

Quail, on the other hand, are usually sought in relatively good weather and during "gentlemen's hours"—from the time it is warm enough for birds to leave their tight ground roost to feed until sundown or shortly thereafter, when they call each other to reassemble for the night. Also, these are upland birds, most likely found outside the swamps and deep woods. After being flushed, of course, quail will often plummet into the thickest cover, in which case it is usually fruitless to follow them very far. To minimize walking or to cover larger fields, hunters frequently ride on horseback or in Jeeps while the dogs do the hard work. Appropriate chaps are standard dress against the briers and brambles that are an integral element of quail habitat. This leg protection also offers some limited impediment to the fangs of rattlesnakes, who might be encountered during the warmer days when they are out of their winter burrows.

All these attractions are exceeded by the relationship between the hunter and his bird dogs. Although the natural quail-hunting instincts have been carefully bred into some species of dogs for centuries, it still takes a lot of time and effort to train a dog well. I have had a dozen or so bird dogs since we came back home from the navy; two outstanding ones, most of them adequate, and a few failures.

There is no doubt that watching good dogs perform is the most enjoyable facet of the sport. They are quietly efficient, ranging within a reasonable area in front of the hunters, obeying what few audible or visual signals are necessary. The best dogs cover the ground rapidly and thoroughly; when they scent birds, they circle quickly to be downwind from the prey, then move in as close as possible—but never intentionally close enough to flush the quail. If the dog is already very near the birds when it first detects their scent, it will freeze almost in midair, landing on the ground alert and erect, and with its nose—in fact, its entire body—indicating the direction of the covey.

A well-trained dog holds a staunch point with an intensely alert demeanor, honors the points of a brace mate, and follows a prescribed discipline when the birds are flushed and shot. Some are taught to hold their point "to wing and shot": to stand absolutely immobile until released by the dog handler after the shooting is over. I've never tried to train any this way, but prefer that my dogs move immediately after the guns are fired in order to find the downed birds and bring them to me. Hunting dogs are expected to mark the fall of a bird, to stay in the vicinity long enough to locate it, and to retrieve the game and bring it to the dog's master. However, it is not easy to restrain eager bird dogs for long. After a short time most of them will resume hunting, whether or not the dead birds have been found.

It's hard to describe how exciting it is to have one's own young dog perform well. Rosalynn and I have raised four children of our own and we now have six grandchildren. As every parent knows, it is a great thrill when a baby stands alone, takes a faltering step, or first mumbles "Da-da." I have to admit that it is equally thrilling when a puppy makes the same kind of progress. My youngest dog, a lemon-spot English pointer named Sadie, is learning how to hunt. I have worked with her in my yard since she was a tiny pup, letting her repeatedly chase and then point a bunch of quail feathers that I flipped back and forth on the end of a fishing line, and also find and retrieve some rags wrapped around a small block of wood. Later, I took her into a nearby field on several occasions just to acquaint her with some of the simplest commands, such as "Whoa" and "Here." Her behavior was erratic at best.

In December 1987, I carried her with me for the first time in public, on a plantation where there were several hunters, two skilled dog trainers, and a number of outstanding older dogs. My heart pounded as I rode my horse, watching Sadie dash furiously ahead among the scattered pine trees, exploring every scent that issued from the briers, gallberry bushes, and scrub oak thickets. Suddenly she froze in a classical point, nose forward, eyes fixed intently ahead, and tail held high. An older dog, her hunting companion at the time, stopped at a distance and pointed at Sadie, honoring her preeminent role. Two of us dismounted, loaded our shotguns, and moved toward her. It seemed that it took us forever; I just knew she wouldn't hold long enough for us to reach her. As we walked carefully past my dog, saying "Whoa, Sadie," over and over, she fidgeted and finally jumped forward. A covey flared up, and we downed two birds. My puppy dashed forward, found one of the quail, brought it directly to me, and dropped it at my feet. I was breathless with joy and pride, savoring the congratulations that poured in from all sides. Her performance had not been perfect; she should not have moved as we passed by on the way to the birds. But to see my puppy find a covey herself, hold for several minutes until we could reach her, then retrieve a bird—it was one of life's most joyous moments!

Every hunter has his own extraordinary dog stories to tell; the remarkable thing is that most of them do not need to be embellished. There is no way to explain how a bird dog can be retrieving a still-fluttering bird and, on the way back to the hunter, stop on a firm point, having scented other quail. I have seen this happen many times but still can't understand how it's possible.

Some bird dogs are remarkably intelligent, able to communicate with their owners in their own way. Oftentimes, for instance, a dog detects quail scent that remains on the ground after the birds have flown away. The dog will hold the point until the hunters arrive, but with varying mannerisms indicate to its master that the birds have already flushed. I have hunted with one dog, a former field trial champion, who would hold his point but give a couple of quiet barks as we approached him, to tell us that birds had been where he was pointing but were now gone. When his trainer spoke or touched him, the dog would resume hunting, attempting to discover where the departed covey had flown.

Being surrounded by men, other dogs, wagons, mules, and horses doesn't seem to interfere with the natural ability of a good dog to do its duty. Once, I was with a group of hunters taking a break from riding our horses. We were standing on the ground discussing the performance of a top dog inside one of the cages on the nearby mule-drawn wagon. All of a sudden, the dog looked toward us and stiffened into a model point. Perplexed at what was happening, we decided to examine the dog more closely. As we walked toward the cage, a quail flushed at our feet!

While hunting recently I lost one of my bird dogs, a black and white English setter named Sport. My companion and I searched for him for half an hour without success. Finally I saw a small patch of white above a fallen log and found that it was Sport—lying flat on his belly with his head propped on the log. He had held an immobile point until he could stand no longer; then, as his muscles tired, he just gradually sank down on the ground. When I patted him on the head he stood up, a little shakily, and moved forward with us. Fifty yards ahead, out of gun range, the covey of quail flushed.

These kinds of experiences happen often and provide never-ending subjects of discussion when bird-dog owners get together.

No matter how many years I have hunted or how many coveys of quail have been pointed and flushed on any particular day, it is still impossible for me to approach an invisible covey without a pounding heart or to avoid being startled when the explosive flush occurs. One fine outdoorsman, Charles Elliott, describes this feeling best: "It's like holding a lighted stick of dynamite; it could go off at any second. The dynamite explodes; although he knew it would, the hunter is never quite ready for it."

Sometimes the dogs and I have walked right over a totally camouflaged covey huddled in the grass and leaves, to have the quail erupt behind me. On other occasions they run ahead, to rise only when far beyond gun range. Although almost invariably found on the ground, quail will sometimes even flush from overhead in a tree when this is least expected. Once airborne, they dart and swoop, climb steeply, or glide horizontally for long distances just above grass level. I have hunted on well-known territory and found four or five coveys around a field. A few days later, a careful search produced absolutely nothing except frustration, and yet the quail would be there again on the next hunt. The unpredictability of quail is one of their sterling attractions.

I have seen quail-hunting bring out the best, or worst, in a hunting companion. The customs and etiquette are well known: to handle shotguns safely, not to rush in ahead of the dogs, to limit shooting to the birds on your own side of the territory ahead, to be restrained in claiming birds that may have been shot by the other fellow, to honor conservation laws, to refrain from criticizing any errant dog except one's own, and to be good-natured and patient about the inevitable disappointments and failures. There are long hours together, walking or riding, when relaxed conversations are possible—more so than in almost any other kind of hunting. Life is just too short to go quail hunting with the wrong people.

Only after I became governor and then President was I ever invited to enjoy the beautiful pageantry of the large plantations south of Plains around Albany and Thomasville, whose prime reason for existence was quail hunting. On these farms of five thousand to thirty thousand acres, wealthy industrialists from "up north" came to live for a few weeks each winter. They and their guests would hunt for several days or just enjoy the natural southern setting of pine trees, live oaks, gallberry bushes, wire grass, cypress swamps, gently rolling hills, winding creeks and rivers, and the diverse wildlife of the area.

In more recent years, the descendants of many of the original owners have had less interest in the hunting and life style of South Georgia and more concern about the economics of owning such a large area of formerly unprofitable land. They now grow a number of cash crops that do not interfere with the quail population, and lease some of the hunting rights during the three-month season in the winter when the working crews on the farm are not busy in the fields. So far, surprisingly few of these original holdings have been subdivided into smaller tracts for family farms or settlements.

On the more genteel plantations, the protocol and procedures are carefully honored by the hosts. Hunters ride either on horseback or on specially built wagons drawn by matched pairs of mules. I have hunted on several of the plantations and have been intrigued by the subtle differences among them. On some, there is a strict dress code for the dog trainers and handlers, and guests are generally advised that evening meals are with jacket and tie. The horses, wagons, and harness are uniformly groomed and maintained, and often the grounds around the main house look like a fine country club's. Other owners, whose plantations may be equally well groomed, go out of their way to emphasize a relaxed atmosphere, with both lunch and supper taken in hunting clothes or similar informal wear.

There are usually twenty or more mature bird dogs on the plantation, a few English setters but mostly pointers, trained during the off-season months to perform their duties in a vigorous and efficient manner. A half dozen or so of them are carried in cages on the wagon for a hunt; a brace of dogs will be on the ground hunting for less than an hour at a time before being replaced by two other dogs.

On these plantations the primary consideration in developing the standing timber and cleared fields is the quail crop. Peanuts, corn, soybeans, and wheat are planted in large fields, while small patches of corn, soybeans, bicolor lespedeza, beggar lice, or other quail food crops are planted in open spaces in the woodland areas. In some instances, noted biologists who adopted the bobwhite quail as their specialty have done research on the plantations and helped to manage the crops and native habitat of the farm. From these definitive studies, begun in 1924 in Georgia, have come many of the conservation measures, land and forest management skills, and wise game laws that have helped to protect and increase the quail population in some parts of our country.

For people who neither own their own land nor have friends who do, there are still opportunities to enjoy high-quality hunting. A few experienced landowners have decided to offer their quail lands and dogs to paying guests. One of the more successful of these entrepreneurs is Frank Pidcock, whose regular profession is growing and warehousing tobacco. More than twenty years ago, Frank acceded to the request of a couple of sportsmen for hunting privileges on his land and charged them a modest fee. Later that same season, he accompanied another group, this time using his own bird dogs. What resulted was the founding of Ashburn Hill Plantation, near Moultrie, Georgia.

Ashburn Hill has developed a relatively small but loyal clientele by offering highly trained dogs, a choice of either Jeeps or horses for riding, and an adequate combination of wild and released quail. There are trap and skeet ranges available for those who wish to improve their skills before going into the field. Nine out of ten of the guests are repeat customers, some of them having returned for more than fifteen successive seasons during the same week of the year. I have enjoyed several nice hunts on this plantation with a guest of my own, shooting two at a time with Frank and perhaps one of his neighbors. Sometimes, as a special privilege, I take along one of my dogs so that the professional trainers can help me correct its faults.

The best measure of the quality of a plantation is the training of the dogs. After just a few minutes in the field, a knowledgeable hunter can size up the dog trainer's commitment and ability. Even after the inevitable mistakes are discounted, there are remarkable differences in standards of obedience and performance, which are evident regardless of how many birds the dogs find. Most good dog trainers prefer to raise their own puppies, with careful attention given to parental bloodlines and field performance. Others just buy semitrained dogs to replace those lost through death or culling and hope that more hunting experience will improve their new purchases.

It can be an embarrassing and almost painful experience to spend a day with incompetent bird dogs. The hunt often degenerates into having many coveys of quail flushed originally by the dogs or horses, the hunters trying to observe where the fast-flying birds settle back to earth, and then hoping to reach the quail before one of the errant dogs flushes them again. A lot of time is wasted searching for the downed birds or for lost dogs, and special retrievers may be nonexistent or as incompetent as the pointers and setters. The air is filled with shouts and the sound of whistles, and then with a stream of excuses for the poor performance. Fortunately, these kinds of experiences are quite rare.

I usually hunt quail close around my home, but I have gone out of the state a couple of times, experiences that have changed my mind about some of the impressions of my earlier years.

One evening in early December 1987, I was sitting near an open fire on a ranch about a hundred miles southwest of Corpus Christi, Texas. The sky was clear and the tranquil scene was illuminated by an almost-full moon. I was with several men gathered around one of the best of fires, chunks of dry mesquite wood burning inside a four-foot oil-rig brake drum that was sunk into a concrete slab. There was not much wind or smoke, so we were able to sit in a complete circle, on folding chairs, watching the flickering flames and talking about other quail hunters and bird dogs we had known.

We were still getting acquainted with one another, since I had really known only one of the men before. This was Sam Walton, probably the most successful retail merchant in the world. He and I had hunted together the previous year in Georgia. His brother Bud was also with us, an associate in their business, who recalled meeting me when he had come to the Oval Office as part of a large delegation of leaders from Arkansas. Walter Schiel, I learned, would be our hunting guide. He was a big man who had been a professional rodeo contestant. Now he grew peanuts on his Texas farm eight months each year and hunted during the winter seasons. Also in the group was Dick Jones, the young owner of the ranch, who was planning to take a rare day off from cattle work to hunt with us the next morning. He and his father leased hunting rights on portions of their land to various people, including the Waltons.

I enjoyed their company for a while, but I was tired. I had left my home in Plains at five o'clock that morning, ridden three hours to Atlanta while doing paperwork in the back seat of a swaying van, spent a while in my Atlanta office, then visited my brother in the hospital before going to board a plane at the Atlanta airport. I had used the air travel time to write the first draft of a major speech on human rights I was to make the following week. There were air traffic delays around Dallas that held up our arrival in Corpus Christi. Just before landing I put my briefcase away, erased the speech notes from my mind, and turned my thoughts to quail hunting. As we made our final approach into the airport shortly before sundown, the pilot gave us the local weather report: clear, strong winds, temperature eighty-two degrees Fahrenheit. The summer warmth was not an encouraging sign for good hunting the next day. I was somewhat disappointed that the two-hour drive to the ranch was mostly after dark, so I was not able to examine the kind of country I would be visiting.

Now, at the camp, I was glad to hear Sam say, "It's late, and breakfast will be at six-thirty. Let's turn in." It was 9:00 P.M., Texas time. In a few minutes I was asleep, lulled by the steady "pat-pat-pat" of the oil well pumps that encircled the camp.

The next morning I could see more clearly that we were staying in several unadorned mobile homes clustered around the fire site, one for cooking and dining and the rest for sleeping. The dog kennels were close alongside. The weather was cool and cloudy, a good omen for our hunt. We sat at a long table eating cereal and fruit and drinking mugs of coffee from a large electric urn. Last night's talk had been about general philosophy and past hunting experiences. But hunting in South Texas would be a new experience for me; this morning I needed answers to a lot of specific questions.

I was told that we would be covering large fields in four-wheel-drive pickup trucks, loaded with dog cages and with an elevated seat behind the cab on which the two or three hunters would sit. From that vantage point we could observe the dogs as they ranged back and forth in front of us. Whenever there was evidence that birds were in the area, two of us hunters would follow the dogs as closely as possible on foot. Walter would be handling the dogs, not shooting.

We were most likely to find quail in the open spaces between the "motts" (which I later discovered was a word from the Spanish *mata,* meaning a clump of bushes) scattered about like small islands in the open grassland. During the 1930s, when parts of Texas and Oklahoma were dust bowls, as described by John Steinbeck in *Grapes of Wrath,* these small sand dunes were formed, perhaps around a clump of vegetation. Over the years, growths of mesquite and cactus covered the mounds, which remained surrounded by a sea of rather sparse native grasses, about knee-high.

The earth was too poor in most places to allow its cultivation or the planting of more nutritious pasture grasses. Attempts to plow the land had merely destroyed what plants were there and permitted the strong prairie winds to blow away the unprotected topsoil. The ranches in this region comprised from 100,000 to almost 1 million acres. This was not too much, my companions explained to me, because it took about 20 acres of the land to support one cow. An average pasture, fenced in by barbed wire, would include 5,000 acres.

I would find that many fields were almost filled with gopher holes, dug by small animals that leave little piles of sand on the surface. The subterranean burrows caused no particular harm unless a horse stepped into a deep one and broke its leg, but we all knew that rattlesnakes often moved in to share the gophers' homes. Predictably, the breakfast conversation turned to the likelihood of our encountering these venomous reptiles, which were more likely to roam around on the surface during the warmer weather we were expecting. My hunting trousers were fairly thick, adequate for repelling the blackberry briers of Georgia, but I had not brought any of the special knee-length boots or leggings designed to provide protection against the more serious danger of snakebite.

I was becoming somewhat concerned, but Walter, our guide, reassured us: "I never wear any snake protection. I've spent my adult life in this part of the country and I've hunted this same ranch for the last eight years without seeing any need to worry about snakes. Let's go hunting!"

Someone said, "If you find yourself too close to a snake, just jump as high as you can—and don't come back down anywhere near him."

We rode several miles on a paved highway, observing the multicolored prairie in the early morning light. I saw a number of redtail hawks and Mexican eagles, a lot of crows and blackbirds, a few of the roadrunners made famous by cartoons, plus a pair of collared peccaries, which a passing automobile had killed. Dick and Walter called them "javelinas." Last year, Sam said, a large javelina, inadvertently cornered, had almost killed one of his best dogs.

We began hunting with two dogs on the ground, one of them a superb young bitch named Streak. She was the daughter of Walter's finest dog, Flash, who was now too old to hunt but not too old to sire puppies. The cloud cover remained, keeping the temperature low, the dogs cooler and better able to perform, and the birds more inclined to be in the open grasses instead of in the shady motts. We followed the normal custom of having two hunters walking at a time when the dogs were indicating that birds were in the vicinity. We found plenty of quail—at least fifteen coveys—and did some better-than-average shooting. Every half hour or so Walter changed dogs, so that none of them would become too tired in the steadily increasing heat.

As midday approached, however, the weather changed abruptly. The sun came out, the morning breeze slackened, and the temperature rose. Hunting was now much more difficult. Our dogs quickly became overheated; they moved more slowly, covered less ground, and came to the truck frequently for drinks of cool water. The plentiful coveys of birds that we had located earlier in the day seemed to have vanished, while those few we found were more likely to be under the scattered growths of mesquite and cactus. We shed as many of our clothes as possible and continued to hunt, looking forward to later in the afternoon when some of these problems would be resolved.

At about one o'clock, bumping along slowly across the gopher mounds, we were watching Streak and commenting on how she was different from most of the other dogs. She never seemed to slacken her pace; always alert, she had the wisdom of an old dog, apparently knowing where the birds were most likely to be in the hot weather. Streak was now concentrating her attention around the motts, whereas earlier she had spent most of her time zigzagging through the open meadow grasses.

All of a sudden she froze, her nose toward the center of a mott and her tail pointed skyward. This clump of bushes was larger in diameter than most, and so we decided quickly that all three of us would spread out and move into the area in front of the dog. Sam went directly into the mott ahead of Streak, while Dick and I went around the bushes to be ready if the quail moved all the way through and came out on the other side. Walter, as usual, stayed close to his dog, not carrying a gun.

We were moving slowly forward, tense, waiting for the unpredictable eruption of quail in flight. Instead, we heard the chilling buzz of a rattlesnake in among the *tasajillo* and prickly pear cactus. Walter, who was nearest the sound, looked all around, and then down near his feet. His right foot was on the snake, just behind its head! It was rattling wildly as it tried to strike him, but his boot had the rattler pinned too tightly to the ground. Walter leaped wildly away, crashing into a mesquite tree. Although Dick and I couldn't see the other men at the time, we saw the bushes moving and heard the exclamations. The most comprehensible was Walter's "Shoot him! Shoot him!" Sam Walton leveled his 28-gauge automatic at the coiled rattlesnake and fired from the hip. Unfortunately, the charge of #8 birdshot hit the wrong end of the reptile, severing about eight inches of its tail.

Streak, apparently thinking this was a wounded quail, dashed in to retrieve it, and the snake struck her and clung there while discharging its poison into her left jaw. Walter kicked the snake loose, permitting Sam to dispatch it with a more carefully aimed shot. Streak, with two small drops of blood left on her face, immediately began hunting again.

Walter caught her as quickly as possible, then brought her to the truck. We stood around discussing whether or not to give her an anti-venom shot, which can sometimes have damaging side effects. Dick advised against this treatment, recounting to us a magazine article he had read about treating poisonous snakebites with electric shock. He and Walter shocked the dog's jaw a few times with an electric training collar; then we watched her closely for a few minutes as she lay quietly in the shade of the truck. When her jaw began to swell, Walter decided to inject the serum.

We loaded up and proceeded back to camp. Sam was distressed that he had only wounded the snake with his first shot. Walter said that he'd jumped in the wrong direction, away from his dog, permitting Streak to leap in before he could stop her.

I tried to console him by saying, "It's not easy to do your best thinking when you're standing on a rattlesnake." Dick and I teased Walter by suggesting that the snake might have bitten him through his boot without his having felt it in the excitement and that some electric shock to his ankle and a shot of serum might be good preventive measures.

As we passed the hunting camp of a professional dog trainer, Walter decided to turn in the driveway. "I'm sure Perkins will have some cortisone that we can borrow. It may be what is needed to save Streak's life." Approaching the isolated mobile home and dog kennels, Walter exclaimed, "Whatta ya know! The veterinarian is here."

The vet examined Streak, approved the treatment we had already given her, and announced that the dog would surely recover. "If the bite had been on her body instead of her head, she would already be dead," he said.

When we resumed hunting after lunch, we were all much more careful about where we stepped. Despite the heat, I had put on a thick pair of Levi's under my hunting pants to stop the fangs of the rattlesnake I could imagine striking at my leg from out of the grass. Our more cautious movements did not diminish our enjoyment of the hunt, although we frequently expressed concern about how Streak might be getting along. That night her head swelled to twice its normal size, but Walter's ice packs helped to ease her pain. When we went to see her early next morning, she was alert and her tail was pounding on the floor of her kennel. Streak struggled to her feet and came forward, apparently eager to join the hunt. It was obvious that she would be all right.

I was impressed with the extraordinary quail population in this part of Texas. The number of wild coveys on the prairie in its natural state was equal to those on the most carefully tended plantations in other regions where I have hunted. During our two days of hunting we discussed the reasons for so many quail: wild partridge peas, grass seeds, and mesquite pods provide a good diet; animal predators seem to pose minimal threats; and I never saw any of the fire ants that kill so many newly hatched birds in Georgia and most of the rest of the nation. Other important benefits are that few pesticides are used in the meadows and only rarely does cultivation of the land or other machinery operation disturb the nesting and feeding birds. In fact, on this enormous ranch there were only two small tractors, used almost exclusively for controlling wild fire.

Pressure from hunters is a relatively small factor in the eighteen-month life cycle of quail on properly managed land. According to wildlife experts, the 300,000 hunters in Texas average only a dozen birds each per season. (There are usually 60,000 hunters in Georgia, whose annual harvest is about twenty quail each.) Since much of the land is not hunted, most quail are never discovered. We took an average of only two birds out of each Texas covey, some of which contained more than thirty quail, with an average size of at least fifteen birds per covey.

I had to return home the morning of the third day, and Sam was scheduled to fly his plane to Alabama, where he would be visiting some of his stores. I have never known any quail hunter more enthusiastic than he, nor more keen to honor the courtesies of hunting and the principles of quail management. He not only owns a half-dozen dogs that have been well trained by him, but keeps them with him in his small private plane as he flies around the country on business. It is no accident that during winter months he is much more likely to visit stores located near good quail territory.

I was not surprised on our last night at the camp when he said, "We don't have to leave until midmorning. If you and I can be in the field at daybreak, perhaps we could find a few birds before we have to take off."

The next morning it was still quite dark when we had finished breakfast. After getting the dogs ready, we stood at the corner of the camp area and listened to the quail calling as first daylight brightened the eastern sky. We began hunting a few minutes later, walking through thicker grass than I had seen before on the ranch, and found five coveys of quail before sunrise, then several more before we had to quit hunting at 9:00 A.M. in time to pack. It was the end of an unforgettable experience.

I am concerned that with large machine cultivation from fence to fence, the increased use of pesticides, and the replacement of much of the hardwood lands with the almost sterile close-planted pine tree forests, much of the best quail habitat in Georgia has been lost; the population of this game bird has continued to fall. As governor, I attempted to stop this decline by promoting the publication of a book, *Prince of Game Birds: The Bobwhite Quail*, by Charles Elliott, and by urging my fellow farmers to join me in following Elliott's suggestions about quail habitat improvement on our farms and timberlands.

Although I still go duck hunting, usually two mornings a year, and hunt turkeys on my farm for a few days in the springtime, my most persistent interest is in quail hunting. Unfortunately, I don't hunt nearly as often as in earlier years. I have to admit that my two bird dogs are not very well trained; they obviously need to be hunted several times a week. This is one task that I am always intending to perform better next year.

Even in times when I'm too busy to go hunting, I can still savor the memories of past outings and anticipate with plea-sure more frequent chances to enjoy the companionship, ex-citement, and challenge that have been associated since my early childhood with bobwhite quail.

CROSSING
BORDERS

SALMO SALAR

Above my desk in our home in Plains, Georgia, is a prized photograph of Richard Adams alongside a waterfall on the Matapédia River in Quebec. A small man, he stands in over-sized hip boots, a rain slicker, and a felt slouch hat, with a bemused expression on his weather-beaten face. The photo is captioned CHAIRMAN OF THE BOARD, ADAMS FISH AND PACKING CO. LTD.

    Richard is one of the most famous salmon-fishing guides in North America, not only because of his intimate knowledge of *Salmo salar* and its Gaspé Peninsula spawning streams but also because of his character, wit, and intelligence.

The "proprietor" of the Fish and Packing Co. was my guide on our first Atlantic-salmon fishing trip, when Rosalynn and I joined sportscaster Curt Gowdy and fishing editor Art Lee during the third week in June 1982. Accompanying us was an ABC camera crew, there to film the television program *American Sportsman*.

When we arrived at the airport in Causapscal, Quebec, officials of the Canadian sports fisheries department presented us with four specially crafted #8 graphite fly rods, inscribed with our names. The reel seats were made of beautiful burled maple wood, similar to that used for the bowls of the most expensive pipes. After a brief ceremony for the assembled news media, we drove to our destination for the week: Auberge de la Montagne, Routhierville, about twenty-five miles upstream from where the waters of the Matapédia join those of the Restigouche and then flow into Chaleur Bay.

The river ran between the railroad and the highway, with a good salmon pool right at our doorstep. On one side of the road was a small and picturesque hotel, which would have been at home in the old "Toonerville Trolley" comic strip. Rosalynn and I were assigned a bunk in the tiny railroad station on the other side of the stream, just a few feet from the tracks. Only three or four trains came through each day, but the engineers knew we were there and never failed to whistle a salute to us—even at four o'clock in the morning. The first time the shrill blast of the whistle and the pounding roar of the onrushing engine interrupted our sleep, we jumped a foot off the bed. For a few moments it seemed that the train would come through our bunk room. It was a horrendous shock, and we decided that we would have to find another place to sleep. Yet only a day or two later we had become so accustomed to the sound of the trains flying by that we hardly noticed them, even in the night.

Our lodging was in the unrestricted public fishing area, open to anyone who held a proper license from the Province of Quebec. A few miles downstream was the private part of the river, available to the ten people each day who were lucky enough to win the right to pay $200 for a canoe, a guide, and exclusive access to four or five pools where the salmon were accustomed to hold for a while on their journey upstream to spawn. These rights are allocated each year by the government of Quebec on a first-come, first-served basis.

Of the total, only one third of the permits were available to nonresidents, and the competition for them was intense. The procedure was for applicants to dial into headquarters at a given time on a day in January to request the fishing reservations. The telephone circuits were jammed with hundreds of simultaneous calls, of course, but a fraction of the callers got through and their names were listed for the choice dates. We were told that some fishermen would arrange for dozens of their friends to call for them, and in large companies all the secretaries would be assigned this task for an hour or two each year. The rights, once assigned, were not transferable. If a chosen fisherman died, for instance, before his fishing day, a surviving spouse or children could not use the permit but had to forfeit the fishing opportunity to the next person on the waiting list.

We were to fish in the public waters for the first two days, and then move down to the private area, where we would have two boats for three days. Somehow, the ABC Television Network had obtained these permits to film us for the TV program. From what we could hear, fishing recently had been just as good, if not better, in the public areas upstream. Fly-fishers had a choice of casting from boats, usually near the middle of the stream, or wading out from shore. Since all of us would be fishing from boats the last three days and I wanted to learn both methods, we decided that Curt and Rosalynn would take the boat and Art and I would do the wading. The water was quite deep in most of the holding pools, and much of the bottom was covered with very large and slick rocks, so it would be difficult to fish in many of the most promising places. Steel cleats on the bottom of our waders and a stout staff would be necessary to prevent our going head over heels in the swift and icy water.

Rosalynn and I had done a lot of reading about Atlantic salmon, and we listened carefully throughout this visit as Curt, Art, and Richard Adams described what we might expect. The salmon is anadromous, one of the few species of fish that can move from fresh water to the salt sea and back again. Then, after spawning, the Atlantic salmon returns to the ocean, its metabolism changing with the habitat. Some have been known to make as many as five spawning runs during a lifetime. The five general species of Pacific salmon, on the other hand, always die in their freshwater stream after completing the first spawning run.

Richard explained that the young salmon (known as parr), are mostly born in the early spring and live in the rivers, much as do trout. Their most common food is aquatic and airborne insects and, later, small fish. The growing salmon remain in their freshwater home for at least a year, and sometimes for a year or two longer. Finally, the 10 percent who survive after birth are ready to go to sea. Almost miraculously, they begin to change color—from the darker mottled sides that provide camouflage in the stream to the dark backs and silver sides and bellies that will hide them best in the open sea. As they move down the river toward the ocean their names are changed, from parr to smolt and, after about a year of feeding at sea, to grilse.

No one seems to know what happens to the smolts during this first year in the ocean. They feed on the abundant sea life, and their weight increases from two or three ounces to several pounds. As grilse, they either return to the river to spawn or stay at sea for another year or two. Their weight can double each year, to twenty pounds or more after they have fed for three years at sea; some fish grow to as much as forty pounds after their fourth year. The largest Atlantic salmon known to have been taken in North America on rod and reel was a fifty-five pounder, caught in 1939. Larger ones have been caught in Europe, including one in Norway that weighed seventy-nine pounds!

The salmon's major sea-feeding grounds off the coast of Greenland have been fairly well known (and heavily fished) for the past twenty-five years. To reach this area the fish must swim a thousand miles or more from their spawning grounds, and yet even after staying in these distant reaches of the open sea for many months, each of the salmon knows the way back to its own place of birth.

The returning fish are fat and strong, driven on by an irresistible urge to procreate. Salmon have almost unbelievable strength and determination. They've been known to leap as high as twelve feet upstream to clear a waterfall that stands in the path to the spawning grounds of their birth.

And yet, the attrition rate among salmon is fearsome, from man-made pollution, natural predators, commercial fishermen at sea and in the estuaries, and sport fishermen in the streams. Most of the great salmon rivers of the northeastern states are now barren of the fish, and the rivers of eastern Canada have nothing like the salmon population of fifty years ago. Stricter limits on commercial catches, water-pollution control laws, and the initiation of special fly-fishing restraints have resulted in some success, but salmon runs in recent years still seem to be decreasing. One hopeful development is that hatchery spawn has been planted in some newly purified streams, including the Penobscot in Maine, and a few salmon are now returning to them. It takes four years or more of the salmon's cycle of existence to assess the result of such an effort.

Sport fishermen have fought for many years to protect the salmon from pollution, from obstructions that prevent the migration to spawning grounds, and from excessive catches both at sea and in the streams. The number of fish entering each river is monitored every season, and the limit of salmon that can be taken by fishermen is adjusted accordingly. A good portion of revenue from fishing licenses is allotted to programs that replenish salmon hatches in suitable streams.

While the spawning fish are in the rivers, another miracle takes place. Most fish, including salmon, are cannibalistic; if they continued to feed as voraciously as they do at sea, the majority of the parr and smolts would be consumed. The wonder is that the large salmon do not eat anything during the several months they are in the stream to which they return; they customarily lose almost half their original weight. As a result, the salmon are very weak on their return trip to the sea after spawning and can do little more than head into the moving stream and let it carry them backward down and into the salt water. They become highly vulnerable during this time of weakness, often exposed in quite shallow water to bear, otter, eagle, osprey, mink, or eel. Only about 10 percent of those spawning ever enter the stream to spawn again.

*　　*　　*

Rosalynn and I also got some last-minute advice about tackle, flies, casting technique, and stream strategy. Our hopes were brightened as each of the others regaled us with wonderful success stories about previous fishing excursions. On his last visit to the same area, a couple of years earlier, Art had gotten the limit of two salmon almost every day for a week. However, all of us were more sobered when we learned about the dismal statistics for the current season. Quebec was not having a good fishing year, and so far there had been only one salmon caught for every thirty days of fishing on the Matapédia. Some quick calculations indicated that if the four of us fished for six days, we had not much more than an 80 percent chance of taking a total of one salmon!

It was steadily drizzling, the wind was blowing hard, and it was unbelievably cold for late June. We had not come prepared for such weather—which was to continue all week. Even with all the clothes we could borrow, the rain still penetrated our rain gear and trickled down our shivering bodies. Curt and I were to agree many times that we had never been colder for as long a period of time. However, no matter how bad the weather was, it never prevented our fishing the maximum time possible every day.

We thought that Curt had harvested our group's quota the first afternoon, when he landed a nice eleven-pound fish in the railroad station pool. That night around the supper table, he tried to be a good sport by downplaying his achievement and reassuring us that all of us would share his luck during the remaining days.

The next morning he caught another of about the same size. When Art and I heard the news we just cast more doggedly and with renewed confidence that the fishing was going to improve. We calculated that each of us was casting an average of more than three thousand times a day but so far neither of us had raised a fish of any kind.

At noon, when we moved downstream to join the others for lunch, we encountered Curt Gowdy beside the trail. He was so excited that he could hardly speak coherently. At first, I was worried about Rosalynn, who was nowhere to be seen, but we soon understood that she was all right and had gone to look for me.

"I've just seen the greatest sporting event of my life," he exclaimed, over and over. "I can hardly believe it!"

We tried to calm him down and turned to the young guide, Steve Levesque, for an explanation. He couldn't speak a word of English, but just pointed down to a tremendous salmon lying in the bow of the boat. Finally, Curt and other bystanders were able to tell us what had happened.

Rosalynn had been casting with the new fly rod we had received on our arrival and had hooked a large salmon. The fish jumped once or twice as he moved downstream, and when the rod bent with maximum pressure, it broke in two, right at the reel seat where the burled wood had failed. For some reason, as we discovered later, the stainless-steel core designed to provide strength had not been connected well. The loose reel then fell down in the bottom of the boat. Rosalynn had continued to clutch the deeply bent rod with one hand, trying to keep its jagged end from injuring her chest and stomach, while she cupped the spinning reel clumsily in her other hand. Desperately, she let the rod go, concentrated on clutching the reel and continued to play the fighting fish. Fortunately, the salmon soon stopped running and went to the bottom of the stream, where he tugged powerfully and steadily on the line.

As the battle continued, the boat was moved in closer to the shore and Curt shouted to a camera crew to bring out a roll of tape. After struggling for a while, Curt finally got both parts of the rod together while the guide managed to tape the reel back on in the general area of the seat. After all this, Rosalynn discovered that the reel was on backward. As it was untaped to be turned around, the huge fish began moving downstream again.

When the reel was eventually secured properly to the stub of the rod and Rosalynn cranked in line and put pressure on the salmon, he began to leap and run, soon stripping off all the fly line and a good portion of the nylon backing. The boat followed downstream for several hundred yards. Only after another half hour of struggling was the salmon finally netted.

Rosalynn had returned by the time the exciting tale was told, and then we heard it all again from a chorus of spectators who had witnessed any portion of the epic battle. At the hotel, the fish was measured and weighed: thirty-nine inches in length, twenty-five pounds. Pride and jealousy struggled in my breast, but pride won an unchallenged victory! Rosalynn was characteristically modest and concerned about me. "I'm sure you'll catch a salmon eventually, Jimmy," she said, "even though it will probably be much smaller than this one."

That same day, Art hooked a fine salmon while casting from a large exposed rock a few yards from the bank. Holding a net, I chased him and the fish far downstream. While Curt and Rosalynn looked on from their boat, we stumbled from one pile of submerged rocks to another. After missing the thrashing fish twice, I finally netted it. Art thought it would weigh more than thirty pounds, but it turned out to be a twenty-two-pounder.

Now everyone had a salmon . . . except me.

We had several rounds of toasts that evening at supper, at first honoring those fishermen who had been successful; then drinks of condolence and to accomplishments yet to come. Some referred to good luck and some to superior skill. Throughout the meal, everyone was ostentatiously nice to me, but the wine flowed freely, and the increasingly humorous solicitude made it more and more difficult for me to keep a genuine smile on my face and to maintain the sincerity of my congratulations to the others. It is not easy for an unsuccessful fisherman to be generous with those who have caught large fish in the same waters.

Since Richard Adams had joined us now, I took him aside from the revelers to talk about the next day, when we would all move to the private waters farther downstream. In his honesty he was not very reassuring, reporting that the fishing had been much slower than he had expected in the larger pools, probably not as good as where we had already been fishing. However, I was adequately confident when, long after midnight, we finally went to bed.

The next morning was my first experience fishing for salmon from a boat. Contrary to the normal procedure of having one fisherman in a boat, we had been granted special permission for two of us and the guide to occupy each craft, but with only one person fishing at a time. This was the only way all four of us could fish the two beats (stretches of stream) we were allotted. There was obviously some tension within our group of fishermen and guides because I had not caught a fish. We had swapped partners for our last days of fishing, and so I was with Curt Gowdy for the first time. The cold and driving rain continued, but all of us enjoyed the habitual optimism of dedicated fishermen.

The bow of the long and narrow boat was kept heading upstream. The anchor, located forward, could be raised and lowered, through a system of pulleys, by the guide, who sat in the stern. At each stop, one of us would stand and begin casting, placing the fly across- and downstream, at an angle of a little more than forty-five degrees to the current, just as we had done while wading. The line would then be borne around by the stream to directly astern, with the small fly clearly visible either on the surface or an inch or two under it.

Our first casts, made on both sides of the boat, were with only a yard of line beyond the tip of the rod, but with each cast the line was lengthened a foot or two until we reached our maximum casting distance. Then Richard raised the anchor and let the boat drift downstream as far as our fly had covered. The other angler repeated the procedure in the new location. In this way we covered a broad swath through the pool, with the fly passing not more than a foot above any salmon that happened to be lying there. No weighted lures were permitted, so the flies were always within an inch or two of the surface.

At each spot, Richard would tell us about the interesting things that had happened there during the previous forty years, both about the fish that had been caught and the idiosyncrasies of the fishermen he had guided. He also gave us constant advice: "Let your line be straight when it hits the water." "Cast a little farther upstream." "Let's change flies and try this stretch again." "If you get a strike, don't snatch it out of his mouth before he's got it. If he misses, give him a little line so he can hit it again."

On occasion, we saw a salmon rise somewhere in the pool, a few times quite close to the boat. Then we would cast dozens of times over the spot, using both wet and dry flies. With some of the dry flies we used the "Portland hitch," taking a half hitch around the eye of the hook to make the fly skeet across the surface of the water like a little boat as it was retrieved or was borne by the current.

181

Richard could see things that were invisible to us, and sometimes we could not understand why he moved the boat in a peculiar way or asked us to fish with a different technique. During the many long hours of casting, I plied him with hundreds of questions about his life as a guide and about Atlantic salmon. The habits of this finest of freshwater fighting fish are almost impossible to understand, and many of them are still unknown or unexplained even by scientists who spend their lives trying to solve some of the mysteries.

The fish we were seeking now in the Gaspé Peninsula were strong and heavy, plentiful enough to permit the survivors to replenish the population of salmon for the seasons to come. They were wary, however, and I was having no luck with them. We fished all day and until suppertime without raising a fish. It was time to quit, but Richard suggested that I might want to continue fishing for another few hours until dark. I accepted his invitation, eager to expand my chances of success.

Now, as the only fisherman in the boat, I could cast fulltime. We tried a lot of different flies, places, and techniques, but the fish were not interested in what I had to present. I remembered my mother teasing me: "Jimmy, when you get behind you pull too quick." On this trip I had not had a chance to pull at all. We gave up when it was no longer light enough to see. And I had still not raised a fish!

The weather was worse the next day, still raining and even colder than it had been all that week. When not casting, we huddled in the boat trying to minimize the rivulets of water that ran down our necks and to thaw out our stiffened fingers. Curt had a good strike by what appeared to be a fifteen-pounder, but it escaped. As I was still unable to entice a salmon to take my fly, the situation was very discouraging. At noon, almost freezing, we decided to join Rosalynn and Art on the bank, build a fire, drink some hot coffee, and eat a snack. We could see them waiting for us in a grove of trees as we rounded a bend in the river.

Richard maneuvered the boat a little to the left of the main stream and anchored. "Try over near the low rocks," he said. I flexed my sore right arm, wiggled my fingers, and initiated the routine of covering the water on both sides of the craft with my fly, a Rusty Rat. Making my final pair of casts, as far as I could propel the line, I sat down to wait for the boat to be moved again. Then Richard said quietly, "Try the same thing once more, but skip the short casts. I think I saw something move."

I began a new series with about thirty feet of line, increasing the length out to near my maximum casting distance. Suddenly there was a tremendous thrashing on the surface, as a salmon charged directly toward me and struck at my fly. I restrained my natural inclination to snatch the line in and instead stretched forward to create some slack in the line. The small fly lay still on the surface. After a second or two, the fish struck again, repeating a charge that reminded me of a hungry alligator after its prey. This time he was hooked and soon dashed madly upstream. I knew he was a big one.

Richard poled the boat against the current in an attempt to stay abreast of the fish. At the same time, he watched the bent rod and gave me quiet advice on how much tension I could keep on the line without exceeding the limits of my tackle. Several times the salmon changed direction and leaped on occasion, to the cheers of the gathering spectators on the bank. I was hardly aware of these events, my mind concentrated exclusively on the fish and the guide's voice. Finally, after another half hour, as the salmon weakened and came ever closer, Richard beached the boat on a gravel bar and stepped into the water with his long-handled net. When the fish was landed, our happy guide let loose a weird, high-pitched cry of triumph, and then held the beautiful salmon up by its tail.

"How much does he weigh?"

"It's any weight you want, Mr. President."

We poled over to the waiting crowd, and someone shouted, "I've got some accurate scales." Our eyes and the cameras focused on the dial as the pointer settled at 29½ pounds.

Although we fished hard for another day and a half, I had only one other strike, a fish of about twelve pounds that was hooked just long enough to make one leap and then was free. Both Art Lee and Curt Gowdy caught a salmon of about this size before we had to pack our gear and head home.

It had been a wonderful week—cold, raining, tiresome, monotonous, frustrating, even dangerous at times on the slippery rocks in deep water, but still a most challenging and exciting time. At last I had joined the ranks of those who admired, caught, and were determined to preserve and protect *Salmo salar,* the leaper, king of sport fishes.

QUEEN CHARLOTTE STEELHEADS

One of the best things that ever happened to our state was that Jack Crockford came to Georgia from Michigan about thirty years ago to work in game and fish management. Jack is a small, quiet woodsman who moves swiftly and silently through the forests or along a stream, noticing everything around him and recognizing most of the plants, rocks, insects, and small animals by name. One of his earliest assignments was to try to restore the deer population in the southeastern states which had been almost completely decimated in our area.

Although I spent most of my early life in the fields and

woods, I saw only two deer during the eighteen years before I went off to college. Wild turkey were more plentiful; we even came across a black bear every now and then, but to see a white-tailed deer was a momentous event. There were a few within the protected areas on the coastal islands of Georgia, and a lot of dedicated biologists joined in the concerted and expensive attempt to trap some of them and release them in the wilder areas on the mainland—mostly without success.

Eventually, Crockford developed the now widely used tranquilizer projectile, utilizing almost pure nicotine as a fast-acting narcotic. This device made it possible to capture large numbers of wild deer and to transfer them without harm to hundreds of new homes. The restocking program has been so successful that now there are substantially more deer in the Southeast than there were before white men came to this continent. In many of the small rural counties of our state several thousand bucks are harvested each season by hunters, and still the deer population continues to grow.

Recently retired as director of Georgia's Game and Fish Department, Crockford supplements his income as a craftsman and artist, producing for necessarily patient customers and friends a few muzzle-loading rifles and knives of great beauty, ornamented with engraving or scrimshaw figures of birds, fish, and animals. He is one of my favorite hunting and fishing companions, having been the first person to introduce me to fly-fishing and to the pursuit of woodcock—both along the Chattahoochee River.

One damp and chilly night near the end of May 1983, Jack, Wayne Harpster, and I were sitting around a table in the Spruce Creek cottage after a relatively disappointing day of fishing. We were bent over a disassembled tranquilizer bullet, as Jack described his experiments with the projectile and how the final patented design evolved. Wayne asked if we wanted to ride around the farm and see if there were any deer feeding in the woods and fields. Soon we were bouncing along wildly in his pickup truck. Wayne had planted the grain, corn, and alfalfa as much for the deer as for his dairy cows, and was as proud of their size and number as of his state record in milk production. At each place we stopped, we would enter the field as rapidly and as quietly as possible, and then dash across the open area, swinging the truck lights and a strong spotlight around to examine the startled deer. They were in all the fields, sometimes as many as fifteen or twenty grazing together. Most of them were does, fawns, or young bucks; among almost two hundred we saw that night, less than half a dozen were mature males. Jack and Wayne explained that the males tended to stay alone except during rutting season and could seldom be found grazing in open places with other deer.

After we returned to the warm fireplace and the murmur of Spruce Creek, our thoughts and conversation turned back to fishing. Jack and I had come up to Pennsylvania for the annual Green Drake hatch, but it was late this year because of the unseasonably cold weather. As we had to leave the next morning, we were naturally making plans for our next excursion. Both my friends were extolling the excitement and challenge of fishing for steelhead. I listened with growing interest as they described their experiences in the Michigan and Oregon rivers, mostly fishing from boats using light bait-casting or spinning equipment, with spoons and salmon eggs as bait.

I wanted to try fly-fishing in streams small enough for wading. Jack's eyes lit up as he began to tell us about his recent visit to the Queen Charlotte Islands of British Columbia, off the west coast of Canada just a short distance south of Alaska. Before the night was over we had commissioned Jack to make arrangements for the following spring.

Now, almost a year later, we were on our way. Wayne was to meet us in Canada, and Rosalynn would come a day or so later after she finished the first week of publicizing her new autobiography. All of us were well equipped with chest waders, #8 fly rods, and sinking tip lines. I had swapped George Harvey a package of quail feathers for some of his beautiful steelhead flies and had also brought a dozen or so of my own. To supplement my already bulging library, Wayne had sent me his favorite book about steelhead. After studying it I got another copy and sent it to Jack; on the flight from Atlanta to Vancouver we shared what we had learned.

Anyone who reads or listens a lot to fishermen will soon discover that there is one never-ending argument: What is America's greatest fighting fish? Bass, tarpon, bonefish, trout, and other types all have their champions, but the sharpest debates are between the Atlantic salmon *(Salmo salar)* and the steelhead *(Salmo gairdneri),* the anadromous or migratory rainbow trout. The steelhead spend a good portion of their lives in the Pacific Ocean or in the Great Lakes, returning to the streams of their birth to spawn. A mature fish will repeat this cycle several times over a period of six or seven years. In most rivers the average size of a steelhead is about seven or eight pounds, with the world record being a forty-two-pounder taken off the coast of Alaska.

A steelhead or Atlantic salmon of half these maximum weights is considered a trophy catch. Since I had caught my large Atlantic salmon on my same tackle, I was sure it would handle the steelhead we would meet. However, I was worried about my right arm. I had recently injured it cutting heavy brush with a bush hook, and it was badly swollen and painful. X-rays had not revealed a serious fracture, but I thought I could feel one of the bones move on occasion. I'd wrapped the arm tightly in an Ace bandage and tested it at home in my backyard. I thought—I hoped—I could still crank the single-action fly reel as long as the weight of the rod and fish would be on my left side. A normal person would never have taken the trip under these circumstances, but fly-fishermen aren't always normal.

There was only one flight each day to Sandspit, our destination on the east coast of the Queen Charlotte Islands, and so we had to spend an afternoon and night in Vancouver. We decided to visit a local sporting-goods store for advice and a few supplies, and then go to the anthropology museum to learn as much as possible about the history and indigenous people of the area we were to visit.

At Bob's Tackle Shop we got our most fervent comments and advice: "Fly-fishing? Don't waste your time trying to catch steelhead on flies." One customer said he had been fishing for steelhead for five years with all kinds of bait and had not yet caught his first fish. After I bought a fly line for Rosalynn, the proprietor gave me a small book, *How to Catch Steelhead.* Illustrated with amusing cartoons, the book advised that heavy spinning tackle and salmon roe (spawn) be offered on or near the bottom of the stream, kept deep in the currents by heavy lead weights. The store's owner also reported that of the twenty thousand British Columbian steelhead fishermen who stalked their prey every year, fewer than five thousand were successful.

Maintaining both our composure and our resolve, we left for the museum to enjoy learning about Queen Charlotte's Haida Indians, whose ancient and regionally dominant civilization is now survived only by some impressive totem poles from the previous century and by two small villages still occupied in the islands. The totem carvings were very similar to those of the Maoris, a Polynesian group whom Rosalynn and I had visited in New Zealand. I was particularly impressed by the beautifully sculptured canoes, each carved with hand adzes from a single large cedar tree.

The next morning we took the daily commercial flight about 450 miles northwest to Sandspit. I walked down the aisle of the plane and talked to the other passengers: a few Indians and a number of loggers returning to their island work after a brief vacation with friends and families in the more-populated areas of British Columbia. For the final few miles I rode in the cockpit, watching the pilot evade some of the prevalent rainstorms along the east coast of the Queen Charlotte Islands. Suddenly the pilot said, "That's Copper Bay, where you'll be staying, over to the left." I could see one small cottage and another building that appeared to be a garage or storehouse, perched on a bluff overlooking a wave-torn beach. He also gestured at the rain squalls all around, commenting that the "misty isles" really earned their name.

Sandspit turned out to be about the size of Plains, inhabited by fewer than eight hundred souls, and so it did not take us long to drive through it on the way to the cottage.

Our host and guide was Walter Ernst, an Austrian who had been an outfitter in the Yukon and then moved to the Queen Charlotte Islands thirteen years ago. His wife, Maria, was a nurse, originally from East Germany, whom we would come to know as a fine cook and gracious hostess.

Walter told us that because of the steady rain the two closest streams, the Copper and Pallant, were too high to wade or fish, but that we might travel to a more distant creek on the northern coast of the island. Although it was already midafternoon, we changed into our fishing clothes and began the one-hour drive to Deena Creek, whose flooded condition always receded more quickly because it drained a smaller geographical region, and no large lakes were in its headwaters. Parts of the area were being heavily logged, and the large clear-cut zones left terrible scars on the mountainsides. At best, they would not be healed even within the next forty years.

The bald eagles along the coastal road were either sitting on rocks near the sea or in the tops of the few Sitka spruce, hemlock, or cedar trees that had been left standing. We also saw hundreds of brant and Canada geese and ducks of many species flying and swimming in the bays and inlets, and a few seals around the rocks.

The dirt roads in the region were quite narrow, reserved for the enormous trucks that rushed from the cutting areas on the mountains down to the sheltered basin on the coasts. There the twenty or more logs in each load were dumped into the sea for water transport to the distant paper mills and sawmills. Then the empty trailer was unhooked and lifted onto the main truck bed by a huge crane, to provide needed traction for the rear wheels on the steep and muddy roads and to permit the shortened truck to turn around in the forest before its trailer was reattached and more logs were loaded.

It would have been a disaster to meet one of the empty or loaded trucks head-on, because the drivers assumed there would be no oncoming traffic, and the roads, only wide enough for one vehicle, had no shoulders. The truck drivers all used radios to monitor each other's movements, and we had to wait each time at the unloading point or creek until we could follow one of these behemoths from the coast to and from our fishing place. During the week it became routine for us to wait our turn patiently, trusting our lives to these drivers. On one or two occasions we had to detour because of delays in the logging operation; a detour could be as long as thirty miles—at least an hour's extra travel time. It was clear that this territory was primarily for loggers, not tourists or fishermen. This pleased me; the last thing I wanted was to be surrounded by a crowd of other seekers of the same fish in the relatively tiny stream.

✵   ✵   ✵

We found the Deena a little higher than normal and slightly stained with tannin, like the streams in our southeastern states. This was better, Walter said, than having the stream crystal-clear, when the fish could be spooked even with long leaders and light tippets.

Jack and Wayne had fished here last October for coho salmon and were familiar with the creek, so they moved confidently downstream. I went upstream with Walter for my first experience with steelhead. We were thankful that the remaining virgin timber in this narrow valley area was not being cut, destroying the beauty of the area and filling the creek with debris from the logging operation. The banks of the stream were quite steep and often overgrown. On occasion we had to circumvent enormous logjams; the tops of the intertwined logs were often twice as high as my head. The surrounding woods were like rain forests, with moss-covered ground and fallen trees surrounding the enormous stumps that had been left from the harvest of a few of the virgin trees many years earlier. Some of the huge logs, after being felled by the sawyers, simply could not be moved to the nearby ocean without the jumbo trucks and roads to accommodate them. They were still lying there intact, some spanning the stream, so large that dozens of second-growth saplings as much as eight inches in diameter had sprouted and were growing out of the ancient bark and moss. Having been raised in the Georgia woods, I was most startled that there were no briers or thorns of any kind. None of us understood why, and no one has ever explained it.

We fished hard, using mostly a Skyomish Sunrise fly or other patterns similar to it, but with no takers. It was not easy fishing with a fly rod, wading in the rough stream without being upended or spooking any fish, placing the fly as far as possible up under the overhanging logs and accumulated debris and having it drift naturally, while trying at the same time to prevent the swift currents from fouling the line or embedding the hook on the myriad underwater snags. Furthermore, it was bitterly cold and a steady rain was falling.

Needless to say, after a couple of hours without a strike I was discouraged. Walter had been fishing downstream from me, and now he drew near. I said to him: "I guess there just aren't any steelhead running now." He came over, removed my artificial fly, tied on a plain #6 hook, and applied a few salmon eggs from a bunch in his raincoat pocket, which was full of water. Before we had to leave because of darkness, I had caught three silvery steelhead, one five-pounder and two eight-pounders. We released two of them and kept one of the larger ones to eat during the week.

The next morning, April 14, was clear and cold. I got up early, before the others, to walk down to the sea in Copper Bay. There were twenty-seven-foot tides and vast expanses of exposed rocks between the water and the cliff on which the Ernst cottage was built. The entire shore was lined with hundreds of large logs, either lost or abandoned by the Queen Charlotte logging crews. One mystery that I couldn't resolve was that of the numerous blacktail-deer tracks going down to the surf, with none coming back up that I could find anywhere along the beach for a mile or more. I could only presume that the deer had swum or waded farther down the shore than I had walked.

I was impatient to go fishing, even when the cold rain resumed, but it was after 10:00 A.M. before we had any lines in the water. When Rosalynn arrived, we advised her to try salmon roe for a while instead of artificial flies—at least until she had caught one fish. On her first cast, she landed a six-pound steelhead, almost more than she could handle because she had underestimated the power of the fish. She was upended in the icy water before the contest was over, but she didn't seem to mind. After putting on a dry woolen shirt, she continued fishing, with Walter staying in sight of her to help if she needed his advice.

Having already caught several the previous day on natural bait, I decided to stick with flies for today. On the creek bank that morning we'd met a young man named Bob Long, who, hearing I was there, had brought us three dozen of his special flies, small patterns made of a multicolored woolen blend—red, pink, green, and yellow—which he exchanged for our promise to join the Steelhead Society.

Late that afternoon, having had two strikes but no fish, I was floating one of the small woolen flies under a great log lying diagonally across the Deena. We had lost many of the flies to the swift current, rocks, and snags. Now I was hung up again, about ready to give up on the fly altogether as a lost cause. Just then, the "snag" began to move. I had a fish on my line, large enough that for a few minutes he was uncontrollable. I could only try to conserve as much line on my reel as possible while the steelhead did as he wished.

I tried to remember what I had learned about handling big fish on relatively light tackle. After getting the slack out of my line and on my reel, I maintained steady but firm pressure, moving down the shallow side of the creek whenever possible until I was downstream of the steelhead. Nevertheless, I almost lost him as he made two hard runs, one up a small tributary stream for a short distance. I applied as much restraint as the tackle would bear, although at other times I tried to moderate the tension to prevent the frantic runs.

Time dragged on. The fish and I moved slowly but inexorably down the stream. Fortunately, I was able to follow him, using the bank when possible and wading at other times. At this point the other fishermen came together to watch our *pas de deux*. On occasion they gave me some quiet encouragement— or laughed rather impolitely when I stumbled or fell. The steelhead jumped several times, and we could see from its bright colors that this one had been out of the sea for a number of days. I was mostly worried about the line getting fouled on one of the many snags in the stream, but each time the fish swam into an old treetop or among some roots the line later came clear. Because of the difficult footing and cluttered bank, I was engaged in a more sustained and difficult contest than I'd had with the much larger Atlantic salmon, but after half an hour the fish was obviously tiring. Finally, Walter was able to slip his net under the big male. We let him rest for a few minutes heading upstream and then watched him swim away, estimating his weight at fourteen pounds.

Clearly, it was the climax of this day's fishing. For a while I had forgotten about the rain and cold. Now, trembling with excitement and fatigue, I decided to rest on my laurels and watch Rosalynn and the others fish for a while.

On the way back home we talked about the different fish that spawned in these Queen Charlotte streams. The biologists who monitored their movements estimated that each year there were about thirty thousand chum salmon and eight thousand coho, but fewer than one thousand steelhead. Since the rivers are relatively small and have a short run between their sources in the high mountains and the sea, without careful conservation practices the steelhead population could quite easily be decimated.

The next morning it was storming, with a gale blowing from the southeast. Rosalynn was hesitant, but we decided to go fishing despite the weather and found that in the river valley the big trees blocked the wind enough for us to manage our tackle well—although at one point a large tree did fall within twenty feet of us. Rosalynn and I each caught a couple of steelhead. For one of mine, a six-pounder, its mate (or, probably, schoolmate) circled and followed my hooked fish around in its evasive maneuvers and right up to the net. After release, they swam off together.

So far, in a day's fishing I usually had a half-dozen steelhead on, landing one or two. When I fished with the fly rod but used salmon roe instead of flies, I could catch two or three times as many, but it was not nearly as much of a challenge. Also, because the fish was more likely to swallow natural bait, the artificial fly was safer for the fish.

The weather stayed cold and wet, with hail substituting for rain every now and then. Our spirits were high, however, because of the good fishing and the wildlife that was so prevalent. Sometimes we could see a pair of bald eagles circling overhead, building their nests and giving the high-pitched cries of love, excitement, or warning. On the way to the river one morning, we stopped to watch a gray whale moving slowly along the coast, only a few yards offshore, spouting regularly. Large otter were in the river, and we saw uncounted numbers of blacktail deer. We also saw the tracks and scat of black bear often, sighting three of them during the week.

One morning we received word that a logging company had offered to let us use one of its helicopters to visit the southern part of the Queen Charlottes. The next day we loaded our tackle and took off for a flight down the east coast. It was obvious from the air that the Copper and Pallant rivers were still too high from the constant rain for wading or convenient fishing. On small Skedans Island, just a rocky cliff jutting out of the waves a mile or so off the coast, we saw a large colony of sea lions. Keeping far enough away not to disturb them, we watched as they dived into the sea from a height of fifteen or twenty feet, moving over the rocky ledges with ease for creatures of such a cumbersome appearance.

We then landed on Lyell Island to observe the logging operation. There were sixty men and forty women and children at the camp, located on the shore of a small and protected bay. They were busy clear-cutting the sometimes virgin stands of spruce, hemlock, and red and white cedar. Earlier loggers had been able to harvest the trees conveniently near the sea, close enough to drag them down to the water with long cable rigs known as skidders. Now, with modern equipment, even the most remote trees could be cut and moved down for loading on barges and ships. A crew of "fallers" could cut down an average of thirty trees a day, but some of the trees were so large that it took a full day of work to cut one tree. The logs were loaded on the huge trucks and hauled down and dumped into the bay, where they were kept confined until the barges arrived to haul the timber to sawmills on the mainland. While we toured the recently completed recreation lodge we realized how enormous some of the trees were: The center table had been made from a single slab of spruce burl—nine feet in diameter.

It was really disturbing to see this virgin stand of timber harvested. The denuded areas were to be replanted as soon as possible, but several decades would pass before the slow-growing trees would be large enough to provide full cover again. It was an unforgettable reminder of how wasteful we are in our use of paper, containers, and other wood products, and what a responsibility we have to prevent timber harvests altogether in some of the most beautiful sites.

After lunch we flew down to the southern tip of the islands, to Ninstints, an ancient village of the Kunghit tribe of Haida Indians. Along the shore enormous totem poles were lined up, each carved from a single cedar tree. Some were still erect; others had fallen over and were in various stages of decay. Stone foundations of old buildings outlined the pattern of the village. The site had long been abandoned, most of the native population having succumbed to European diseases. They had been fierce warriors with an advanced civilization in their day.

An 1840 census showed 308 people living here in twenty houses, with eleven other Kunghit villages in the islands. Now there were only two small settlements left.

Coming back up the west coast of the Charlottes, we decided to head east and stop on Louise Island to try the fishing. Jack and Wayne went to Mathers Creek, while Rosalynn, Walter, and I tried nearby Skedans Creek. The current was dangerously strong, and many of the large round rocks on the bottom were covered with slime. After falling in twice, I decided to confine my wading to places near the shore where I could maintain a relatively firm footing.

Within a few minutes I had a heavy strike on the small multicolored fly. I quickly realized that this fish was by far the largest one yet. I could see his bright-silver color as he leaped three times far downstream. Because of the deep water and dangerous currents I could not move far from where I was, and yet in spite of maximum pressure on my tackle, the steelhead continued to head toward the sea at a steady pace. Even with my most vigorous efforts, when all the backing was gone from my reel the leader broke and the fish was free. This was a fish so strong that there was never a real contest, and I could only stand there and admire one who had conquered me so easily. We had been in the stream for a long time; I was too cold and exhausted to fish anymore, and soon we were on our way back to a fisherman's cherished destination: a fire, hot shower, and some dry clothes.

That evening we decided to go into town and accept an invitation to be guests at the Sandspit Inn for supper. The seafood platter we ordered included shrimp, octopus, razor clams, spring salmon, oysters, scallops, and Alaska crab legs, along with all the necessary trimmings. While we were enjoying it, a group of men from the 442nd Rescue Squadron sent us over a bottle of white wine and their business card, which read:

ALWAYS READY — QUICK RESPONSE — GOOD ENDURANCE — HARD WORKING — ANY TIME, ANY PLACE — BUSH JUMPS — EXTRA PUMPS — BIG BUNDLES INTO TIGHT PLACES — CELESTIAL POSITIONING — AURAL HOMING — ILLUMINATING PATTERNS — THE SEARCH AND RESCUE SPECIALISTS THAT SMART PEOPLE IN DISTRESS CONTACT IN B.C. AND THE YUKON.

After reading this (and laughing) I felt much safer about the dangers of stormy weather, falling trees, swift currents, wild animals, enormous log trucks, and being lost in the forests.

Our last day, when we fished inland on the Pallant River, was the best day of all. It was blustery again, with winds reported in excess of sixty knots, but we caught and released eleven large and heavy steelhead. It had been a stormy week. Although we'd never felt at risk, when we arrived back in Vancouver we learned that two fishing trawlers and one sailing sloop had been lost at sea off the Queen Charlotte Islands. None of the crews was ever found.

Later, when I thought back to the trip, remembering the beauty and fragility of the wilderness, the denuded hills stuck in my mind. As a timber grower myself, I knew that all harvesting could not be prohibited, but I felt strongly that some of the more precious places, especially lovely or retaining the ancient history of the indigenous people, had to be preserved. I joined many other interested citizens who wrote to the Prime Minister of Canada, urging the government to protect the river valleys and especially scenic sites from logging operations.

Two years later, it was announced that special legislation had been passed by the Canadian Parliament, restricting logging operations throughout the southern part of the Queen Charlotte Islands, including the Haida Indian village and its carved totems.

BONEFISHING
ON
ANEGADA

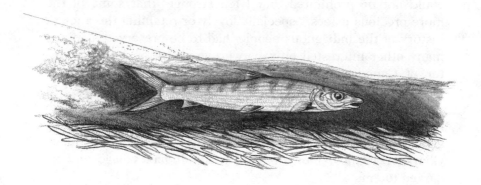

A thin white streak just above the waves indicated that our destination was less than ten miles away. Unlike the other Virgin Islands we had left far behind in the west, Anegada Island in the British Virgins had no mountains or hills. The highest dune was less than thirty feet above sea level.

As we cruised slowly and carefully through the coral reefs approaching the shallow harbor, Jack Crockford and I looked eagerly to the right and left for some sign of bonefish, either their tails above the surface or discolored water from their feeding on the bottom. Neither of us had ever seen one; all we knew was what we had read in sporting articles or learned in recent telephone conversations with some of our fly-fishing friends. Still, we knew more than anyone else on the forty-two-foot *Jambalaya.* Our hosts were weekend sailors from San Juan, deep-sea fishermen who did not understand how we could possibly be interested in the small and seldom-eaten denizens of the reefs when some of the best blue marlin fishing in the world was within sight of this very island.

I remembered some of the phrases about the fish from McClane's *New Standard Fishing Encyclopedia:* "It usually makes an incredibly swift run of 50–100 yards or more, and even a small fish has power out of proportion to its size. Bonefish live in a constant state of alarm. Sometimes it would seem that if you breathe too hard the whole flat erupts in fleeing schools." We were convinced from many conversations with experienced anglers that stalking bonefish feeding on the Caribbean flats was one of the ultimate challenges of fly-fishing.

It was late afternoon of an early summer day in 1986 when we anchored in the crystal-clear water. Some of the islanders asked if we would like to bring our tackle to one of the shallow inlets and help them catch some baitfish. Soon we were knee-deep in the tidal pools with our #5 fly rods, casting small bright-colored flies out into the currents and up into a labyrinth of mangrove roots for ladyfish.

They struck savagely, with aerial acrobatic displays that exceeded those of any freshwater fish I had ever seen. In a short time we had several dozen of them in a large Fiberglas drum for the grateful fishermen. Already, our introduction to the remote island felt auspicious indeed.

The next morning the wind was blowing strongly. White-caps, even in the sheltered coves throughout the reef area, indicated that it would not be a good day for novice bone-fishermen to learn new skills. Since our hosts had been eager for us to try the deep shelf just to the north of the island, we decided to troll in the deep sea until about noon and then come back in to the shallow reefs.

At 8:30 A.M. we headed west in the thirty-two foot *Marlin* (owned by another Anegada visitor named Marlin Fitch) in water just deep enough to float our boat safely. As we cleared the tip of the island the wind and waves hit us full force—a nearby Coast Guard cutter reported up to twelve-foot seas. I took the helm in order to take my mind off the waves and to help ward off seasickness. In just a few minutes we were at the hundred-fathom shelf, beyond which the ocean depth increased rapidly. We zigzagged eastward along this line, approaching shore in a southerly direction until the depth finder indicated about thirty fathoms, then turning and heading northward until the water was too deep to get a reading on the instrument. On the bridge with me were Marlin Fitch and Herman Groezinger, a permanent resident of Anegada who had just yesterday taken two marlin—a 120-pound white and a 280-pound blue.

At about ten o'clock we sighted a flock of sea birds off toward the island. I steered toward them, knowing that they and large fish often fed on the same schools of baitfish. Just as we passed through the birds, the right outrigger rig tripped. We could hear the #80 Penn reel singing. The indicator showed forty-five fathoms. We shouted for Jack Crockford to take the rod, but he was not able to move from his heaving bunk. When I jumped down and took the bent rod, I received a tremendous shock. In all my life, the biggest fish I had fought was a twenty-nine-pound Atlantic salmon, and yet now I almost went overboard while Herman struggled on the slippery and pitching deck to help me into the small white seat.

"How big is it?" he asked.

Through clenched teeth, I replied, "I don't have any idea, but I know it's a hell of a lot bigger than I am."

Marlin was backing the boat down as fast as possible, but the great fish was still staying deep and moving away, apparently without effort. After a few minutes Herman got a small harness around my back and shoulders, then snapped it into an eye on top of the singing reel. This took a lot of pressure off my arms and hands and gave me some hope for the first time that I might eventually be able to match my unseen adversary.

After a while I was able to take in a few turns of line, as the fish apparently stopped his descent. Everyone was guessing what it was: "a big shark," "a bluefin tuna," "white marlin," "blue marlin." After each possibility there was a general discussion. Most of the bluefins had probably moved north; the tuna and shark would stay deep; it seemed bigger than a white marlin; a blue would likely have come up near the surface and stayed there: The speculation continued. I was just listening, trying to hold on and keep from getting drowned by the waves breaking over the fantail in my face.

Then the fish moved up to the surface, quite a distance from the boat, and we caught a glimpse of a dark dorsal fin or tail in the waves. "Shark!" "Tuna!" "Blue!" were the exclamations. When the fish sounded, going quite deep, there was a consensus among the observers that this was unlike a blue marlin, who usually stayed nearer the surface this early in a battle.

By now I was soaking wet with spray and sweat. Every muscle from my neck to my toes seemed weak and painful. My hands were cramped like claws on the rod and the reel handle as I tried to keep the strong rod up away from the gunwale and to take in a few turns whenever possible. Although the minutes seemed to drag by, someone called out, "It's been an hour!" I tried a few swallows of Gatorade, but was afraid too much of it would make me sick in the heavy seas. I had never in my life strained as hard as this for so long a time. It seemed that the line would surely break, and I asked repeatedly—and unsuccessfully—if we shouldn't ease off some on the drag, both to protect the tackle and also my ribs and shoulders. We were all in good spirits, with a lot of joking going on: about whether I was drenched with sweat or spray; if handling big fish was more difficult than the Congress or Menachem Begin; how this experience compared with catching trout, bass, or salmon; whether I would prefer to eat my lunch with chopsticks; or if I wanted to swap places with my seasick fishing partner.

Finally, the line began to cut away from the boat, and I shouted, "He's coming up!" When he hit the surface he just kept on going toward the sky—a big and beautiful blue marlin!

I took in a lot of the relatively slack line, and Herman said quietly, "It won't be long now." The fish rolled a couple of times, not so far away. Strangely, the line seemed to be coming from his back instead of in his mouth. We wondered whether he was foul-hooked or if the line was temporarily caught around his dorsal fin. The marlin sounded again, easily stripping off the precious line that I thought had been won for good.

After a few minutes in the deep, he came back to the

surface. I could hear the cameras clicking as the great blue-and-silver fish made five or six consecutive rolling leaps, crossing from left to right across our stern. He was not so far away. "He'll go three hundred and fifty or four hundred pounds at least!" someone cried.

I listened to this and retorted, "He feels a lot bigger than that."

Then he came straight up, shook his bill, and dived again. We had seen him quite clearly; everyone agreed that he was foul-hooked and did not seem to be getting much weaker. It was going to be a long, hard fight, but I was eager for it. After some consultation, Herman and Marlin decided that it would be better to tighten up a little more on the drag.

Deep within the ocean, I felt something hit the line several times—a sharp, jolting sensation. "He must be whacking the line with his tail or his bill," I shouted.

"Or maybe there are some sharks around him now," someone remarked. I continued to crank, a few feet at a time.

All of a sudden the line went slack. I almost fell over backward. I didn't try to hold back the words of grief and anger that escaped my lips. Everyone stayed quiet for a while, and finally I said, "That was some fish! All I hope is that it was he and not a shark who cut the line."

My shoulders were sagging with fatigue and disappointment. For the first time I realized that I was surrounded by exhaust fumes, which were bubbling up and blowing over the fantail into my face. I felt a wave of nausea coming on. After all of us expressed our heartfelt admiration for the fighting spirit and strength of the marlin, I went up on the bridge and lay down across the seat.

It was almost noon, and time to return to the reefs. I relived the battle in my mind as the small fishing boat traveled with the wind from crest to trough of the big waves. Now I was eager to get back to the pier, where we hoped the bonefish were waiting.

When we inquired around the local bar and restaurant and among the fishermen about a bonefishing guide, we were disappointed to be told that there was none on the island. It did seem a little surprising. However, each respondent was eager to give us free advice on where and how to catch these fish.

Bonefish were very plentiful around Anegada, but few people fished for them. One of a kind, the species is the only survivor of an ancient family dating back perhaps 125 million years. The fish are most prevalent along the Florida coast, throughout the Caribbean, and in equivalent north and south latitudes around the world. The rod and reel record of almost twenty pounds was taken off the coast of Africa, but fish of even half this size are rarely caught in this hemisphere. Bonefish feed by rooting in the bottom of relatively shallow water for shellfish, squid, and small fish. Because the water becomes discolored and at times the fishes' tails stick out of the water as they stand almost on their heads to feed, they can be detected. The idea is for the fisherman to spot the feeding fish, cast carefully in their path without scaring them, and entice the bonefish to take whatever particular lure is offered. This isn't easy to do with shrimp or some of their natural foods and a spinning outfit, and with an artificial fly on a fly rod it is much more difficult. Bonefish are very spooky, and the slightest disturbance can send them all running.

During the next couple of days we waded around the still windswept flats near the shore of Anegada, often sighting the tails of bonefish but never getting close enough to reach them with our flies. The strong winds never slackened. In the shallow water the waves kept the sand stirred up too much to detect any muddying of the bottom by feeding bonefish. One afternoon we traveled over to the northwest corner of the island, where there were some comparatively sheltered areas, but still the sand whipped around our legs and quickly piled up over anything we set down on the beach while we were wading nearby. Some hefty bonefish cruised past us in the open channels between the waterline and the first line of seaweed, but they were not feeding and had no interest in the flies we laid down carefully before them.

We had no luck at all. Late in the afternoon of the day before we had to leave, one of our party came back to the boat to report that he had been drinking beer with an honest-to-goodness guide, Clinton Vanterpool, who offered to fish with us, with one proviso: We had to make the request directly to him. He wasn't volunteering his services. Among the tiny island's inhabitants, there was obviously some competition and jealousy, which perhaps explained the failure of the others, mostly white, to tell us about the black guide. In return, too proud to approach us, he was peeved that we had not come to find him. We quickly made arrangements to meet him shortly after sunrise for a few hours of fishing before our departure. At his suggestion, we were to bring both light spinning rods and fly-fishing gear.

The islanders had said Clinton seemed to be "arrogant and somewhat surly," but on the dock in the early morning light he was quite civil and supremely confident. Confidence was what we needed right then, and I was grateful when he said, "We'll have bonefish within an hour." Soon we were speeding eastward into the choppy swells, heading for some of the offshore reefs. The open eighteen-foot fishing boat had a built-up platform near the bow, covered with a piece of tufted carpet. Jack and I expressed our interest in wading and casting a fly to feeding bonefish, but Clinton said, "It's too deep to wade where we're going, and too muddy in there where it's shallow."

Instead, our guide pointed ahead and said, "Bonefish feeding." We couldn't see anything, even when he told us to look for the light-colored "mud." We were trying to spot small patches of discolored water, but eventually we realized that Clinton was pointing at broad expanses of milky surface, sometimes several acres in size. There seemed to be tremendous schools of the feeding fish in water from eight to ten feet deep.

Clinton pulled the boat up into the windward edge of one of the stained areas and told us to cast upwind while the boat drifted slowly through the feeding area. But our coiled fly lines were blowing off the platform, and our casting distance was disappointing.

We shifted to the ultralight spinning tackle. On the first cast I had a ferocious strike and saw most of my six-pound test line disappear from the reel before I could turn the fish.

"Jack, he must weigh twenty pounds," I shouted with delight.

I finally brought in a three-pound bonefish, Jack netted it, and, after a proud look, I smiled and eased the blue-and-silver speedster back overboard. Pound for pound, it beat anything I had ever caught. Clinton, watching us, said, "I'd like to keep a few. They're good eating."

Soon we were taking bonefish on the fly rods, casting across the wind and letting the line and boat drift together downwind. Our largest ones weighed five or six pounds, but each was a miracle of strength and speed as it moved like a tiny torpedo back and forth beneath the surface.

Before returning to the dock we went into the flats, where wading was possible. There were no bonefish tailing, but Clinton pointed out to us a few of the "gray ghosts" moving among the standing strands of grass. The constant wind and choppy surface made fishing very difficult for two novices, and neither Jack nor I was ever able to stalk a particular fish and then place a desirable fly close enough for a take.

Being typical fishermen, we were certain that if we could have stayed just one more day, knowing what Clinton Vanterpool had now taught us, or if the wind would just ease off by five knots, we would be sure to take bonefish in a more classical manner. In any case we had been among many hundreds of them, had caught enough to be convinced of their extraordinary fighting qualities, and had become personally familiar with some of the difficulties of outwitting what many believe to be the finest game fish on earth.

FISHING
IN
EUROPE

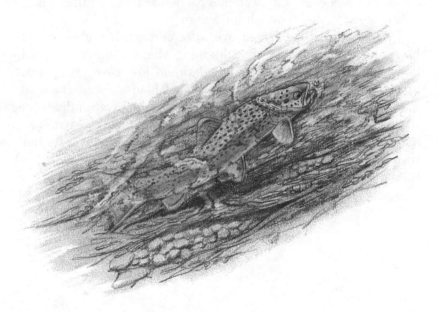

Ever since I took up fly-fishing I have been intrigued by the written history of the sport. Europe is where it all began. From Izaak Walton's treatise *The Compleat Angler, or the Contemplative Man's Recreation,* "Being a Discourse of Rivers Fishponds Fish and Fishing not unworthy the Perusal of most Anglers," thousands of volumes by anglers of all ages have spawned; we look upon Walton as the patriarch of us all. Many people who love the outdoors might, when tempted to write, have best followed the admonition at the bottom of the stained-glass window in Winchester Cathedral, England, dedicated to our patron saint: STUDY TO BE QUIET.

Even before Izaak Walton, there had been a definitive work about fishing, written by Dame Juliana Berners of St. Albans, said to have been a noblewoman and a prioress. Entitled "Treatyse of Fysshynge wyth an Angle," the earliest known copy was written out by a scribe in 1450 and is now in the library of Yale University. Among other information, the author lists twelve different artificial flies known to be effective in the streams around her home. So far as is known, it is the first recorded treatment of fishing as a sport. This little bit of history made the prospect of fysshynge in European streams even more exciting to us.

In June 1986, Rosalynn and I were successful in consolidating a number of business engagements into a long working trip to England, Switzerland, West Germany, Ghana, and Zimbabwe. Along the way, however, we were hoping for a few days of recreation, and so we decided to accept a longstanding invitation from some close friends to spend a few days on their farm in western Wales. Peter Bourne and his wife, Mary King, had sent us a booklet about the region, with an aerial photograph of their home that revealed the site of a first-century Roman fort and hot-water baths on the premises. This ancient military installation was, according to the text, on the bank of the Teifi River, which I had already heard was an excellent fishing stream for brown trout. Of course, it was my interest in the remains of ancient Roman forts that induced us to accept the invitation without delay!

The sheep-raising region around the farm seemed to be settled mostly with Peter's relatives, who had lived there for many generations. Welsh was the native language, but everyone we met also spoke some English. As soon as we'd unpacked and changed clothes we walked the short distance across the flower-strewn meadow to the riverbank and then moved quietly upstream to observe the clear water running from one deep pool to the next, with shallower weed beds between. Although no trout were rising, there appeared to be a fair number of small golden flies clinging to the willow and alder branches over the stream. Peter was not a fly-fisherman, but he was delighted that we were pleased.

Late that afternoon, after supper, Moc Morgan and his son Hywel came by the cottage, eager to introduce us to Welsh fishing. Moc, who had long leased the fishing and hunting rights on the farm, was a noted BBC commentator on his favorite pastime. And Hywel, although only nineteen years old, had won the silver medal in the most recent international distance fly-casting championship, held in Spain. During the few remaining minutes of daylight, we returned to the Teifi (pronounced Tye-vee) with our rods, where Rosalynn, downstream from me, caught a twelve-inch brown trout—while I came up empty-handed. This was becoming a habit of hers.

Early the next morning I redeemed my reputation, and after a few days we had both learned enough about the stream and its currents, the dwelling places and habits of its trout, and the identity and timing of the mayfly hatches to enjoy fairly consistent success. Long leaders, fine tippets, and small flies proved to be the secret. We also managed to arouse Peter's and Mary's interest in fly-fishing. After a few lessons Peter was able to take two nice trout, one by a very elegant presentation in a clear pool.

In the days that followed, we explored the nearby countryside on foot and on hardy Welsh ponies, as well as making longer journeys to other communities, stopping every now and then along the way to visit assorted members of Peter's family. The rolling hills and valleys of Wales are remarkably beautiful, carefully manicured by the flocks of sheep that are the mainstay of the agricultural economy.

Ubiquitous green hedges outline each farm, field, and road. We were fascinated by how they are formed. A row of saplings, one or two inches in diameter, are chopped through almost completely with a diagonal cut, except for a half inch or less that always leaves a strip of bark intact. Then the small trees are bent over parallel to the ground and left to grow. Surprisingly, the deep wound heals and most of the trees survive. During subsequent seasons the growing limbs are trimmed to shape the practically impenetrable hedge. Almost any kind of tree seemed to be suitable for the method. The ancient hedge leading across a bridge to Peter's house was beech, but we saw others of many varieties including hazelnut, oak, alder, holly, and hawthorn.

We asked one of the cousins how long it took to make a good hedge.

"I don't really know," he replied. "I reckon about two hundred years."

One day Moc, Hywel, Peter, and I drove about thirty miles north to a mountain lake, to fish with wet flies for rainbows. As we passed through a small village on the way, Moc said, "There are only thirty homes here, but out of them have come six international anglers."

I had no idea what an international angler might be and finally decided to reveal my ignorance by asking him to explain.

"There are competitions each year to select the fourteen best fly-fishers in Wales. Twelve of them go on the national team, with the other two in reserve. I've been on the team for several years and am now its secretary, or manager. Our team competes with similar groups from England, Ireland, and Scotland.

"The fishing is done in lakes, from freely drifting boats. Weighted fly lines and flies are prohibited, and as many as four flies can be mounted on the leader, at least twenty inches apart. The hardest rule to define and enforce is that flies cannot be stripped in fast enough to imitate a swimming minnow. Furthermore, flies cannot be trolled behind the drifting boat, which may move quite rapidly over the surface in a strong wind. In retrieving the line or working the flies, the rod tip must always be kept above the horizontal.

"There is an oarsman in each boat, and a competitor in the bow and stern from two different nations. They exchange places every two hours, and at the end of ten hours of fishing the catches are weighed to determine the winning team."

There is no such competition among fly-fishermen in America; the contests—for large cash prizes—are limited to bass fishermen. Even among them, everyone is on his own; as far as I know there's no team cooperation.

Since members of the local fishing club were scheduled to meet us, we pressed on over the twisting roads in order to arrive on time. About two miles short of our destination, however, a farmer opened his pasture gate just in front of us and about 150 sheep entered the narrow roadway between two fences. For a half hour we followed at a lamb's pace as the sheep were moved up the trail to a higher pasture. We soon forgot about time, fascinated by the two sheep dogs as they meticulously herded the flock to its destination.

On the lake shore we received a cordial welcome from more than a dozen fellow fly-fishermen, who had some photographers handy to record the event. Then, joining a number of small boats on the lake, we tried to follow the international rules as Moc had outlined them. While a brisk wind drove our boat across the water, we caught a brace of heavy-bodied rainbows. Some of the other fishermen took as many as half a dozen trout. I was not familiar with this kind of fishing, and some of my strikes were so fast and ferocious that my flies were carried away and I was left with a broken leader. No doubt I missed several that an international angler would have caught.

The farm home where we were staying, just south of Tregaron, was not far from the sea. While fishing in the quiet pools of the Teifi, we were startled a number of times by the wild and explosive leap of an Atlantic salmon. One of them, a fifteen-pounder jumped repeatedly at intervals of about five minutes and ten to twenty yards as it moved upstream. It refused our nervous offerings of the few streamers we had on hand.

During our visit the sea trout, or sewin, were just beginning their annual run. We were invited by Colonel Gilbert Chaldecott to visit him at the mouth of the Tywi River (pronounced Tow-ee), near Carmarthen, to try our luck at some evening fishing. The water was high, but a few fish were rising. Wading chest-deep and casting a #10 streamer across and slightly downstream, we fished about a hundred yards of the beautiful water. The good colonel, who hobbled agilely along the steep bank on his one sound leg and a stout cane, shouted constant encouragement and advice. Despite his generous assistance, I caught one two-pound fish.

"When I first came home from military service in India it was not like this," our host apologized. "Some evenings we would catch thirty, averaging three and a half pounds. That was before the acid rain destroyed the streams. But even now, in a week or so there will be some very good fishing here."

Since Rosalynn's waders were leaking, she was soon shivering and had to leave the water. After she dried off and was outfitted in borrowed clothes, we enjoyed a lavish streamside banquet and a recitation of some of the colonel's poems that more than made up for the scarcity of fish.

ॐ

A few days later Rosalynn and I were in the heart of the Swiss Alps, in the beautiful resort center of St. Moritz. It was still early in the season; the Palace Hotel opened for the summer the day we arrived. We had managed to squeeze in a brief visit just before an international health meeting we were attending in Geneva, hoping that we might be able to do some mountain climbing and hiking, with time to fish for a couple of hours late in the afternoons.

In driving from the airport to the hotel we noticed that there were two kinds of streams flowing parallel through the narrow valleys between the mountain peaks. One was clear and the other milky-white, obviously carrying large quantities of suspended soil directly from the many glaciers in the surrounding mountains. The glacial water was directed into a series of small man-made lakes along the main river, where the tiny rock fragments settled to the bottom. I wondered how long it would be before this constant sedimentation filled the lakes.

Our first expedition after we arrived was to the local sporting goods store, where we learned that trout and grayling were plentiful in the area but that the fishing regulations were quite complicated and had to be stringently observed. The hotel manager offered to have fishing licenses and a copy of the regulations delivered to us; by late afternoon the package and a bill were brought to our room. We paid 120 Swiss francs (about $70), regretting that we had not made it clearer that we wanted only a three-day permit, not the one we'd received—for the entire season.

I made a last-minute check of our fishing tackle and, while Rosalynn finished getting into some casual clothes, began to read the booklet, dauntingly entitled *"Fischereibetriebs-vorschriften."* Fortunately, there were French and Italian translations along with the German text, and we were able to use our knowledge of Spanish enough to understand some of the general principles. Still, the complexities were overwhelming:

There were prescribed times for fishing the different waters, the kinds of tackle to be used, and a tiny map of this Swiss region delineating at least one hundred restricted zones. It seemed obvious that the regulations were primarily for lake fishermen and did not encourage fly-fishing on the streams.

Since we had only a couple of hours to fish before dark, we decided to try a small clear stream and lake we'd noticed near the airport when we arrived earlier. Although we never saw a fish rise, I managed to catch and release a ten-inch brown trout before we returned to St. Moritz for supper. At least that gave us hope. The hotel manager encouraged us to bring any future catch to the chef, who would be glad to demonstrate his special recipes for a meal. He also asked if we would need another license. When I replied that we already had two for the season, he smiled and informed us that those we had purchased were for one day only!

The next day we took a cable car to one of the mountain peaks overlooking St. Moritz and hiked back down the steep trail. With binoculars we were able to scan the valley quite thoroughly. We detected some promising stretches along the main river where we thought we might have more success fishing. Later that afternoon we drove upstream from St. Moritz and walked down from the roadway, across a small meadow, through a gravel pit to a relatively smooth stretch of water below the Silvaplana lake. A few fish were rising near the far bank, but we couldn't see any insects on the water. Rosalynn tied on a black ant, and I decided to try a small Dark Hendrickson. Within a few minutes we had taken two nice trout and an eighteen-inch grayling. We decided to keep them for the hotel chef and release any others we might catch.

After a while a lady with a large dog came strolling by. She pointed at my rod and spoke to me pleasantly in German. I presumed she wanted to know if we had any luck, and I told her, in English, that we had caught three fish. She repeated her previous words until I finally understood one of them: *Verboten.* She pointed far upstream to a small sign, which naturally I went up to read. There was a red circle with a fish in the center.

We left carrying our three fish, which we enjoyed for supper that evening. I didn't want to compute what our meal cost, although there is no question that I have often spent much more for a lot fewer fish. The next time we fished in Switzerland, we resolved, we would be better prepared and more familiar with both the restrictions and the opportunities.

ॐ

The following summer, after an exhausting trip to Asia, the Soviet Union, and northern England, Rosalynn and I arrived at Lainston House, near Winchester, in Hampshire, England. It was certainly time for a rest, and what better place than the countryside where both Izaak Walton and Dame Juliana Berners had roamed and fished in the nearby rivers. We drove up a long winding road and were ushered through the rear entrance and then to our corner room on the second floor of this old English manor, which had been converted to a small hotel only about five years before our arrival.

It was a warm Sunday afternoon, and from our window we could see groups of guests having tea on the lawn and under the ancient linden trees. A few of the younger men and women were sunbathing on the manicured front lawn, which extended for almost a half mile to the east. Nearby, a game of croquet was underway, the most strenuous exercise to be seen.

It seemed that our metabolism almost automatically shifted into low gear. We changed into casual clothes, slowly explored all the way to the end of the east lawn, and then had tea in a quiet place in front of the manor. The hotel manager came to inform us that there would be a performance of Shakespeare's *Hamlet* in a natural bowl on the lawn in the late afternoon. We enjoyed the play, with a serving of fresh raspberries and cream during the intermission. Then, after a delicious supper, we threw a Frisbee until John Russell and his wife, Anthea, arrived from their nearby home. They were to be our fishing hosts for two days and, after we got acquainted, gave us some pointers about the nearby streams. When we retired for the night, it was still daylight outside.

Early the next morning we ran for about three miles into Winchester, jogging around the narrow and confusing streets until we came to the cathedral. This beautiful building, begun in A.D. 1079 and finished three centuries later, is famous in its

213

own right. It is also known to millions of young people because of the hit song of the same name, and for many trout fishermen it is special as the burial place of Izaak Walton, who died at the age of ninety, 304 years before we arrived in the churchyard.

It was still early when we returned to our hotel, eager to realize a longtime dream of trying the two most famous chalk streams nearby, the rivers Itchen and Test. At nine o'clock Bill Loader arrived at Lainston House. He would be our gillie (guide) for the day as we fished in the Itchen, just a short distance from his home in Easton. On the drive to the stream he explained that there were no significant daytime fly hatches in July, that we would be fishing upstream to relatively infrequent rises, and that our catches, if any, would be brown trout only—no rainbows or grayling.

"We're a quarter of a mile from where the grayling come," he told us. "You might see the odd salmon, but it would be unlikely to take your fly."

The water was transparent. The river averaged about twenty to twenty-five yards wide, bordered on one side by fields of wheat and barley and on the other by trees and an occasional house and garden. When visible, the bare ground back from the stream was white, composed mostly of the chalk of the Hampshire plains. Many large trout could be seen in the deeper places in the stream, sometimes darting from one hiding place to another. However, ranunculus and other water weeds provided adequate cover when the fish chose to stay hidden.

The Itchen was alive with water birds. Coots, dabchicks, and moorhens could be seen in every stretch of the river; at first glance we often mistook the small diving dabchicks for rising trout. Mallards and other ducks led their orderly young in and out of the quiet pockets along the bank. The most obtrusive creatures of all were a pair of parent swans with five half-grown cygnets. They continually cruised up and down the stream, the male swan often straying far off by himself, then flying back to join his family, splashing noisily on his long takeoffs and his fast landings. Bill explained that swans mated for life, hatching a brood each year, nursing their young carefully, teaching them to fly, and then driving them off as they approached maturity.

For some time we could not see any trout rising, but

finally, in a broad shallow pool with the water broken up into many streams by the waving fronds of ranunculus, we spotted a dimple every now and then. We cast repeatedly, offering several different flies without success, and then Bill and I walked slowly up the stream, leaving Rosalynn to fish alone (which is almost always her strong preference). She continued to experiment with various flies, finally taking a heavy sixteen-inch brown on a small black gnat. When we met at noon in a nearby pub to enjoy a ploughman's lunch and a pint of bitters, I had still not caught a fish.

During the afternoon both Bill and I fished while Rosalynn did some sightseeing in the area. I was lucky enough to take four browns, ranging from fifteen to eighteen inches. Each time, my companion lifted them from the stream with a long-handled net, carefully removed the hook with forceps without grasping the fish, and then gently returned the trout to swim away. It was a delightful fishing experience, and we could understand why for the last five hundred years or more, English fishers, both men and women, have enjoyed the same stretch of stream. When Christopher Columbus was busy discovering America, fishermen were trying to outwit brown trout in these same pools, using pointers from Dame Juliana Berners's treatise.

The following morning we drove early to Stonehenge, where we stood reverently among the huge stones as the sun rose, pondering the mystery of how these enormous monoliths could have been moved from their distant quarries. Of course, I also wondered what devices these innovative people might have used almost four thousand years ago to take trout from the nearby streams!

Then Rosalynn and I returned to The Mill, which is the British Isles headquarters of Orvis Company and the Russells' home. During breakfast we discussed how, through their stores, Orvis met the needs of sportsmen all over the world. Soon thereafter, Charles Brand joined us to be our gillie as we fished on the Test. Charles drove us to Romsey, where we entered a meadow area just above Broadlands, the home of the late Lord Louis Mountbatten. Both Queen Elizabeth and Charles, the Prince of Wales, had taken their spouses there for their honeymoons, and the historic mansion was now a lively tourist spot. As we fished in the broad river, we could look downstream and see groups of visitors strolling about the lawn. The water birds on the Test were the same as those on the Itchen, including, coincidentally, a pair of swans with five cygnets, somewhat larger than the ones we'd seen earlier.

It was a hot, clear day, and again the fish were seldom rising. We spent a lot of time sitting or standing quietly in the meadow, well back from the stream, just waiting for signs of a feeding trout. The Test was a greater stream than the Itchen, at least fifty yards across, and slightly stained. Whenever we saw the rare rise, most often to take a single insect, we cast twenty or thirty times to the spot, using every conceivable type and size of fly. Charles suggested that we might try a nymph, saying that even some of the strictest English clubs encouraged nymph fishing during July. However, we wanted to fish in the "proper" fashion—staying with the dry fly and casting upstream only to a particular rising trout.

About noon, under three enormous plane trees, I had our first modest success of the day, inducing a vicious strike with a small black gnat, the brown leaping two feet out of the water as the fly came free. One strike was better than nothing, but not much.

We ate a picnic lunch alongside the stream, not having caught a single trout. Afterward, Charles said, "Let me show you what they were taking from the Test a hundred years ago." We walked upstream a few yards to a highway bridge, and there in the deep shadow were several outlines of trout cut out of lead sheets and nailed to the bridge. On each was the name of the fisher, the date, the weight of the trout (ranging from thirteen to fifteen pounds), and the pool from which it came. The shapes of the fish were surprisingly short and deep compared to the trout of today. Again, Rosalynn decided to leave us, this time for some shopping in the nearby villages.

A few more fish were rising by midafternoon and both Charles and I were fishing, but neither of us was able to present a fly they would take. Finally I asked him if there were any black ants in the meadows, to which he replied, "No, but perhaps you might try one of your American designs."

I tied on a small winged ant and still failed to entice a

trout, then put on a larger deer-hair ant, applied flotant, and offered it to the next rising fish we saw. There was an instant swirl, and I landed a nice brown.

From then until the end of our fishing day I cast this fly to five other trout. All of them took the black ant as it floated by; I landed four of them. Fishing with barbless hooks, it was easy to release the fish without harm. Of the largest, Charles said, "He'll go three pounds."

That evening Rosalynn and I celebrated our forty-first wedding anniversary with some friends who drove out from London. We had enjoyed our party a little too long, and it was almost dark when we arrived at Kimbridge on the Test to join John Russell. We could see that the surface of the river was steadily broken by circles from feeding trout. "It's a nice hatch of sedges. You call them caddis in America," John said.

By the time we had our tackle ready it was too dark to see the hatching flies or our own artificials on the surface, but we tried to guess how to cast to the constantly rising trout. We each had several fish on, and Rosalynn and I landed three fish each, mine a grayling, a brown, and a rainbow. It was a beautiful wedding anniversary!

NEW ZEALAND ADVENTURE

Ever since I've been reading or hearing about fly-fishing, the reports of enormous trout in the streams and lakes of New Zealand have been fascinating—and tempting—to me. However, the time and expense of so long a trip continued to be prohibitive. Finally, in February 1983, I received invitations to speak to large and distinguished audiences both in Australia and New Zealand. Quickly I examined the world atlas to see how far my forum in Palmerston North, New Zealand, was from Lake Taupo and all its famous tributary streams. Since it was quite close, my civic responsibilities as a former President prevailed. I decided to share my opinions about world affairs with the people "down under," while leaving a couple of days for Rosalynn and me to go fishing.

Our first week was spent along the East Coast of Australia, from Melbourne to the Great Barrier Reef to northern Queensland. The schedule was so crowded that we had little time for recreation other than some sightseeing wedged in among official duties and a quick trip from Dunk Island out to the barrier reef for some snorkeling and a nice catch of "Spanish" mackerel (which appeared very similar to the king mackerel of our country). My entire itinerary was well publicized in Australia, and every time I met New Zealanders there, they always seemed to be from the South Island and deplored my plans to limit my visit to the North. We regretted it, too, having heard about the great fishing and scenery on South Island, but just did not have enough time to divide the precious days between the two places.

By the time we had fulfilled our duties in Palmerston North, the advice we'd received on how to fish the New Zealand waters was too voluminous and contradictory to sort out. Many of our new friends, who had weekend cottages, or "baches" in the nearby Taupo area, regaled us with stories about the five-, six-, and seven-pound rainbow and brown trout they or their fishing partners had caught. They laughed indulgently when we talked about our own catches measured in inches and repeatedly asked us to convert these lengths into weight in pounds so they could compare our fish with theirs. Even my description of a prize nineteen-inch brown trout taken and released in Wyoming brought no reaction other than a quiet but unmistakable expression of something like sympathy. (Note that this New Zealand trip preceded my catching a larger trout in Alaska.) Some of them cautioned me not to use anything less than an untapered fourteen-pound test leader in the larger rivers and the lakes. We attended church services on Sunday, and the prayers and benedictions included supplications to the Lord to "guide the rod and line of Brother Jimmy" and "to let him savor the joy and satisfaction of true New Zealand fishing."

Articles in the local and national newspapers announced that we were finally heading for our long-awaited private angling vacation. As we crossed over the Tongariro River near

Turangi we were somewhat concerned about the excessive publicity and the obvious worry among New Zealanders that our fishing expedition might be disappointing. Consequently, we were quite pleased to arrive a few moments later at the Tongariro Lodge and find no news media there to greet us.

The comfortable and attractive cottages were fairly new, owned and operated by Tony Hayes, fishing guide, and Margaret Coutts, chef and general manager. It was about 4:30 P.M., too late to go to any of the smaller headwater streams, and so Tony immediately asked if we would rather get a good night's rest after all our long-distance traveling and be ready to fish early in the morning.

"We came to fish first; we'll rest later," I replied, and Rosalynn nodded her head in agreement.

Tony said, "We've arranged to spend tomorrow in some of the smaller streams in the remote headwater areas. However, since we have only a few hours left this evening, perhaps you would like to fish in the mouth of the Tongariro. It's just a short distance from here, and the trout come up to feed on the smelt and small freshwater crawfish where the river enters the lake. We'll need to cast fairly long distances, so it will be necessary to use a shooting head on our fly lines."

We had never cast a shooting head before, but it didn't take us long to decide now was the time to learn.

On the way to the small delta area, we saw several ducks and hundreds of beautiful black swans and their little white or light-gray cygnets, stretching their long necks to the bottom of the lake where they fed on grasses. Tony complained: "They're pretty all right, but they pull up the grass and let the currents distribute it increasingly around the lake, where it takes root and spreads even more."

There were a number of small boats fishing in the lake, slowly trolling the depths, but they were prevented by law from coming within three hundred meters of the fly-fishing area where we were headed. Tony explained some other rules: no weighted flies, single hooks only, minimum size of "keepers" fourteen inches from nose to the shortest point of the tail, a limit of eight rainbow, with no limit on browns. Then he asked if I wanted to keep our fish or release them. I followed my usual policy. "Let's release them," I replied.

There were two or three other fishermen casting near our chosen spot when we arrived, but Tony's partner was holding one of the best places for us. None of them had had much luck that day, and we were not overly confident as we stripped off a pile of line and prepared to cast the fast-sinking shooting head as far as possible out into the deep water. We were using #8 rods, with nine-foot leaders and six-pound tippets. It was too much for Rosalynn to handle, and so she let Tony help with her casts until she could learn this new technique. I had a lot of trouble trying not to stand on the line I had stripped off and to prevent its being fouled on some obstacle as the strong northerly breeze moved it around, but was soon casting it a reasonable distance—about one-third less than Tony was sending Rosalynn's line.

The river current helped to carry the fly even farther, and we let it sink slowly into the deep and clear water for about one-half minute before we began the slow and steady retrieves, pulling the fly line in our left hands with a rhythmical figure-eight motion. My fly pattern was a Hairy Dog on a #8 hook, a red chenille body wrapped with gold ribbon, a fairly long brown hair hackle with a tail of darker brown and a touch of blue-green. Rosalynn's fly was a white-and-silver imitation of the small smelt.

Soon I noticed what I thought was an Irish potato floating by in the current, then another and another. I said, "Rosalynn, either those are potatoes or the rocks are floating down here in the bottom part of the world." Tony laughed and explained that the entire region was covered with about a hundred feet of porous rock or pumice from the volcanic explosion that had formed Lake Taupo about 1,800 years ago. When it's dislodged from the stream banks, and until it's completely waterlogged, the pumice floats almost halfway out of the water.

After about twenty minutes of casting, waiting, and the slow retrieve, I shouted to Tony: "I'm caught on the bottom!"

"Retrieve faster," he replied; then: "That's not the bottom!" as the rod bent almost double and the reel sang loudly. As I kept strong tension on the line but watched it run out steadily, I could hardly believe a trout was doing that. Then I saw a silver streak far to the left of where I thought the end of my line would be, and yelled, "Whose fish is that?"

"Yours," said Tony as he lengthened the telescoping net-handle. After a few abortive runs and slow steady retrieves, the beautiful hen rainbow was in the net. Rosalynn asked Tony how big the fish was. "I don't know," he answered, "but I have some good scales."

I was quite disappointed as the pointer settled on 3, and turned to Tony with a smile to say, "Well, I've never caught a three-pound trout before."

"Mr. President, that's three kilograms," he said. "Also, we really need one large fish for supper tonight. Okay to keep this one?"

It didn't take me long to agree, after I finally converted metric weight into more than six and a half pounds of trout. Tony was happier than I was, if that was possible. He told me later that he felt all the responsibility for New Zealand's fishing reputation was resting on his shoulders.

Rosalynn soon landed a three and a half pounder and a few minutes later I got another just a little smaller. Then the sun disappeared behind a high cone-shaped extinct volcano in the west and almost immediately all of us were chilled, hungry, and eager to show our largest fish to the nervous New Zealanders who were waiting to flash the news to our friends in Palmerston North that their prayers had already been answered. Riding along in the gathering dusk, we saw several brightly colored pukekos, or swamp birds, that live around the edge of the lake. Although it was February 13, in the middle of the New Zealand summer, we were shivering when we arrived back at camp. After some photographs, Tony suggested that we spend a few minutes in the hot tub while Margaret cooked supper, and soon we were luxuriating in the steaming and bubbling water. No doubt about it, we were on vacation.

Later, in the lodge, we drank a few toasts to our New Zealand hosts and to the wise men of old who had transferred the first *Salmo gairdneri* eggs from California to Lake Taupo, 101 years before we came to obtain a fine return on this outstanding original investment. Tony and some of the other guests explained that the rainbow and later brown trout (mostly in the South Island) had been disseminated all over New Zealand, flourishing so well that early in this century the lakes and streams became overpopulated and the fish too small. The fish biologists encouraged seining and heavier fishing to reduce the fish population and increase the average weight of fish to about ten pounds. Fishing regulations have been modified to maintain trout size at about three pounds in Lake Taupo. There were never any native trout in New Zealand and, strangely, no indigenous mammals at all except for a few flying bats. Now the country abounds with introduced red deer, wild boar, opossums, rabbits, and other wild animals.

Soon Margaret brought the fish camp menu for the evening—from native mussels in lemon cream sauce to strawberry crêpes with ice cream. On the facing page was written: "Smoked trout served before dinner, courtesy of Mr. Jimmy Carter." She explained to the group that it was illegal for trout to be bought or sold in New Zealand; it could only be served as a gift. I thought that she must be serving a fish caught earlier and smoked over a long period of time, but she assured us that this was indeed my catch of that afternoon.

It was as delicious as any smoked trout or salmon we had ever eaten. When I told her so, Margaret introduced us to their dinner guest John Wells, the man who had invented the smoker and who produced fishing tackle and supplies in nearby Rotorua. With two small cups of cooking alcohol under a shallow tray of sawdust, his smoker produces enough heat and smoke to cook a large trout in about twenty minutes. The trout is first deboned, and the exposed fillets salted, peppered, and then rubbed with brown sugar—to outstanding results.

One of the newly arrived fishermen at the lodge was a magistrate and retired dairyman from the southwestern part of England. He told us that he spent eleven weeks in New Zealand each year, as he found the tightly restricted fly-fishing for trout in his native land a poor substitute for salmon fishing in Scotland or the quest for large browns and rainbows down under. He had already spent two or three weeks in the Southern Island of New Zealand and had not netted a fish. This was extremely unusual, but extraordinary rains had made normal fishing impossible, and he recalled with wonder (and perhaps some exaggeration) one day when it had rained twenty-three inches! Now, he had come up to Lake Taupo to try to change his luck.

He pointed out that New Zealand had just defeated Great Britain in cricket, his country's team had lost a major rugby match in Australia, and he was determined not to let an American catch a larger trout than he. I was intrigued with his ideas about sport, particularly when he opined to the group: "There are two recent developments in competitive games which I can never accept. One of them is the wearing of helmets by athletes to protect their heads. This adds an element of artificiality to manly contact that borders on cowardice. The other is even worse—the clasping of hands or other demonstrations of excitement or pleasure after a goal is scored. In my youth this would have been considered the grossest exhibition of poor sportsmanship—the opposite of a proper display of humility after a triumph." He obviously didn't think much of our recent Super Bowl contest!

Early the next morning we flew by helicopter from the lodge to the northeast, crossing many pristine streams on the way to the Rangitaiki River, which flows within the large Kaingaroa national forest. In most places, the Rangitaiki has steep and well-defined banks, often crowded, unfortunately, with toitoi, a tall grass six to eight feet high with a large bushy head similar to a horse's tail—and an insatiable appetite for our fly lines. The day was cloudy and no trout were rising, so Rosalynn and I fished for a while with nymphs, casting upstream into the deep pools and using a roll cast whenever necessary. We had several good strikes, but by lunchtime I had not landed a fish.

By this time, the sun had come out and the cicadas could be seen and heard around the stream. I shifted to dry flies, using primarily Royal Wulffs furnished by my guide, Gary Kemsley, and some cicada imitations I had brought with me. I was fishing mostly to the infrequent rises. Finally, over against the far bank, I saw a trout that appeared very large. I offered a Royal Wulff to him, and he rose for a look but refused to take. After glimpsing the fish I was quite excited and so I decided to sit down for a while, change to a cicada imitation, and give both me and the fish a chance to rest. It was a difficult cast, the water was clear, and the fish must have grown so big because it was cautious and wily. I figured I had one more good chance. I checked behind me thoroughly, found a place between the toitoi bushes for a back cast, and lucked up on a perfect placement. The fly bobbed along under the overhanging bank without any drag, and I saw a formidable dark-brown shape rise out of the depths to meet it.

It was the biggest trout I had seen so far. As he struck at the fly, I lifted the tip of my rod to set the hook. The fish disappeared under the bank, untouched. Gary was gracious and said I didn't strike too soon, but I had an uneasy feeling that I should have waited a fraction of a second longer. We were both shaken by the size of this fish. Although we returned to the hole a couple of times during the afternoon, we were not to see him again. I did catch and release five or six trout on dry flies, the largest a heavy sixteen-inch female rainbow of about two pounds. Gary was somewhat disappointed that so few fish were rising or taking flies, but for me it had been a delightful experience.

We decided to return to the lodge early enough to fish for a while before dark with wet flies in the much heavier water of the Tongariro. I particularly enjoyed piloting the helicopter over the hills and streams north and then east of Lake Taupo. Circling low over one cleared area in the immense forest, we found a ranch for growing several thousand red deer. Many of them had very large antlers, which, Gary explained, provided a major source of revenue to the ranchers. As with rhinoceros horn, portions of the antlers are considered a powerful aphrodisiac in the Far East, where there is a ready market for them. Some of the sheep growers in New Zealand have also begun to produce red deer, but primarily for the venison.

Soon Tony and I had arrived in the large river pools a mile or so above the lake, but had no luck during the short remainder of the day. We had promised to be back at camp in time for the scheduled supper, hoping that our English friend had been able to supply the smoked trout for the premeal festivities. Fortunately for all of us, he had brought in a six-pound rainbow. I helped with the cooking and later enjoyed the vivid descriptions of his fishing prowess, scoffing at his determination to catch a larger fish than mine.

Since we would have to leave before noon the next day for Auckland, I made arrangements with Tony to go out quite early the next morning for one more session of fishing. We were to leave the lodge at about 5:15 A.M. so that we could be back at the river mouth by daybreak. Later, I overheard the magistrate discussing our very early morning plans with his dinner companion. "I like fishing as much as anyone," he said, "but I deplore fanaticism in any form."

Well, in my case fanaticism prevailed. That morning Tony and I were casting our small flies into a slight breeze from the north long before we were able to see the many frantic trout that were splashing all around us, apparently feeding on smelt near the surface. I thought a dry fly might be appropriate, but Tony insisted that we stick with the nymphs and sinking lines. At daylight we could see the fish leaping among the wavelets, but we didn't have a strike for a time. As we waited, Tony weighed the landing net so that we would be able to determine the size of any fish without having to handle it, but this was all we accomplished for quite a while.

Before sunrise, Tony had on a nice trout, but before he could bring it near the surface it was off the hook. A few minutes later I had a ferocious strike and could only hold the rod high and put as much pressure on the reel rim as possible without permitting the fish to break the line.

"I'm sure," I said through clenched teeth, "this is the biggest one yet."

"I can tell by looking at the rod—and your face," replied Tony.

The monster went deeper and deeper, and I began to despair of ever turning it enough to bring it close to the waiting net. Suddenly the line went slack. I felt stricken with disappointment. I reeled in several yards of line and then felt renewed pressure as the rod bent again. The fish had simply been running upstream against the current toward me. It was now much closer to us but still firmly hooked. We continued the seesaw battle for about ten minutes more and finally glimpsed the rainbow as it rolled near the surface. The beautiful fish was soon in the net, weighing eight pounds. I told Tony to let it go, but he said that sometimes his fishing guests would go as long as a month without catching anything over seven pounds. Could he keep the fish to display at the lodge? he asked. "It's yours," I said, and we resumed fishing.

When we'd caught two more trout, it was time for us to return to camp and prepare for our departure. The sun was now well up, and on the west side of the lake the bright rays illuminated one of the most beautiful little towns I've ever seen. Populated by about ten Maori families, the hamlet was built around a boat landing and a lovely little church. Just to the north was a breathtaking waterfall, perhaps a hundred feet in height, which came pouring down the steep mountainside. As we observed this lovely site, two fishermen approached us from up the river and asked if we'd had any luck. We had caught two or three, we told them. It seems they had fished all night with wet flies and had about half a dozen.

I started to raise my eight-pounder when one of the men held up an enormous brown trout with the hooked jaw of an elderly male. Later, it weighed in at twelve pounds, two ounces. That huge trout against the backdrop of the beautiful Maori village exemplified our brief stay in New Zealand, which will always be one of my most memorable fishing experiences.

A
VISIT TO
NEPAL

We could hardly believe it. Rain beat against the plane window as we prepared to land in Kathmandu in the fall of 1985, defying all the odds and weather history. Mid-October was almost guaranteed to be dry, at least a month removed from the monsoon season. The rain and snowfall come during the early summer months, so that's when the photographs of snow-covered peaks must be taken. True, we'd seen a brief report in the Bangkok newspaper about an unseasonable cyclone centered over the Bay of Bengal, but we'd had no premonition that its effects might be felt in Nepal. Now we were dismayed to learn that fog and driving rains were likely to persist for an indefinite period.

For years Rosalynn and I had been making tentative plans for this trip, even while we were still in Washington. We had discussed the possibilities with Richard Blum, a friend and accomplished mountain climber, when he visited the White House with his wife, Dianne Feinstein, mayor of San Francisco. Finally I realized that Rosalynn was serious about the adventure when, early in 1985, she told me that October would be a good time for us to go. After blocking out the time, we read some of the books we had accumulated about Nepal and the challenge of trekking with the Sherpas in the high Himalaya Mountains. In addition to our routine jogging and cycling, she and I spent several months working out with weights for an hour or so each day, determined to strengthen the muscles we would need in carrying a backpack over the steep trails. I had recently turned sixty and saw this as a worthwhile physical challenge and also a chance to learn something about the remarkable history of the country.

Hearing about our possible visit, King Birendra extended an official welcome to his kingdom. He offered the services of the Nepalese Air Force to expedite our travel to the starting point of our trek—provided we paid the cost of the helicopter operations. And so we devised an ambitious itinerary, based on the good weather everyone guaranteed for this time of year.

We were to spend one day in Nepal's capital and fly west about 120 miles to Ghasa, on the banks of the Kali Gandhaki river. Then we would follow this stream through the deepest gorge on earth, more than 22,000 feet below the Dhaulagiri range on the west and the Annapurna range to the east, trekking as far as Kagbeni. During these four or five days we would ascend from Kathmandu's 4,600 feet to twice that altitude, slowly becoming acclimated to the atmospheric changes.

Then we would fly to Namche Bazar, at an altitude of 11,300 feet, about a hundred miles northeast of Kathmandu in the region that encompasses Mount Everest and its drainage area. After a two-day side trip to Thami monastery we would attempt to trek north to Pheriche, at 14,000 feet or perhaps a little higher, in whatever time remained in our visit. Weather permitting, we might then be able to helicopter to the Everest base camp, at about 17,500 feet.

Our ambitious schedule was heavily dependent on air transportation, but now the weather throughout Nepal made flying almost impossible—and threatened all our trekking plans. The rain and fog in the lowlands were accompanied by heavy snow at greater altitudes. Expedition teams in the high mountains were in serious jeopardy, and we began to hear reports of deaths among them from avalanches and exposure to the elements. The expedition leader and four other members of an Indian expedition on Everest had perished; a Sherpa was killed in an avalanche that struck a Japanese group attempting to scale Manaslu, one of the Nepalese peaks that exceed 8,000 meters in height; and in separate expeditions on Annapurna South, a West German and two Greeks had died.

We monitored the news every hour, waiting for favorable weather reports. Instead, we were distressed to learn that not far from where we planned to go but a mile higher, a team of thirty-two New Zealanders was trapped between two high and now impenetrable passes north of the Annapurna range. A small group of seven men had volunteered to bring news of their plight to rescue teams, but four of them died in an avalanche. Helicopters of the Royal Army of Nepal were trying to locate the isolated trekkers and give them aid. Our ambitions paled into insignificance compared to the need to rescue these lost trekkers. We were told that if the fog lifted the next morning, the rescuers in French-built Puma and smaller Alouette helicopters would be flying around the west side of Annapurna past Ghasa, our first destination. Since they were going our way with empty aircraft, the pilots offered us a ride to that point.

It seemed a risky venture to us, but the air controllers showed me maps of the route we would follow, which was well clear of any threatening peaks. When Stan Armington, who was coordinating our Nepalese travels, assured us that it would be a safe flight, which could be terminated at any time for a return to Kathmandu, Richard, Rosalynn, and I agreed: it would be better than spending even more time in our hotel rooms. After some delay, we took off in one of the larger helicopters, heading west. Visibility remained at zero while we climbed and then leveled off at above 12,000 feet, well above any peaks that were near our path. As we peered out the windows into thick fog, Rosalynn commented, "I would rather spend the rest of our lives in Kathmandu than be here."

The weather did not improve, and so after we cleared the first mountain range, we descended into Pokhara, where there was a rudimentary instrument landing signal. It was apparent that we could go no farther. After an overnight stay in nearby Fishtail Lodge, we were faced with an uncomfortable choice. Despite the daily official weather forecast of "clearing in the afternoon," it might be several days before we could proceed with our original trekking plan. Even then, if the weather prevented further flying we were likely to be isolated in the Annapurna region and forced to abandon any hopes of trekking up toward Mount Everest in the eastern portion of Nepal.

Although it had now been raining in Nepal during seven of the last eight days, the weather in Kathmandu was said to be improving. We decided to cancel our Annapurna trek and fly directly to Namche Bazar, where we had planned to start the second part of our trek in the higher altitude. We sent word ahead to our chief Sherpas, asking them to allow us an extra day to become acclimatized to the heights before beginning our somewhat rapid climb to the north. If everything went well, there was a chance now that we might trek as far as the Everest base camp—and salvage at least part of our trip.

After an uneventful flight we landed at Shyangboche airstrip on a flat peak about 1,300 feet above Namche Bazar. Waiting for us as we disembarked from the Puma was Pasang Kami Sherpa, who lived in Namche. After introductions, he smiled and said in excellent English, "Just call me P.K." He and another Sherpa named Ang Tsering, a hero among his peers for his Mount Everest exploits, were to be our chief guides, or *sirdars*, during our trek toward Everest. "You have come the easy way," P.K. said. "It takes seventeen days for the mailman to walk here from Kathmandu."

We descended a precipitous trail into Namche Bazar, and then proceeded to P.K.'s trekker's lodge, where a sign on the door informed us that the lodge was CLOSED 3 DAYS. PRESIDENT CARTER VISIT. In a small room usually occupied by Pasang Kami and his wife, Namdu, we found our luggage already deposited on the floor, and sleeping bags arranged on a wooden platform. It was still foggy and cold, so in a few minutes we joined Richard and Stan Armington in the dining area for some hot tea.

Richard was very experienced in mountain climbing, having spent six weeks in Tibet in 1981 as a member of the first team attempting to scale Everest from the northeast. Although unsuccessful, Dick had intended to return for another attempt. In the meantime, however, he had married, which had put some restraints on his former free-roving mountaineering habits. He missed the successful climb two years later, but at least knew that the team's first attempt had helped to make possible this triumph on the mountain.

Stan, a former instructor in the technical aspects of climbing, was now an owner and manager of Himalayan Journeys, the outfit in charge of our trip. Author of *Trekking in the Himalayas,* he had decided to join our group, actually hiking himself for the first time in almost two years. Not incidentally, Stan was also the owner of the Rum Doodle in Kathmandu, described by *Newsweek* magazine as one of the thirty best taverns in the world.

As though they were responsible for the weather, Stan and Dick repeatedly assured Rosalynn and me that there really were beautiful days in Nepal, that the scenery was magnificent, and that trekking was an exhilarating experience. We teased them by denying all these claims.

It was obvious that the dining room of the lodge was also used for worship. A statue of the Buddha was enclosed in a cabinet near our table, and an enlarged outline of Buddha's footprints were attached to the ceiling. In precisely arranged racks overhead were stored several dozen religious books, each one consisting of a stack of separate printed or inscribed pages wrapped in silk and tied carefully between two thin wooden boards. Although Nepal is now the only Hindu kingdom in the world, it was for centuries a Buddhist nation. About 10 percent of Nepalese are still Buddhists, including almost all of these mountain people, who are heavily influenced by the culture of nearby Tibet. P.K. and his family were devout believers; they often read the scriptures themselves, and on special days they invited monks or lamas into their home to lead the religious services.

Our trekking party would consist of eight other Americans in addition to Rosalynn, Dick, Stan, and me. Rosalynn and I decided to take a quick look at Namche Bazar and found that the small village had a surprising number of shops and hostels. Since many of the trails into the high mountains had been closed since the heavy snows of a few days ago, there was something of a trekker traffic jam in Namche. A group of young climbers told me that staying in one of the hostels cost only 2 rupees (about 12 cents) a night, with some proprietors offering free lodging if they could sell guests meals as well. The trekkers' only complaint was that the charge of 1 rupee for a large cup of hot tea was excessive.

The shops were filled with handicrafts from Tibet, locally produced yak-wool mittens, socks, hats, and blankets, and an amazing array of trekking equipment and food items. P.K. and Ang Tsering explained that after every international expedition, successful or not, there were a lot of unused supplies to be sold or given away rather than toted back down to Kathmandu. Both here at the trekking crossroads and farther up among the more isolated settlements, the most exotic items could be found. Caviar, candy of all kinds, smoked seafood delicacies, canned meats, U.S. freeze-dried meals, and specialty foods with labels from many nations were displayed on the shelves of the small shops.

We ate supper early, in anticipation of our first hike the following day. Throughout our time with him, P.K. always insisted that we wash our hands thoroughly in a potassium permanganate solution before eating any food. The water we drank was always boiled first, fresh vegetables and meat were cooked thoroughly, fruits were restricted to those we could peel ourselves, and canned goods were handled carefully to avoid any possibility of contamination. Because of such precautions, stomach ailments among P.K.'s trekkers are almost nonexistent, although some members of our party had already suffered from diarrhea during their brief stay in Kathmandu.

Pasang brought us an open-mouthed pitcher to be used as a welcome alternative to cold visits to the outdoor privy during the night. (Because of the large quantity of hot tea we would consume to prevent dehydration in the dry air, this turned out to be a precious gift, although somewhat small at times!) We took off our shoes and crawled into the sleeping bags, fully dressed. The weather outside was dull, gray, cold, and wet. Inside, it was also cold, but at least it was dry. This was our third night in Nepal, and we still had not seen a mountain.

The tremulous sounds of Buddhist ceremonial instruments woke me at first daylight. I opened the window a crack for a look outside. The view was breathtaking, with the 22,000-foot Thamserku peak towering over us in the east, shimmering white with its cloak of new-fallen snow. I focused my camera on the scene as Dick Blum pounded on the thin wall. "Look out," he urged, "and see if I was lying about the high mountains."

We hurried to repack our duffel bags with just those items necessary for an overnight trek to Thame, usually a five-hour journey westward along the Bhote Kosi River, following an ancient trade route into Tibet. The yaks, loaded with tents and other larger bundles, left first to meet us at our destination. Just for a two-day trip, there were heavy burdens for the animals and porters. After breakfast we followed with our small day packs, accompanied by Sherpanis (women Sherpas) and other bearers, who in the days to come would often be toting sixty pounds of food, extra clothing, and other supplies that might be needed on the trail. The more heavily laden helped to support the burden on their backs with a flat strap across their foreheads.

For an hour or two as we walked we had a clear view of Khumbila, the sacred mountain of the Sherpas. Not much more than three miles north of Namche, this beautiful 19,000-foot peak has never been climbed, and no Sherpa would ever assist anyone who sought to scale its heights.

One of the first things we learned was always to walk on the left side of the Buddhist prayer offerings. Sometimes these were carvings on a large rock; more often they were enormous piles of individual prayer stones, each covered with long prayers or repetitions of the standard mantra OM MANI PADME HUM. Some of them were quite old, eroded by the weather and covered with lichens; others were recently chiseled. Less frequently, there was a small temple, or *chorten,* surrounded by the flat prayer stones. All these had to be circumambulated in a clockwise direction in order to send the prayers to heaven. (The presumption was that as travelers went up and down the trail, always passing on the left side of the stones, their movements eventually resulted in properly walking all the way around them.) At times the left-hand trail could be quite inconvenient, but the Sherpas took great care to ensure that we observed the custom. We talked about this among ourselves, finally deciding that to violate this rule of worship might be ten times worse than walking under a ladder or having a black cat cross our path.

When we stopped for lunch, Rosalynn entertained some of the small children with a bubble-blowing kit. The children were fascinated as they blew streams of the shiny spheres into the mountain air, and stood in line over and over again awaiting their turn. I also provided some entertainment by letting them speak into my small tape recorder, then playing back their tinkling words and laughter.

The old trail to Thame was quite well defined and reasonably smooth as it paralleled the river bed. However, after a few hours we began to see the ravages of a terrible flood that had profoundly changed the valley the previous August. A small hydroelectric project being built by Austrian engineers and near completion had been permanently destroyed. The former deep canyons where the lake would have been were now filled level with white stones and debris. The trail, yak pastures, potato fields, and homes had disappeared into the gorge, and the new and temporary paths were very difficult to follow. In many places near the river there was no trail at all, and we traversed back and forth along ruts that had been left by yaks, goats, wild animals, or down-rushing rainwater or melting snow. Perhaps because of the recent rains, we saw a series of small avalanches still pouring down into the wide stream bed, carrying portions of fields and paths. The rumble of falling rocks and earth drowned out the roar of the milk-colored mountain stream and reminded us to be careful as we picked out a new place for each step.

Although it was past normal harvesttime, many of the native families were still gathering their crops. With small hoes or mattocks, the women carefully dug up each entire field to a depth of about six inches, flicking the exposed potatoes behind them with deft movements. Other women sorted the tubers by size, the larger ones destined for cash sale at the market, the others to be consumed by the family. During the winter, if there was no grass or hay available, the yaks and other live-stock would be nourished by the same food. The potatoes kept for the family were buried in deep holes in the fields nearest the villages and covered with layers of straw and earth as protection from freezing. This was the people's staple crop, the only life-sustaining one that could grow at such altitudes. Al-though some buckwheat was also grown, it was only with the introduction of the potato in about 1850 that the Sherpas had found it possible to live at such high altitudes.

Even with our light packs it was hard going. To us it seemed almost impossible that the farmers we met carried their heavy bags of potatoes all the way to Namche for next week's market. Each man would have to make several of the long trips during the week to sell this portion of their farm products next Saturday for a good bit less than $5. All those we encountered smiled brightly, put their hands together before their faces in a prayerlike gesture, and returned our greeting. *"Namaste."* If the path was quite narrow, they would take advantage of our meeting for a brief rest, removing the heavy strap from their foreheads and easing their loads down where they could resume the burden most conveniently. Many of the men we met on the trail were spinning a batch of already-carded yak hair into yarn, using a simple device of three six-inch-long sticks fixed at right angles, like a three-dimensional star. The crossed sticks were twirled until about a foot of yarn was spun, and then this yarn was wrapped on the sticks and the process repeated. It was a productive way to pass the lonely hours of a solitary walk.

When we arrived at Lower Thame, we saw that the village was located on a relatively broad plain covered mostly with potato fields and circumscribed by almost vertical snow- and ice-covered walls rising more than two miles into the sky. We were glad to find that our dome-shaped tents were already pitched alongside a small stream, with our duffel bags inside. Cold and bone-tired, we prepared to snuggle down in our sleep-ing bags for a long rest. After warming up with cups of hot lemon tea, however, we contemplated hiking up the side of a sharp ridge to the monastery, or *gompa,* overlooking the valley. Rosalynn was appalled at the thought of even more climbing, but eventually decided to go with us. None of us would have been very disappointed if she had been able to talk all of us out of it, but this was our first day of trekking, after all, and we were looking for a challenge.

As we approached the *gompa* after a long and steep ascent, we saw some large and exquisite birds feeding under the nearby rhododendron and juniper trees. They were blood pheasants, found only within a narrow range of altitude from 11,000 to 13,500 feet. A few moments later we were startled to see three birds—even larger and with much more beautiful, iridescent colors—scratching in a small potato field. They flushed and swooped down over us, one of them, a cock, narrowly missing Rosalynn's head. The Sherpas exclaimed, "Those are *danphes,* which we rarely see." Known otherwise as impeyan pheasants, they are the Nepalese national bird, with feathers of nine different colors, varying from a tan tail to a shiny-blue topknot. The *danphes* range as high as 15,000 feet, but move down into forests at half that altitude to spend the winter.

We were welcomed at the ancient monastery but informed that a visit was inappropriate because the high lama was in Namche for a few days, leading a special service in one of the homes. Despite our desire to see the place, this brief stay did give us a chance to get back to camp earlier and to have a longer night's sleep in our tents.

As we crossed the river the next morning on the way back to Namche, we witnessed an unforgettable scene. As in many developing countries, the people can no longer afford costly petroleum fuels for heating and cooking, and much of the original forest land is now denuded. The native families, having no alternative, must spend an increasing portion of their daylight hours in gathering wood. Now, on the side of the steep avalanche area, we saw women and children digging the limbs and newly exposed roots out of the earth and rocks, chopping them into short pieces that could be carried on their backs, and attempting to haul the precious cargo up the sliding face of the cliff to the remaining trails far above them. The workers were constantly avoiding the stones and debris that slid or flew down into the river past their heads. It was the most difficult and dangerous work I had ever seen, and it made me glad that trekking parties are forbidden to use wood and must bring in their own kerosene for fuel.

Before making our final descent to the lodge, P.K. and I decided to visit the Sherpa museum, located a few hundred feet above the village. The others preferred to get some rest. There was a small flat field on the hill from which we caught our first glimpse of the Mount Everest peak, almost hidden by the somewhat nearer 28,000-foot Lhotse. As is my custom on long trips, I had brought a Frisbee along. Now I wanted to test it in the rarefied atmosphere. We were about two and a half miles above sea level, but the Frisbee performed perfectly. P.K. was surprisingly adept at throwing it; after the test, I gave it to him for his children.

Back at P.K.'s lodge, we discussed our plans for the night. All of us were quite tired from our long trek and needed to rest, but decided to accept invitations to attend a Buddhist worship service and a Sherpa party—both in private homes. In one, two high lamas and about twenty monks were praying and chanting from daybreak until late at night for twelve days. Now we knew why no lamas had been at home in the *gompa* we had visited. In anticipation of their own approaching death, an aged and relatively affluent couple had sold most of their yaks and other possessions in order to finance the elaborate ceremony, at a cost of several thousand rupees. None of the Sherpas in our group doubted the wisdom of this devout act as a proper way to prepare for the next life.

We entered the upstairs room quietly and found it similar in arrangement and configuration to some of the monasteries we had seen in Kathmandu and in other countries. The family had completely rearranged and decorated it for the occasion. The repetitive service was hypnotic in its effect, with a slow and inexorable rhythm of chanting followed by the strangely pleasing cacophony of the standard array of instruments: a large drum, some buglelike brasses, cymbals of different sizes and tones, and the two ten-foot bass horns. The lamas and monks seemed unaware of our presence, but the owners of the home seated us near the stove and served us Tibetan tea laced with yak butter and salt and tasting similar to bouillon. We stayed for about half an hour (not drinking much tea), and I

recorded the ceremony on a pocket-size tape recorder to bring
to my daughter, Amy, who was studying comparative religions
and Eastern culture.

We then moved a couple of doors down the street to attend
the Sherpas' party, which was planned to celebrate the return
of some members of their family from two or three months of
trekking in distant mountains. One of those who attended was
a relative of Ang Tsering named Ila Tsering. He had climbed
Everest in the early 1960s and had later visited the United
States and Europe. In Washington he'd had an audience at the
White House with a leader whom he called "King" Kennedy.

The party was already well under way when we arrived.
We were served fruit, nuts, cookies, and glasses of *chang,* a
homemade rice beer that tasted like Japanese *sake.* Led by
some of the younger Sherpanis, a group of little children sang
and danced. Later, an hour or so after the children were ordered to retire for the night, the adults began to sing. Then
they formed a single line with arms clasped around one another's waists, the women together on the left with all the men to
their right. It was very difficult for us to anticipate the music's
beat or to understand the complicated foot movements. Going
back and forth in front of the dancers were our hostess and
other women, serving mugs of *chang* and small glasses of
rakshi, a much stronger rice liquor. We tried some of it, which
gave us the courage to join the dancers. After some awkward
shuffling, it seemed—at least to us—that our performance improved. The dancers were still going when we left for bed.

Outside our lodge we met a group of Japanese trekkers
who said they had just returned from the Everest base camp,
which was our own final destination. When I asked them how
deep the snow was there, one of them put her hand just under
her chin. Not very encouraging.

At breakfast we prepared to take the high and more difficult
trail so that we could visit the Kunde Hospital and the Hillary
School at Khumjung. Afterward, we would come back down to
the lower trail, cross the river, and then climb again to
Tengboche monastery. Stan and Dick guaranteed us that it
would be a day we would never forget.

As we began this long trek, we were surprised to learn that

our total entourage would include fifteen yaks, forty porters, and twenty Sherpas and Sherpanis. Most of them would leave each morning well ahead of us trekkers, so that only a few would ever be within view except when we were in camp. The cost to each trekker with this kind of service amounts to about $40 a day. Our support group seemed excessive until I recalled the account of the Japanese expedition in 1978, when Yuiichi Miura had skied down the south col of Mount Everest. Requiring large quantities of photographic equipment and other supplies, Miura's group had begun their trek with a great herd of yaks and eight hundred porters (six of whom later perished in the broken ice above the base camp).

After a long and steep climb, we visited the Kunde Hospital, built and funded by the Edmund Hillary Himalayan Foundation. At about 12,500 feet we could see the highest line of trees just 500 feet above us—and one of the most breathtaking views in the Himalayas. Our destination, the Tengboche monastery, was visible in the distance across the Dudh Kosi river; we also gazed for several minutes at Ama Dablam, Kantega, and Thamserku, three beautiful mountains. If I were a mountain worshiper, Ama Dablam would be the focal point for my prayers.

As we were a little behind schedule, P.K. and I picked up the pace on a slight downhill grade leading from the hospital to the Khumjung school. When we arrived there, Rosalynn was lagging behind us, slightly nauseated. She had tried to move too quickly in the thin air. It was our first augury of the difficulties that would soon beset many of us.

The headmaster and about forty of the students were lined up with the traditional white scarves, or *katas,* to give us a royal welcome. By the time the tiniest students had completed their happy duty, I was completely covered with the *katas,* from my shoulders over the top of my head. There were 341 students enrolled in ten grades at Khumjung, another Edmund Hillary project. About one third of them hiked both ways every day from Namche Bazar, excellent training for their future careers as professional trekkers, for which the schooling—except for learning English—could take place only on the mountainsides. Even playing along the way, the children were able to make the trip in about half the time it had taken us.

Tengboche was at around the same altitude as Kunde, but

we had to descend about 2,000 feet to the river, cross it at Phunki Thankhka, and then climb back up to the monastery. It was a discouraging prospect. We soon met some Japanese trekkers who had been as far as Pheriche, our destination for the following day. They said the snow was about two feet deep at the 14,000-foot altitude, and they had decided not to go any farther.

A mile or so below Khumjung, a wide selection of Tibetan artifacts and handicrafts was displayed alongside the trail on platforms of flat rocks. Rosalynn bought an antique Tibetan silver belt buckle for Amy but, uncharacteristically, she did not feel like shopping more than a few minutes. As we walked, she fell behind, moving quite slowly. We decided to let her lead our procession. On the steep trail all of us were thankful for the slower pace. We asked one traveler who had preceded us up the mountain if he had any advice for us. He said, only half jokingly, "Turn back! Turn back!"

Tengboche is known as one of the most beautiful places in the world. Built during the early part of this century, the 12,500-foot-high monastery is on a promontory above the Imja Khola River with a clear view of some of the world's highest mountains, including Nuptse, Lhotse, and Everest. We were welcomed by the high lama, or *rimpoche,* and a long line of monks, ranging in age down to small boys five or six years old. Again, I was covered with *katas* after I honored Buddhist tradition by placing one of the scarves in the outstretched hands of the lama.

Escorted into the recessed courtyard of the *gompa,* we sat on a stone slab and sipped hot tea while the monks played their horns, cymbals, and drums. Then we were given a preview of the annual *Hemis Tsichu,* a festival dance usually conducted at Tengboche only during a special holiday in November. It was a strange dance of masked figures who performed their ancient ritual around a central courtyard pole from which a vertical sheaf of prayer flags flapped in the wind.

In a quiet moment, I asked the young-looking *rimpoche* how long he had been high lama at Tengboche. He replied, "Fifty-two years." Although he had not been identified as the reincarnation of his deceased predecessor until he was four years old, the presumption was that he had held the position since birth. Later in the evening we attended the regular Buddhist service, a much more complete ceremony than we had seen before. From time to time attendants delivered to the assembled monks different headgear, shawls, and other accoutrements, which were donned in unison at the proper time. I sat next to the *rimpoche* again and noticed that he did not participate in the chanting and playing of instruments. The ritual was obviously in his honor. Immediately in front of him was a special prayer book, of the highest quality, lettered in gold, and obviously quite old. I asked my host who had written the manuscript. "I did," he replied. I thought he did not understand my question, but P.K. leaned over and explained, "He did it in a previous life."

Although the temperature outside was below freezing, there was no heat in the room. We were buried in our down-filled parkas and still shivering, but our host and the monks who served us a private supper wore only their red or yellow robes draped over one shoulder. Their heads were shaven, and their right arms were exposed to the cold air.

Rosalynn and I were offered two matted platforms in a nearby building for our sleeping bags, but we decided to spend the night in our tent below the monastery in a small pasture. For the first time, we managed to zip our two sleeping bags together, covering the entire arrangement with a heavy yak-hair blanket that P.K.'s wife, Namdu, had woven for us. "You will need this on the cold nights," she had said.

She was right. Removing only our shoes, we slept fairly well, but it was bitterly cold during the night, down to fifteen degrees Fahrenheit. The next morning we found our water flasks frozen in the tent. Still, we never doubted that we were much warmer there than we would have been in the drafty building on the hill.

Soon after daybreak a young monk brought us two beautiful paintings, one of Tengboche and the other a panorama of the mountains, villages, and monasteries in the region. In both scenes, there was a prominent Yeti, or Abominable Snowman, scaling the peaks. The monk requested of us and Dick Blum that he be considered for further education in English, either in Kathmandu or in the United States. Soon another young monk, who had served as our interpreter, came to make the same request. We had a brief meeting with the *rimpoche* to seek his advice. He thought for a while and responded that he would like to meditate on the question until some time the next year, at which time he would decide whether anyone needed to go off to a distant school and, if so, which of his monks would be most worthy. We later explained the lama's decision to both of the ambitious young men, and they accepted without dissent.

After the sun had been up between Ama Dablam and Kantega for about an hour, we left Tengboche, taking the trail northward. By then the temperature had risen to twenty-one degrees Fahrenheit. Less than two hours later we crossed back to the west side of the Imja Khola River. Dick and I decided to take a side trip and climb to Upper Pangboche monastery to see the famous Yeti scalp, which the monks exhibited proudly to visitors. We took photographs of the seamless relic—representing a large pointed head, bald on top with reddish hair around the sides. It looked authentic, but we understood that it had been given other identifications by scientists who had analyzed it, such as the scalp of a blue bear or the stretched and molded hide of a large wild boar. In that particular environment, we preferred to think of it as genuine.

We were now well above 13,000 feet. Several of our party were experiencing headaches and some nausea, and so we paused frequently as we climbed upward, sometimes stopping for just thirty seconds to take a number of deep breaths. At other times we sat on rocks to rest, enjoying the scenery, drinking hot tea, and taking photographs. We had passed through the highest villages that are inhabited year around. Those above us consisted mostly of sod- or rock-enclosed yak pastures, with a few buildings that were occupied only during the warmer months.

As we approached Pheriche, we heard the cry of birds in distress and looked over to see a golden eagle swooping down upon more than a dozen Himalayan snow cocks. Two or three at a time, the chirping birds sailed down the mountainside and disappeared into a narrow ravine. The eagle almost caught one, but eventually all escaped. Each time we stopped on the trail to eat lunch, ravens and yellow-billed choughs would come within two or three feet of us. They have been known to attack climbers' food packages on the highest reaches of the Himalayas.

As we approached the 14,000-foot level, some of our group were feeling even worse. We were thankful that there was a Himalayan Rescue Station in Pheriche, where we would be staying. After checking the distances and time remaining, I now saw that it might be possible to climb all the way to the Everest base camp, after spending two nights in Pheriche to become acclimatized. The snow here was about a foot deep but melting slowly for a couple of hours each day when the sun was warmest.

Pheriche consisted mostly of yak pastures, enclosed by two-toned walls made of alternating layers of white stones and black sod. Soon after we arrived, Rosalynn and I received an invitation from Jill Riegel to stay that night in the clinic instead of our tents. It was doubtful that we would be any more comfortable, but we were reluctant to reject this offer of hospitality. As we entered the snow-covered compound, we were greeted by Dr. Riegel, of Jackson, Wyoming, and Cathy Olsen, a registered nurse from Pocatello, Idaho, who had volunteered to serve here for three months during the trekking season. The clinic had no running water, heat, or toilet facilities, but these two women were glad to be able to serve the Sherpa families in the area, along with the steady stream of trekkers who suffered from altitude sickness, snow blindness, and other ailments.

At Jill's insistence, Rosalynn and I moved into the doctor's room, which had a wooden shelf wide enough for two sleeping bags. We then returned to the tiny reception area, where a fire was burning in a small stove in honor of our visit. This was the first time the doctor and nurse had been authorized by their director in Kathmandu to have a fire in several weeks. It was a welcome respite for all of us from the frigid night air.

Rosalynn and I felt fine while we were in Pheriche, but other members of our team continued to suffer from altitude sickness. When we made short hikes up and down the nearby hills, several of our companions chose to stay in their bunks. By now we had all learned to recognize the early symptoms: loss of appetite, sleeplessness, headache, and nausea—all signs for alarm, because unless there is sufficient acclimatization, usually requiring the trekker's quick descent to a lower altitude, fluids can build up in the lungs or brain, with fatal results.

During the first day, three of our group developed the symptoms of acute illness; Dr. Riegel recommended that they be evacuated. Although one of the men was a 2:38 marathoner and another competed regularly in Hawaii's Ironman triathlon, surprisingly they were completely debilitated. We carried a small transmitter that, through a U.S. Navy satellite over the Indian Ocean, ensured that we had good communications with Kathmandu, and so we called there for an army helicopter to come for the sick men.

When they arrived at the hospital in the nation's capital, we learned, the American embassy physician determined that all three had fluid in their lungs and that one of them was also suffering from cerebral edema. After a short time at the lower altitude the patients felt better, but the aftereffects of their illness lasted for a week or two.

We thought our troubles were over for a while, but that night Dr. Riegel came in late to join us for supper and said, "Another of your party is extremely ill, the worst case of altitude sickness I have ever seen. It has developed very rapidly, and I am not sure he can survive the night." We were shocked. Immediately we forgot about food and began to discuss plans to put our sick friend on a stretcher and quickly carry him down to a lower altitude.

But the doctor interrupted us. "He should not be moved right now," she said. "There would be no way to treat him properly if he were bouncing down the mountainside in the dark. He's receiving intravenous nourishment and I've just put him on pure oxygen. The next hour or so will determine how he reacts. We can only hope for the best."

Luckily, when we hurried up to the clinic we found the patient lucid, more cheerful, and responding well to the treatment. He continued to improve through the night and was flown out early the next morning. The size of our party was steadily decreasing. We began to feel as if we were in an Agatha Christie novel.

*　　*　　*

As soon as the helicopter departed, we headed north toward the tiny villages of Dughla and Lobuje, planning to travel several miles and to climb more than 2,000 feet before nightfall. As the sun rose higher, the air grew very warm and we began to shed our parkas and jackets. In some of the narrow trails the snow turned to a slick slush, making walking very difficult. It was impossible to avoid losing our balance and falling often into the snow on either side of the path.

When we were not more than twenty steps from our lunch stop at Dughla, Rosalynn became nauseated. We were at 15,200 feet, and she had gone as far as she could at our rapid pace. After she lay down in the shade for a while, with her head in my lap, Rosalynn, Richard, and I discussed our options. We had a steep climb to Lobuje ahead of us that afternoon, and we knew that the following day would be the most difficult of all. If we were to make it to the base camp, or still higher to one of the peaks of Kala Pattar, we had to begin our trek long before dawn and to return at least as far as Dughla before nightfall. With an early and fast walk, we could then make it back to Pheriche the following morning in time to catch our planned helicopter flight to Kathmandu.

Although Rosalynn was feeling better and would be all right at a lower altitude, it seemed unlikely that she could continue to climb rapidly. After quite an argument, we finally convinced her that she had already performed heroically but it would be better for her to return to Pheriche, be treated for her early symptoms of altitude sickness, and wait for us there. Had we been moving at a more leisurely rate, I had no doubt that she could have stayed with us.

By then we had lost more than half our original party, and three of those remaining were not feeling well. I hated for us to be separated, but was relieved to see her descending the mountain at a strong and steady pace before we resumed our climb.

On top of a ridge above Dughla we passed a group of seventeen snow-covered cairns. Richard and Stan explained that these monuments honored Sherpas who had been killed on expeditions to Mount Everest, beginning with the six who had died with the Japanese skiing group. All of us were sobered by these reminders of human courage and the dangers of the high mountain peaks.

The snow was about three feet deep as we approached Lobuje. Walking along a small stream at the bottom of a steep hill, we heard the snow and ice cracking above us. When we stopped for a moment to look closely at the surface a few feet above our heads, we could detect downward movements of an inch or two at a time. P.K. advised us to move steadily onward, trying not to make any noise that might disturb the hillside. At 16,000 feet, none of us felt like hurrying, even with an incipient avalanche above us. At the time, we were more worried about our toes freezing in our sodden socks.

In Lobuje some of us squeezed into the tiny kitchen of the hostel proprietor and tried to thaw out in the smoky interior. Cold and wet as we were, our spirits were low. For me, it wasn't the same without Rosalynn. When we found that one of the rooms was completely vacant, we decided to spend the night indoors instead of in our tents. P.K. produced a can of charcoal from somewhere which generated enough heat to warm and partially dry our wet boots. After treating them with waterproofing solution, we ate supper and planned our goals for the next day.

We would leave before daybreak, hike to Gorak Shep near the Everest base camp, and—if possible—attempt to climb up to Kala Pattar peak. At best, this would take six hours of steady hiking. We all knew that the trail would be less traveled, the snow deeper, the air thinner, and the climbing steeper than what we had already seen. Furthermore, we had absolutely no time to waste; successful or not, we would have to begin our return journey no later than noon, moving much more rapidly downhill in order to reach Pheriche before it was too dark to see the path.

There was not much enthusiasm or confidence about the next day—a lot of silence, none of the usual bantering among us as we crawled into our sleeping bags, all crowded together on narrow shelves, one above another. Still completely clothed, I shivered for several hours before warming enough to go to sleep. After that, the loud snores from all around awakened me frequently during the night. I was in an uncharacteristically bad mood, declaring to myself that I would rather have been in my tent where it was quiet!

We got up at 4:20 to eat our standard breakfast of hot tea,

cookies, and rice porridge laced with granola and raisins, and were on the narrow frozen trail by 5:15 A.M. The sky was the most beautiful I had seen in the thirty years since I had left the navy. The Milky Way and constellations from Ursa Major to Orion stood out with surprising brilliance, each star clear and distinct. The almost-full moon had just set and it was quite dark, but after half an hour dawn began to break and we were able to see well enough to walk without our flashlights.

We were traveling on a moraine of dirt and rocks atop the Khumbu glacier, which extended from high on the slopes of Everest and Lhotse down past Lobuje and halfway to Dughla. The snow varied from one to four feet deep; in most places the trail was no wider than a footprint. One behind another, we stumbled forward. Using a single ski pole, I was able to balance well enough to minimize the number of times I fell. Slowly, the scenery unfolded ahead of us. After two hours we got a clear glimpse of Everest, hidden the previous three days by the nearer Nuptse and Lhotse peaks. Now, as we climbed, more and more of the world's highest mountain became visible, surrounded by its mighty neighbors. The atmosphere was crystalline. Perhaps for the first time, we could understand what the word "breathtaking" meant.

By the time we reached Gorak Shep (which means "dead crow") Ang Tsering and I were several hundred yards ahead of P.K., Dick, and Stan. We decided to go almost straight up the westward cliff toward Kala Pattar, or "black pinnacle." As we neared the top, the *sirdah* put his hand on my elbow. He pointed ahead and we saw nine Himalayan snow cocks sitting just above us on a horizontal ledge. They flew back out of our sight as we moved forward, but after a few minutes sailed down past us toward the small lake between Gorak Shep and the Everest base camp. It was a beautiful and eerie sight. The brown, white, and gray birds seemed to have a bluish tinge against the bright white snow as they flashed by.

We climbed over some very difficult terrain and finally arrived at the top, well ahead of most members of our group. We were exhausted, but proud and greatly relieved that our climbing was over. As we sat down to catch our breath and look over at Everest and the other mountains, we could also see far below us the red and yellow tents of the Indian and Japanese expeditions arrayed at the base camp. After a few moments, Ang Tsering said, "This is really not the top. Most people stop here, but the top peak of Kala Pattar is several hundred feet above us." He pointed farther to the west; we could barely see a tiny point of rock far above. Shocked to know that there was more climbing to do to reach our goal, I didn't know whether to faint or throw up. However, we resolved to go for it, and so began a slow and extremely dangerous climb upward. It was one of the most foolish decisions I've ever made.

Knowing nothing about the technical aspects of mountain climbing, I was extremely uncomfortable as we clung to the large and often loose rocks with our fingers, thighs, and toes. On our left was a precipitous drop of several hundred feet. We were not equipped with crampons or even a rope, and the snow and coating of newly frozen ice made each foothold uncertain. At that altitude the temperature was almost always below freezing, but in the midday sun some of the snow would melt in small patches on the south side of rocks, then freeze hard as soon as the sun set below the western mountaintops. These sheets of ice made firm footing and handholds impossible. I could not imagine how I had ever gotten myself into such a predicament.

Halfway up we discerned two people on the peak, which gave me some encouragement. Still, it took us two hours to climb the short distance. At first I was more angry with my lack of judgment than pleased with our accomplishment when we reached the pinnacle. We were at 5,630 meters, or almost exactly 18,500 feet above sea level. At that moment I had taxed my maximum endurance and ability and felt no desire to climb any higher—ever!

Far below us we saw P.K. coming our way, alone, the others in our party having wisely decided to remain on the lower peak. We now had a magnificent view of Everest, including the south col, where the Indian climbers were still encamped. The two people we had seen at the top of Kala Pattar were part of the same expedition. One of them was making observations and photographs across the intervening chasm with a celestial-type telescope, and the other was manning a motion picture camera and a radio.

The Indians recognized me with amazement and urged me

to speak to the new expedition leader on the south col. Radio fidelity was excellent. I expressed my condolences about the loss of their five men, my admiration for the Indians' courage in continuing the effort to reach the peak, and my best wishes during their final assault scheduled for the next day. I didn't envy them.

We had no time to lose; our daylight hours, during which we could traverse the steep mountainside with safety, were waning. We decided to descend by a circuitous but much safer route through the snow. After I picked up a few small stones for souvenirs for my grandchildren, we began our journey back down to Gorak Shep. The trail was not very steep but quite treacherous, and all of us fell more than once into the deep snow that surrounded us. At the base of the cliff I lay down to rest and thought I would never be able to get up again, but after some hot lemon tea, a piece of bread, and a bowl of soup, we were on our way back down the way we had come.

It was soon dark. One of our party was quite ill, and so we put him in front, with a lantern on his head so he could see the trail. He moved slowly, taking only a few steps at a time between periods of rest, but we knew it might be fatal for him if he fell without our seeing him or was inadvertently left behind. While we crossed the many small streams by stepping carefully from one rock to another, he waded straight through, often knee-deep in the icy water. He was obviously disoriented, not knowing what he was doing other than plodding spasmodically ahead.

We arrived in Pheriche at about 9:00 P.M., all totally exhausted. What a relief to have our sick companion under Dr. Riegel's care! After receiving some medication and oxygen, he felt much better, recovering rapidly at the lower altitude. Rosalynn, feeling fine, had already flown to Kathmandu. I drank some hot tea, climbed into my sleeping bag without supper, and slept soundly through the night under Namdu's heavy blanket.

When I woke up next morning I was surprised to find that my fingernails were split, my hands were bleeding, both shins were skinned, and I had bruises inside my thighs and on my buttocks. I bathed in a tin pan of hot water, shaved, put on clean clothes, and waited for the helicopter to take us to

Kathmandu. When we heard it coming we told everyone good-bye and hurried out to the landing spot.

We had an emotional exchange of *katas* and expressions of *"Namaste"* with our Sherpas and the medical staff. The helicopter, however, flew past us and landed a few hundred yards away in the middle of the valley. Two or three people emerged whom P.K. recognized. "Those are two Italian women," he told us. "A number of years ago both their husbands died here from altitude sickness on the same day and are buried in that place. Every two years their wives come to place a wreath on the graves and then return to Italy." After a few minutes the women reentered the helicopter, which soon disappeared toward the south.

When our small Alouette helicopter came, we had to leave our Sherpas and porters, who would have a long and difficult two-day trek back to their homes in Namche Bazar. We left Pheriche at 8:45 A.M. and landed at the airport above Namche at 8:53. In those eight minutes we had flashed over Pangboche, Tengboche, Khumjung, and Kunde. It had taken us three days to cover those distances on foot. Trekking in the high Himala-yas had been an incredibly exciting and gratifying experience, testing all of us to the maximum of our abilities. We had set a formidable goal and reached it. Now we looked forward to another Nepalese adventure, quite different—and, thank good-ness, much less demanding.

ॐ

About two hours after leaving Namche Bazar we landed at Meghauli airport, in the Royal Chitwan National Park, where we were met by five large elephants with howdahs on their backs and drivers sitting astride the huge necks. Palm trees waved and water buffalo plowed the rice paddies. It was hard to believe that twenty-four hours ago we had been on top of Kala Pattar, in more than three feet of snow. As we walked toward the elephants, the largest one, named Shamsher Bahadur, moved over and, at a command from his driver, knelt beside an eight-foot platform. Rosalynn and I climbed up and took our places on a padded howdah, a wooden platform about three feet wide and four feet long.

We were soon trying to act nonchalant as our mount waded across a broad river, then pushed his way through thick elephant grass which towered high above our heads.

We had come to see as many Asian animals as possible in their native habitat, hopefully including the Bengal tiger. "It is possible that we might see a rhinoceros between here and the lodge," said Yam, our guide. "There are now more than four hundred in the park, averaging about one for each square mile. However, they are not easy to find during the heat of the day."

Beneath us were some of the three-toed rhino prints in the soft mud, and a deep straight track about four inches wide leading from the grass into some stagnant water, which we thought might be from a young crocodile.

"No, a python," said Yam. "Unlike other snakes, they do not weave from side to side as they crawl. The muscles and skin of their abdomen move to propel them straight ahead."

When we emerged on the bank of a smaller stream, the driver stopped his mount and pointed down. "Tiger prints," Yam told us. There were a number of them, made by at least two different Bengal tigers.

The howdah became more comfortable after an hour or so, as we learned to synchronize our own swaying body movements with the elephant's rolling gait. We left the path and advanced through thick undergrowth. Shamsher had an uncanny ability to stay just far enough away from trees so that our dangling legs would not be crushed and to pick his way through the easiest route. Trees of three or four inches were assessed by his trunk and carefully bradded to the ground by one of his front feet. I thought about the women and children desperately searching for the few roots and splinters on the landslide near Thame and what they would have given for the wood being trodden here and left behind.

We sighted spotted deer and some crocodiles as we approached the lodge where we would be staying overnight. It was long after noon; we had been on the elephant now more than two hours. Just as we mentioned that lunchtime was near, we heard a high-pitched "Ho!" in the distance. "Might be a rhino," the driver said. We turned toward the sound and Shamsher moved into high gear. Soon we heard crashing in front of us and could see the high grass moving a hundred yards away.

"That's one of our elephants, coming this way," said Yam.

After a minute or two something else moved the grass very slightly, and much nearer. A male rhinoceros emerged, stopped short when he saw us, and then turned slowly to his right. To us, the rhino seemed very large at that close range, but Yam said, "He is much larger than he looks—at least six feet at his shoulders—and he weighs more than two tons." The rhinoceros watched us closely for about five minutes, then began to walk slowly away from us. Finally Yam declared, "It's time to eat."

At the camp, Shamsher Bahadur maneuvered easily up to an unloading platform, ten feet above the ground and on a level with the lowest row of guest rooms. Yam gave a perfect explanation about why the lodge was on such high stilts. "It is easier this way to keep the animals, snakes, and spiders out of the bedrooms."

"Are pythons poisonous?"

"No, but there are a few cobras around. The most dangerous snake is the small common krait. Its venom is extremely toxic. It's unlikely that they will be in your room, but you should be careful while on the ground."

In the midst of so much beauty, it was easy to forget the lurking hazards.

There was no electricity in the camp, but the kerosene lanterns and candles were adequate. A two-man reciprocal pump pushed water to a high tank, so there was warm and cold running water. More important, we had toilets on which we could sit down—a luxury we had almost forgotten.

During lunch, Yam said, "Although it is not likely, there is some chance that you might see a Bengal tiger tonight. We are successful about twice a week in inducing one to come and take our bait, but even then they frequently disappear before we can reach them. We don't feed them often, so that they never become dependent on the food we provide. For at least three months, during the monsoon season, we don't give them anything."

He explained that individual tigers are easily identified by the patterns of their stripes. During the past two years six different males and four females had been observed at this particular site, indicating that in a given area the turnover was quite rapid. Males were dominant and more mobile, each serving from two to four females. The population had been growing and was now at maximum density in Chitwan, with about one tiger for every ten square miles. The younger tigers, when mature, were forced by the dominant ones to move out into other surrounding areas.

"We offer them a live young water buffalo weighing about one hundred and fifty pounds; if two tigers feed on the same night, the buffalo is totally consumed. We also have a few leopards in the area, but the tigers rule this jungle. Since they are at the apex of the entire ecosystem, we must carefully balance our conservation practices in order for them to flourish."

That night, shortly after supper, we were called to the door of our room with the whispered news: "A tiger has come!" After a short Jeep ride we walked up a steep hill in the jungle for about 350 yards. At a small clearing we were asked to extinguish our flashlights and remove our shoes; then for another five minutes we walked silently, in single file, up a jungle trail. When we stopped, we found ourselves inside a closely thatched blind, with a row of small openings at eye level on one side. We took our places, absolutely silent, one person at each slot. Suddenly a cleared mound in the dense forest about fifty yards away was brilliantly illuminated by battery-operated spotlights. We caught our breath when we saw the majestic tiger, then shared binoculars to examine her more closely.

A whispering voice said, "It is a female, about four years old. She has been here before, but we haven't seen her in quite a while." The crouching tiger continued her feeding, undisturbed by the attention she was getting. "For some reason, the lights have never driven them away, even the first time we turn them on a new tiger."

We walked back in the dark, sobered by the sight of the rare and savage beast feeding so ferociously. Rosalynn was disturbed by the sacrifice of the water buffalo. "Would you rather she had dined on one of the spotted deer?" I asked. "And besides, we were eating yak meat several times last week." Rosalynn was not placated.

✻   ✻   ✻

From our final visit to the Kathmandu valley the next morning, where we returned before noon, there remains a kaleidoscope of vivid images in my mind's eye: ancient palaces of four previously competing kingdoms; intimate wooden carvings of surprising eroticism; religious temples, prayer wheels, and flags, bloody sacrifices, and statues of fierce gods and their consorts—a strange but pervasive mixture of Hinduism and Buddhism, melded over the centuries so that each accommodates the symbols and trappings of the other. There was also a beautiful young Living Goddess, now seven years old and certified by priests to be totally unblemished since birth, publicly worshipped even by the king and queen of Nepal; a nearby town populated almost entirely by ceramicists, producing pottery of every description for sale throughout the country; a hostel for young daughters of some of Nepal's 110,000 lepers; the holy Bagmati River, on whose banks continuous cremations are under way, each wooden pyre being tended carefully for six or seven hours by bereaved relatives with shaven heads as the body is slowly consumed in the flames; and a heterogeneous population of Negroid, Mongol, and Indo-Aryan races who comprise the only Hindu kingdom on earth, governed by a king educated at Eton and Harvard who is accepted by many as the reincarnation of the god Shiva.

Our visit to Nepal had been more wondrous and exotic, as well as more arduous, than we ever envisioned in all our years of planning. Here, on the other side of the world, everything Rosalynn and I had seen was as different as possible from our lives at home. I would never have imagined, as a boy in rural Georgia, that I'd climb near Everest, ride an elephant, or watch a wild Bengal tiger feed in the jungle—except in a dream.

FULL CIRCLE

ON
TURNIPTOWN
CREEK

I have written most of this book sitting at an open picture window in the loft of our small log cabin on the banks of a stream in the North Georgia mountains. Below me, perhaps fifty feet away, is a quiet pool, rock strewn, from which multiple gushes of white water flow over and through large granite boulders. The pool is fed by a series of waterfalls that drop about thirty feet in all, tumbling down the stream bed from an almost horizontal rocky ledge just about level with my eyes. Now, in early September, I can barely see the highest falls through the leafy branches of rhododendron, red maple, white pine, black gum, alder, hemlock, dogwood, and wild honey-suckle. The first leaves are just beginning to fall, and after each gust of wind through the narrow valley we can see a few of them floating down the creek like small red and yellow boats. In a few weeks the leaves will be gone, and the upper waterfall will be in full view.

This is Turniptown Creek, which rises five miles east of our cabin and continues on a fairly straight course until it runs into the Ellijay River. Rosalynn and I have walked the entire distance, during different seasons of the year, and I confess it is gratifying to find that our waterfalls are twice as high as and more beautiful than any others on the creek. There are a number of houses, mostly weekend cottages, built far upstream from us, but when we go downstream we see no buildings of any kind. In most places there is not even a path; when the water is high during the winter and early spring it is impossible to wade down the creek and very difficult to make much progress at all without frequent detours up the steep hills to get around the precipitous rock formations that keep the water in its bounds.

After leaving the White House in 1980 we were burdened with duties and overrun with visitors. Rosalynn and I had not spent more than two or three days at a time either alone or without pressing responsibilities for more than fifteen years. When some friends, John and Betty Pope, showed us this property, there was no doubt that it was a place where we could nurture our privacy.

With the Popes as partners we made the plans for our cabin. The buried electric power lines, drinking water supply, and waste disposal system were designed to change the natural site as little as possible. Today even the traces of these are gone, and we believe that the place is as beautiful as it was when we found it.

While we were still building, I asked the state game and fish biologists if there were any trout in the stream. They reported that it was too small to have been stocked with hatchery trout, but they would be glad to bring a few fish to the stream if I ever wanted them. Brook trout were about gone in this region, they said, and rainbows very rarely reproduced naturally in North Georgia. This was disheartening news, but did not detract from my pleasure in the site's natural loveliness.

The following July, when we finished construction, we went up to spend our first few days at the small cabin. It was remarkably cool, often fifteen degrees less than reported on the Chattanooga radio stations, and delightful to sit on the front porch that extends out toward the bank of the stream.

On this visit I was able to examine the creek more closely. I found a good population of mayfly, caddis, and stonefly nymphs under the stones in the creekbed, so I knew the water was pure and cold enough for trout. Late one afternoon Rosalynn and I were observing a small hatch of white mayflies. When I referred to my entomology book, *Stenonema ithaca,* easily imitated by a small Light Cahill fly pattern, was the nearest match I could make. Somewhat disappointed because there were no wild trout in the stream, I went down and sat on a large rock at the base of the pool and watched the small insects emerging from the water and fluttering on top. A few of them were darting back and forth, three or four inches above the surface of the water. Suddenly, there was an explosive rise not ten feet away, and an eight-inch trout came up out of the water to take one of the airborne mayflies. In all my life, it was the most memorable rise of a wild fish, exceeding in my mind even the soaring leap of a mighty blue marlin off the coast of Anegada Island in the eastern Caribbean.

When I reported this momentous event to one of the old-time fishermen in the community, he replied, "Yep. Turniptown has always had a pretty good crop of native rainbows."

A few weeks later I had a call from my young Montana friend Rich McIntyre, whose Timberline company specialized in the rehabilitation of trout habitat. After exchanging pleasantries, he said, "I hear you've built a mountain cabin on a creek, and I want to make a small contribution to the enterprise. I'll be on the East Coast soon with one of my biologists. If you like, I'll take a look at your stream and give you some advice on how to improve it."

Of course I accepted his offer immediately. Within a few weeks we were together in our creek. To inventory the fish, Rich had brought along a small electric shocking outfit whose generator was powered by a gasoline motor carried in his backpack. With the two electrodes and a dip net, we moved upstream from one pool or crevasse to another. The weak electric current was not strong enough to injure the fish but would stun them for a moment so that, if we were very quick, we could scoop up some of them before they recovered.

Within a couple of hours we had caught ninety-nine trout, all rainbows, ranging in size from three to ten inches. We saw a few larger ones, but they escaped. Rich examined each fish, weighed and measured it, took a scale or two to determine its age, and quickly returned it to the water. He also assessed the population of insects, sculpin, minnows, creek chubs, and other potential trout food. Although quite pure and with a fair population of insects, Turniptown Creek could not support many trout, or very large ones, because the granite stream bed produced minimal nutrients, unlike those where limestone or chalk deposits would always provide a much richer menu and water that was less acidic. At least the many bubbling waterfalls kept the oxygen content high.

All in all, I was pleased. I later followed Rich's advice by arranging small rock dams to deepen some of the pools in order to make better holding basins for the times during the late summer when the stream was at its lowest and warmest stage.

Since then, Rosalynn and I have enjoyed fishing and also observing the creek closely at different times of the year. We've learned more about trout habits and insect hatches in addition to studying the bird and animal population along its banks. Two black bear came down the valley while the cabin was being built, and sometimes we see their tracks on the sand and gravel bars. There are also some ruffed grouse and a number of white-tailed deer. Late one evening we opened the cabin door and watched a small flock of wild turkeys calmly walk just in front of us, not thirty feet away, cross the water, and disappear up the mountain.

Turniptown Creek is in what was once the gold-producing area of Georgia, and there are many legends recorded in the county history books about an Indian chief named White Path, who owned a number of black slaves in the early nineteenth century and became quite wealthy from his mining operations.

Some of these tales seem far-fetched, but it's interesting to stretch one's imagination enough to believe them. In any case, several miles below us, not far from our stream, was the large cabin where White Path lived before he and other members of his tribe were forced to leave the Southeast on the "Trail of Tears" and suffer a torturous migration to the government's Indian reservations in Oklahoma. The chief died on this march, never to reach the unwanted destination.

One morning we were hiking up a steep incline in front of our cabin when we came to a strange path in the forest. Unlike the numerous old logging trails that crisscross all the woodlands in North Georgia, this one was shaped more like a ditch and seemed to follow a level contour around the mountain. We decided to follow its generally westward direction and soon realized that it was descending very gradually but at a constant rate. At a few places where it crossed a small stream or drain, there was a kind of viaduct constructed of rock, with the man-made ditch continuing across it. This path was obviously a sluice of some kind, quite old, with some trees as large as eighteen inches in diameter growing in it.

As we followed the waterway farther and farther on subsequent exploratory visits we finally reached the point where it disappeared into the ground, about ten feet below a huge oak tree. We were perplexed, disappointed that our theories about a long waterway had been disproved. But when we scraped away some loose dirt, a tunnel was revealed.

I felt like a kid in an adventure story. We searched the other side of the hill and, about a hundred yards away, found where the sluice emerged. After some reluctance and half-bantering remarks about bear dens and snake condominiums, we crawled down into the tunnel and, bending over, walked safely through to the other end. Farther westward there were three other similar arteries dug through the hills.

Eventually the waterway ended near, but high above, Turniptown Creek, overlooking excavations that had obviously been ancient placer mines. It now seemed obvious that the channeled water, at high pressure, had been used to wash the dirt and stones from the gold flakes and nuggets. Later, when we described our explorations to the proprietor of a nearby antique shop, she gave us a large and ancient nozzle that she said was used for this very purpose. Now on the ground along-side our cabin, it is a reminder of mountain history.

With telephones, mail delivery, and word processors, our days at the cabin are usually about as busy as those in Plains, but there are no passers-by and visitors are rare. In this different atmosphere we find more time to read, meditate, study, and explore. With field guides to trees, birds, mammals, nests, mushrooms, wild flowers, ferns, rocks, and minerals and a good collection of other nature books, it is much easier to learn about the relatively isolated community around us.

We have especially enjoyed getting to know some of our neighbors, who are friendly but taciturn, inclined to respect the privacy of others, worshipping in religious services that are more emotional and fundamental in character than those to which we are accustomed. We have been to a few square dances and other social events, and we shop at the country stores and nearby roadside stands to buy fresh corn, tomatoes, apples, and cider. On our long hikes we often stop by to visit families who greet us from their yards, and sometimes leave with fresh vegetables, some blackberry preserves, sourwood honey, a woven basket, or maybe an invitation to fish in their pond.

Just over the mountain from our cabin, within easy walk-ing distance, is the Turniptown Missionary Baptist Church, where we have worshipped on some of the first and third Sundays. There is a regular membership of about fifty, most of whom have amazing musical ability. On our first visit, the pastor began calling on various people to leave their pews and come to the front to play instruments or sing. Before the service was over, almost every member had participated in the extem-poraneous program, often with the performers and congrega-tion laughing, choked with tears, or, on a few occasions, actually racked with loud sobbing. They knew each other and related the words of a selected hymn to either a happy event or a tragedy in the lives of those who were singing. One lady sitting behind us leaned forward every now and then to whisper: "That man gave up drinking and was saved last month," or "They just lost their Mama," or "They've been separated but are living to-gether again," or "The little girl up there has leukemia." Although we didn't know the people personally, we responded with a few tears of our own.

After two hours it was time for some invited guests to arrive at our cabin, and so we had to leave, long before the service was over. I stood to apologize to the congregation for our premature departure, and, partially to compensate, I later turned for them on my lathe a pair of mahogany collection plates.

Walking the steep trail back among the tall trees, Rosalynn and I wondered why the service in the little mountain church had moved us so profoundly. It seemed that we had participated in a ceremony from olden times. Some of the hymns were little changed from their origin in England or prerevolutionary days, preserved down through the generations by the unshakable religious beliefs and customs of mountaineer ancestors. The surprising public display of unabashed laughter and tears—deep emotions that resonated among all their Christian brothers and sisters—had demonstrated the closeness of family members and their ties with others in this isolated rural community.

In such a setting, companionship from family or caring neighbors was available whenever it was needed, but total solitude could always be found just a few steps from one's door. We felt that meditation among the rolling mountains and deep valleys, the cathedral-like forests and pristine bubbling brooks, all served to keep these people especially close to nature and reminded them unceasingly of God's miraculous creation. Regardless of one's faith or beliefs, it would not be possible to absorb these impressions without being moved.

In some ways, our place on Turniptown Creek completes a circle in my life, bringing me back to many of the outdoor experiences of childhood in South Georgia that I enjoyed with my mother and father. Our children and grandchildren are already sharing this love for the outdoors. It multiplies our pleasure to have them picnicking with us on a flat rock in the middle of the creek, with the small babies in their bassinets shaded from the sun by an overhanging ledge of stone. Together, our older grandchildren stand with us under a waterfall; help to identify the mountain trees, shrubs, and flowers; explore the hills and swamps; pull a trout from the stream; or sit on the front porch to hear recollections of bygone times and loved ones long gone. All of us know that this place will be theirs someday, perhaps to share with later generations.

Here in this mountain valley even the awareness of our own mortality does not detract from the reassuring contemplation of the cycles of nature. The words of Ecclesiastes come to mind:

> A generation goes and a generation comes,
> But the earth remains forever.
> Also, the sun rises and the sun sets;
> And hastening to its place it rises there again.
> Blowing toward the south,
> Then turning toward the north,
> The wind continues swirling along;
> And on its circular courses the wind returns.
> All the rivers flow into the sea,
> Yet the sea is not full.
> To the place where the rivers flow,
> There they flow again.
> . . .
> That which has been is that which will be,
> And that which has been done is that which will be done.
> So, there is nothing new under the sun.

It is good to realize that, if love and peace can prevail on earth, and if we can teach our children to honor nature's gifts, the joys and beauties of the outdoors will be here forever.

INDEX

A

ABC Television Network, 174, 175
Adams, Richard, 173, 175–176, 180–183
Alabama, 145, 147–151
Alaska, 76, 113–129
Aleuts, 113
Allen, Ross, 54–55
Alligator gar, 30
Alligators, 30, 34–35
Altitude sickness, 244–245, 246, 250, 251
Ama Dablam Mountain (Himalayas), 240
American Sportsman magazine, 10
American Sportsman TV show, 174
Andrews, Rupert, 114
Andrus, Cecil, 114, 116
Anegada (British Virgin Islands), 198–205
Annapurna Range (Nepal), 229, 230, 231
Argentina, 66, 67
Arkansas, 83–90
Armington, Stan, 230, 232, 233
Arthur, Chester, 7

Ashburn Hill Plantation (Ga.), 161
Aspen, 107–108
Atlantic salmon, 14–15, 66, 174–184, 188, 210
Australia, 219

B

Bagmati River (Nepal), 255
Bait, 26, 27, 28
 see also Lures
Bald eagles, 190, 194
Bass, 145
 in Alabama, 147–151
 in Georgia, 27, 28, 31
 striped, 64
Bass Anglers Sportsman Society, 145–146
Battle River (Alaska), 126–127
Bears, 126, 262
Bengal tigers, 252, 253
Berners, Dame Juliana, 207, 213, 215
Billy's Lake (Okefenokee Swamp), 30
Bird dogs. *See* Dogs, hunting
Birds
 in Okefenokee Swamp, 31

Birds (*Cont.*)
see also Hunting; specific
birds
Birendra, King (Nepal), 229
Blacks, 20, 45
Bluegills, 32–33, 34
Blue marlin, 200–202
Blum, Richard, 229, 230–233,
234, 242, 243, 246
Bobcats, 47
Bobwhite quail. *See* Quail
Bonefish, 198–199, 202–205
Bourne, Peter, 207, 208–209
Boy's Life magazine, 10
Brand, Charles, 215, 216, 217
Bream. *See* Bluegills
British Columbia (Canada),
188–197
British Virgin Islands, 198–205
Broadlands (England), 215–216
Brooks, Charlie, 93, 96, 97, 98
Brooks, D. W., 11
Brooks River (Alaska), 126
Buddhism, 232, 234–235, 238,
241–242
Bull Sluice (waterfall), 16
Butterflies, 17

C

Caddis flies, 67–68, 69
in Alaska, 121, 125, 128
in England, 217
and "gulpers," 93
Camp David, 7, 70, 71, 76
Canada
British Columbia, 188–197
Quebec, 173–184
Queen Charlotte Islands,
189–197
Canada geese, 17, 149, 190
Canoeing, 15–16
Caribou, 127
Carp, 27, 100
Carter, Amy, 74, 239
Carter, Chip, 79, 93, 98

Carter, Don, 106
Carter, Earl, 12, 13
and bird dogs, 40–42
as disciplinarian, 19
family life, 20
and fishing, 21, 29, 31–32,
33–34
and hunting, 36–39, 43, 44
Carter, Gloria, 19
Carter, Hugh, 52
Carter, Jack, 56, 117
Carter, Jason, 116–121, 125–129
Carter, Jeffrey, 38
Carter, Jimmy
in Alaska, 113–129
in British Virgin Islands,
198–205
in Canada, 174–184, 187–197
canoeing and kayaking, 15–16
childhood, 9–10, 16–17,
18–53, 55–56
in China, 99–100
duck hunting, 56–58, 83–90
in England, 213–217
fishing, 11, 63–82, 92–102,
147–151; see also specific
locations
grouse hunting, 103–112
in Japan, 100–102
lost in woods, 56–58
mountain climbing, 228–253
and nature, 8, 17
Navy career, 6–7
in Nepal, 228–255
in New Zealand, 218–227
quail hunting, 153–169
reading material, 8, 10
shooting skills, 10
skiing, 7–8
in Switzerland, 211–213
turkey hunting, 134–144
at Turniptown Creek, 259–266
in Wales, 206–211
Carter, Lillian, 12, 16–17, 19
Carter, Rosalynn
in Canada, 174, 175, 178–180,
192, 194

Carter, Rosalynn (*Cont.*)
canoeing, 15–16
in China, 99
in England, 213, 215, 217
fishing, 11, 65, 66, 67, 70, 71, 73–75, 77, 78, 79, 93, 96, 178–180, 192, 194, 208, 210, 215, 221, 222
in Japan, 100–102
lost in woods, 58
in Nepal, 229, 230, 232, 233, 235, 237, 240, 241, 242, 244, 246, 250, 254
in New Zealand, 220, 221, 222
skiing, 8
snakes, encounters with, 53–54
in Switzerland, 211–213
in Wales, 208, 210
Casting, 31, 64, 80
Caveney, Ned, 107, 111
Chaldecott, Colonel Gilbert, 210
Chattahoochee River (Ga.), 15, 103
Chattahoochee Valley Wildlife Conservation program, 13
Chattooga River (Ga.), 16
China, 99–100
Chinook salmon, 115
Choctawhatchee Creek (Ga.), 22, 24, 55
Clarence Lake (Alaska), 114
Clark, Jack, 21, 40, 44, 56
Clark, Rachel, 21–23
Cleveland, Grover, 7
Cobras, 253
Collier's magazine, 10
Compleat Angler, The, 206
Confederation of Fly-fishers, 92
Conservation, 13–14, 91, 135, 185–186
Coolidge, Calvin, 7
Coons. *see* Raccoons
Copper Bay (Queen Charlotte Islands), 189, 192
Copperheads. *See* Bluegills

Copper River (Alaska), 116, 118, 119, 125, 127
Copper River (Queen Charlotte Islands), 189, 194
Cottonmouths (water moccasins), 51–52, 53
Coutts, Margaret, 220, 222, 223
Coyotes, 140
Crockford, Jack, 185–186
bonefishing, 198, 200, 204
as fly-fishing instructor, 65
game bird hunting, 103–104, 106–107
"gulper" fishing, Yellowstone, 92–93
steelhead fishing, Canada, 191
turkey conservation under, 135
Crocodiles, 252

D

Danphes (Nepalese pheasants), 237
Daughenbaugh, Don, 77, 78, 79
Davis, A. D., 21
DDT, 149
Deena Creek (Queen Charlotte Islands), 190, 191, 192
Deer, 185–186
in Georgia, 185–186
in New Zealand, 225
nicotine tranquilizer, 186
in Pennsylvania, 186–187
red, 225
spotted, 252
Deliverance (motion picture), 16
Delta Queen (steamboat), 68
Dickey, James, 16
Dogs, hunting, 40–47
electronic beepers, 109–110
and quail, 155–161
and rattlers, 52–53, 165–167
squirrel dog, 43–44
theft of, 41–42
Dolphins, 6

Dougherty, Paul, 97, 98
Doves, 39
Ducks
  in Arkansas, 83–90
  conservation, 91
  in Georgia, 48–49, 56–57
  mallards, 85–91
Ducks Unlimited, 14, 91

E

Eagles, 190, 194, 243–244
Eels, 24
Eisenhower, Dwight, 7
Elephants, 251–252, 253
Elk, 107, 109
Elliott, Charles, 158, 169
England, 213–217
Ernst, Walter, 189, 191, 192,
  193
Eskimos, 113
Everest. See Mount Everest

F

Farm animals, 20–21
Feinstein, Dianne, 229
Field and Stream magazine, 10
Firehole River (Yellowstone), 97
Fishing
  bait, 26, 27, 28
  casting, 31, 64, 80
  childhood, 10–11, 21–35
  dangers and discomforts, 15,
    64
  fly, 63–71, 74–82, 92–99,
    209–210
  history, 15, 206–207
  hooks, 75, 78
  joys of, 11
  lures, 28–29, 69–70, 81, 146,
    148, 150
  moral arguments, 12–14
  rods and reels, 31, 64, 75–76,
    95–96

on television, 147, 148,
    151–152, 174–175
  tournaments, 150–151
  see also specific fish; specific
    locations
Fish World (Ala.), 147–148
Fitch, Marlin, 199, 200, 202
Flat Rock Club (Yellowstone), 97
Flies, 67–70
  see also specific types
Fly fishing, 63–71, 74–82,
    92–99, 209–210
  see also specific fish
Forest. See Woods, dangers of
Forrest, Rembert, 24, 55, 56
Foxes, 44–45
Franklin, Benjamin, 134

G

Gaspé Peninsula (Canada), 173,
  182
Geese, Canada. See Canada
  geese
Georgia, 134
  grouse, 103–105
  plantations, 159–161
  quail, 40, 42–43, 104,
    153–161, 168–169
  turkeys, 134–144
  see also specific areas
Ghasa (Nepal), 229, 230
Godwin, Pete, 10
Goll, Chris, 114, 116–128
Gorak Shep (Nepal), 248, 250
Gowdy, Curt, 15, 174, 175,
    178–183
Grayling, 67
  in Alaska, 67, 114–115
  in Switzerland, 211, 212
  in Yellowstone, 93, 97–98
Gray's Run Rod and Gun Club
  (Pa.), 79
Great Britain. See England;
  Wales
Great Depression, 20, 22, 135

Grebe Lake (Yellowstone), 97–98
Green Drake flies, 73–74
Greenland, 176
Grey, Zane, 10
Griffis, Lem, 29–30
Groezinger, Herman, 200–202
Grouse, 103–112, 262
"Gulpers" (trout), 93, 96
Gypsy moths, 78

H

Haida Indians (Canada), 189,
  195, 197
Hammond, Jay, 114
Hampshire (England), 213
Harpster, Wayne, 71, 73, 74, 77,
  82, 99–101, 186–187, 191
Harvey, George, 74–76, 78, 80,
  81, 92–99, 122, 187
Hawaiian Wiggler lure, 28
Hawks, 38–39
Hayes, Tony, 220–222, 225, 226
Hebgen Lake (Yellowstone), 96
Henry's Fork (Yellowstone), 97
Henry's Lake (Yellowstone), 94
Hillary, Edmund, 240
Himalayan Journeys, 232
Himalayas, 229–251
  see also specific peaks and
    mountains
Hodges, Kaneaster, 84, 86, 87,
  89, 90
Hooks, 75, 78
Hoover, Herbert, 7
Hortense (Ga.), 32–35
How to Catch Steelhead (book),
  188
Humminbird depth finder,
  146–147
Humphreys, Joe, 80
Hunting
  birds, 37–42
  childhood, 36–50
  dogs, 40–47, 53–53, 109–110,
    155–161, 165–167

  ducks, 56–58, 83–90
  headgear, 39
  moral arguments, 12–14
  quail, 153–169
  turkeys, 134–144
Hunting Creek (Md.), 7

I

Indians, 113, 262–263
Insects. See Flies; specific types
Itchen River (England), 214, 216

J

Jitterbug lure, 29
Jones, Dick, 162

K

Kaingaroa national forest (New
  Zealand), 224
Kala Pattar peak (Himalayas),
  248, 249
Kali Gandhaki River (Nepal), 229
Kami, Pasang, 231, 232, 233,
  238, 240, 242, 247, 249
Kantega Mountain (Himalayas),
  240
Kathmandu (Nepal), 229, 231,
  233, 255
Kayaking, 16
Kemsley, Gary, 224–225
Kennedy, John F., 239
Khomeini, Ayatollah, 116
Khumbila Mountain (Himalayas),
  234
Khumjung School (Nepal), 239,
  240
Kinchafoonee Creek (Ga.), 22,
  26
King, Mary, 207, 208
Krait (snake), 253
Kreh, Lefty, 96

Kunde Hospital (Nepal), 239, 240
Kunghit Indians (Canada), 195–196

L

Lake Eufaula (Ala.), 145, 148, 151
Lake Iliamna (Alaska), 118, 127
Lake Kukaklek (Alaska), 126
Lake Okeechobee, 150
Lake Taupo (New Zealand), 218, 221–223
Lee, Art, 174, 175, 178, 180
Leonard, H. L., Co., 76
Levesque, Steve, 179
Lhotse, Mount. *See* Mount Lhotse
Light Cahill flies, 69
Light Gray Drake flies, 69
Little Satilla River (Ga.), 32
Living River, The (Brooks), 97
Loader, Bill, 214–215
Lobuje (Nepal), 247
Logging, 195, 197
London, Jack, 10
Long, Bob, 192
Loons, 127
Louise Island (Queen Charlotte Islands), 196
Ludie's Lake (Ga.), 32
Lures, 28–29, 69–70, 81, 146, 148, 150
Lyell Island (Queen Charlotte Islands), 195

M

Mackerel, 219
Madison River (Yellowstone), 97
Magazines, 10
Mallards, 85, 86, 87–88, 89, 90–91
Mann, Ann, 146, 147–148
Mann, Tom, 145–152
Maori, 189, 227
Marlin, 200–202
Marsh hen, 14
Maryland, 7
Matapédia River (Quebec), 173, 174, 178
Maxwell, Tom, 76
Mayflies, 67–69, 73–74, 75, 93, 261
McIntyre, Richard, 97, 98, 99, 261–262
Metz, Bucky, 81, 93
Michigan, 106–111
Millponds, 27–28
Miura, Yuiichi, 240
Monarch butterflies, 17
Monasteries, 237, 238, 241–242
Moonshine, 48
Moore, Frank, 84, 88, 89
Moose, 125, 126
Morgan, Hywel, 207–208, 209
Morgan, Moc, 207–210
Moths, 78
Mountain climbing, 229, 230–253
Mount Everest, 229–232, 238–240, 244, 246, 248, 249
Mount Lhotse (Nepal), 248
Muir, John, 10
Muskie, Edmund, 13, 114

N

Namche Bazar (Nepal), 231, 233
Nanuktuk Creek (Alaska), 126
Nature, 8
Naval Academy, U.S., 6
Navy, U.S., 6–7
Nepal, 228–255
New Standard Fishing Encyclopedia (McClane), 199
New Zealand, 218–227

Nicotine, as deer tranquilizer, 186
Ninstints (Queen Charlotte Islands), 195–196

O

Okefenokee Swamp (Ga.), 29–31
Olsen, Cathy, 244
Opossums, 45
Orvis Company, 215
Osprey, 149
Outdoor Life magazine, 10

P

Pallant River (Queen Charlotte Islands), 189, 194, 197
Peccaries, 164–165
Penn State University, 74, 80
Pennsylvania, 7, 71–82, 186–187
Penobscot River (Maine), 177
Pesticides, 167, 168
Pheasants, 237
Pheriche (Nepal), 241, 244, 250–251
Pidcock, Frank, 161
Pike, 128
Pike Lake (Alaska), 118, 119
Pileated woodpeckers, 140
Plains (Ga.), 9, 19
Plantations, 159–161
Poindexter Slough (Mont.), 98
Poinsett County (Ark.), 84
Pokhara (Nepal), 231
Pomfret (U.S.S.), 63
Pope, John and Betty, 260
Possum. *See* Opossums
Potatoes, 235–236
Prince of Game Birds (Elliott), 169
Pythons, 252, 253

Q

Quail
    in Georgia, 40, 42–43, 104, 153–161, 168–169
    grouse, comparison to, 104
    killing of, 13
    in Texas, 162–168
Quebec (Canada), 173–184
Queen Charlotte Islands (British Columbia), 189–197

R

Rabbits, 44
Raccoons, 45–47
Rail (marsh hen), 14
Rainbow River Lodge (Alaska), 116, 119
Rainbow trout. *See* Steelhead trout; Trout, rainbow
Rangitaiki River (New Zealand), 224
Rattlesnakes, 52–53, 54, 166–167
Reading, nature material, 8, 10
Red Rock Lakes (Yellowstone), 94
Redtail hawks, 38
Reels. *See* Rods and reels
Rhinoceros, 252, 253
Riegel, Jill, 244–245, 250
Riss, Lloyd, 74–75
Rods and reels, 27, 31, 64, 75–76, 95–96
Royal Chitwan National Park (Nepal), 251
Ruffed grouse, 110–111, 262
Rum Doodle tavern (Nepal), 232
Russell, John, 213, 215, 217

S

St. Moritz (Switzerland), 211–213
Salmon, 115, 125
    Atlantic, 14–15, 66, 174–184, 188, 210

Salmon (*Cont.*)
  Chinook, 115
  sockeye, 125
Salmon River (Ida.), 65
Sandspit (Queen Charlotte
  Islands), 189
Saturday Evening Post magazine,
  10
Schiel, Walter, 162–167
Schwiebert, Ernest, 96
Sea lions, 195
Sea trout, 210
Seehorn, Monte, 105
Sewin, 210
Sheridan Ranch (Yellowstone),
  94–95
Sherpas, 229, 231, 234–240, 246
Shooting, 10
  see also Hunting
Shrimp, 6
Sitzer, Leonard, 83–84, 86–90
Skedans Creek (Queen Charlotte
  Islands), 196
Skedans Island (Queen Charlotte
  Islands), 194
Skiing, 7–8
Snakes, 54–55, 164
  cobras, 253
  krait, 253
  pythons, 252, 253
  rattlers, 52–53, 54, 166–167
  water moccasins (cotton-
    mouths), 51–52, 53
Snow cocks, 243, 248
Sockeye salmon, 125
Sonar, 6, 146–147
Spruce Creek (Pa.), 7, 71,
  72–79, 81–82, 186–187
Squirrels, 43
Steelhead Society, 192
Steelhead trout, 66–67, 187–188,
  191–194, 196–197
Stoneflies, 67–68, 69, 128
Stonehenge (England), 215
Streams, 64–66
Strickland, Joe, 32–35
Submarines, 6

Suckers, 25–27
Swamps, 49, 51, 56
Swans, 214, 216
Switzerland, 211–213

T

Teifi River (Wales), 207–208,
  210
Television, 147, 148, 151–152,
  174–175
Tengboche (Nepal), 240–243
Test River (England), 214,
  215–216, 217
Texas, 162–168
Thame (Nepal), 234, 235, 236
Thamserku peak (Himalayas),
  234, 240
Thoreau, Henry David, 10, 17
Tibet, 232–233, 241
Tigers, 252, 253–254
Timber, 195, 197
Timberline, Inc., 97, 261
*Tom Mann's Methods for
  Catching Bass* (Mann),
  145
Tongariro River (New Zealand),
  219–220, 225
Trekking in the Himalayas
  (Armington), 232
Tricorythodes flies, 69, 75
Trout
  in Alaska, 116, 118, 121–124,
    128–129
  brook, 66, 79
  brown, 66, 67, 216, 217, 219,
    220, 222
  in Canada, 187–188, 191–194,
    196–197
  cooking of, 223
  in England, 214–215,
    216–217
  feeding habits, 65, 67–70
  fly-fishing for, 65, 78–80,
    82
  "gulpers," 93, 96

Trout (*Cont.*)
  hooks, 75
  killing of, 12
  in Montana, 98–99
  in New Zealand, 219, 220–225,
    226–227
  in Pennsylvania, 73–80, 82
  rainbow, 66, 93, 95, 116,
    118, 121–125, 129, 219,
    220, 222, 225, 226,
    260–262
  releasing, 70, 75, 124,
    220
  sea, 210
  size, 67
  steelhead, 66–67, 187–188,
    191–194, 196–197
  in Switzerland, 211, 212
  tracking, 70
  in Turniptown Creek, 260–262
  in Wales, 210
  in Yellowstone, 93–98
Trout Tactics (Humphreys),
  80
Trout Unlimited, 14
Tsering, Ang, 231, 233,
  248–249
Tsering, Ila, 239
Turkeys, wild, 14, 104–105,
  134–144, 262
Turniptown Creek (Ga.), 105,
  259–266
Turniptown Missionary Baptist
  Church (Ga.), 264–265
Turtles, 23, 31, 55–56
Tywi River (Wales), 210

U

Udall, Morris, 116

V

Vancouver (British Columbia),
  188–189
Vanterpool, Clinton, 203–205
Virgin Islands, 198–205

W

Walden Pond, 10
Wales, 207–211
Walton, Bud, 162
Walton, Izaak, 11, 27, 206, 213,
  214
Walton, Sam, 162, 163, 165,
  166, 168
Washington, George, 7
Water buffalo, 254
Water moccasins, 51–52, 53
Webster County (Ga.), 16
Wells, John, 223
Whales, 6, 118
Whiskey, 48
Whitefish, 96
White Path (Indian chief),
  262–263
White-tailed deer, 14, 186
Whitlock, Dave, 93, 95
Wild turkeys. *See* Turkeys, wild
Winchester (England), 213–214
Woodcock, 103, 104, 109
Woodpeckers, 140
Woods, dangers of, 51–59
Wolves, 127

Y

Yellowstone, 93–98
Yeti, 242, 243